CAMBRIDGE ENGLISH PROSE TEXTS

Revolutionary Prose of the English Civil War

CAMBRIDGE ENGLISH PROSE TEXTS

General editor: GRAHAM STOREY

OTHER BOOKS IN THE SERIES
The Evangelical and Oxford Movements, edited by Elisabeth Jay

FORTHCOMING
Science and Religion in the Nineteenth Century,
edited by Tess Cosslett
Romantic Critical Essays, edited by David Bromwich
Burke, Godwin, Paine and the Revolution Controversy,
edited by Marilyn Butler
American Colonial Prose: John Smith to Thomas Jefferson,
edited by Mary Radzinowicz

Revolutionary Prose of the English Civil War

edited by
HOWARD ERSKINE-HILL
Fellow of Pembroke College, Cambridge and
University Lecturer in English

and
GRAHAM STOREY
Fellow of Trinity Hall, Cambridge and
Reader in English

CAMBRIDGE UNIVERSITY PRESS

Cambridge
London   New York   New Rochelle
Melbourne   Sydney

Published by the Press Syndicate of the University of Cambridge
The Pitt Building, Trumpington Street, Cambridge CB2 1RP
32 East 57th Street, New York, NY 10022, USA
296 Beaconsfield Parade, Middle Park, Melbourne 3206, Australia

First published 1983

Printed in Great Britain at The Pitman Press, Bath

Library of Congress catalogue card number: 82-12904

British Library cataloguing in publication data

Revolutionary prose of the English Civil War.–
(Cambridge English prose texts)
1. English prose literature–Early modern,
1500–1700
I. Erskine-Hill, Howard   II. Storey, Graham
828'.4'08   PR1293

ISBN 0 521 24404 8 hard covers
ISBN 0 521 28670 0 paperback

Contents

List of illustrations   *page* vi
Acknowledgments   vii
Introduction   I
    History   I
    Biography   12
    Political thought   21
    Style   29

Prologue. Letter from Cromwell to his brother-in-law,
    Colonel Valentine Walton, 5 July 1644   33
1 HENRY PARKER, *Observations Upon Some of His Majesties
    Late Answers and Expresses*, 1642 (second edition,
    corrected)   35
2 Extracts from the Army Debates, October 1647   64
3 WILLIAM WALWYN, *The Bloody Project*, August 1648   89
4 JOHN LILBURNE, *Englands New Chains Discovered*,
    February 1649   101
5 JOHN MILTON, *The Tenure of Kings and Magistrates*,
    February 1649   116
6 RICHARD OVERTON, *The Baiting of the Great Bull of
    Bashan*, July 1649   145
7 GERRARD WINSTANLEY, *A New-Yeers Gift Sent to the
    Parliament and Armie*, December 1649 (first part) 155
8 JAMES HARRINGTON, *Valerius and Publicola*, 1659   176
9 JOHN MILTON, *The Readie and Easie Way to Establish
    A Free Commonwealth*, April 1660 (second edition,
    enlarged)   203
Epilogue. *Queres and Conjectures, Concerning the present state
    of this Kingdome*, 1643   230
Appendix. *An Agreement of the People*, composed October
    1647   237

Notes   247
A select booklist   262

Illustrations

1   *Englands New Chains Discovered,*
    February 1649, by John Lilburne,
    title-page   *page* 102
2   *The Baiting of the Great Bull of Bashan,*
    July 1649, by Richard Overton, title-page   146
3   *The Readie and Easie Way to Establish*
    A Free Commonwealth, April 1660, by
    John Milton, title-page   204

Acknowledgments

We are very grateful to Dr Richard Tuck for
advice on some of the issues raised by Henry
Parker's *Observations*; to Mrs Audrey Daughton
for her assistance in the preparation of our editions
of two of the pamphlets; to Dr Blair Worden for
his advice on the introduction; and to Andrew
Brown and Terence Moore, of Cambridge University Press, for their meticulous editing and helpful suggestions. We have also benefited greatly
from the interest taken in this period by several
generations of seminar pupils at Cambridge.

H.H.E-H.
G.S.

Introduction

History

The English Civil War period – twenty years of violent political turmoil in the history of what was then a marginal and second-rate European power – has proved a seminal event in an English-speaking civilisation that has subsequently become world-wide. Crucial episodes of this kind are soon transformed into myth. The image of the martyr-king falling before the malign forces of faction and destructive rebellion held sway for a century or more, before yielding to an evolutionary myth according to which the forces of progress among the Puritans broke open the archaic forms of the State to march confidently off in the direction of John Locke, the American Constitution and the quasi-scientific propositions of Marxist theories of history. In our time the more recent myth perpetuates itself through the potent word 'revolution', used here in its modern sense of a violent creative outbreak of the new and progressive, a sense unknown to the people who lived through those events.

The historian must be ready to test the myth, and to de-mythologise where necessary. With events of such importance we want to know what really happened, and what the men who shaped the history thought they were doing at the time. The captivating term 'revolution' has to be defined, for in the older sense of a sudden reversal in government the word is certainly one which participants in the Civil War used to describe what was going on around them.[1] In this sense there were four revolutions between 1640 and 1660: the Civil War which culminated with the defeat and execution of the King; the curtailing of Parliamentarian power to establish the quasi-monarchical Cromwellian protectorate; the final republican bid for mastery which brought down Richard Cromwell and briefly defied a rising demand for a restoration of the Stuart monarchy; and that restoration itself in 1660.

This distinction is important because within these revolutions something else was happening, or trying to happen, a revolution in a more modern sense: a bid to move from the extraordinary events of the First Civil War to a society in which power no longer derived primarily from property but from the people.[2] The proposals put forward by the Levellers[a] in the Army Debates, and in tracts by men such as Lilburne, Walwyn and Overton, can seem so close to the ideals of modern representative democracy that it is hard not to succumb to some form of evolutionary myth. As S. R. Gardiner said in 1893, 'the modern reader finds himself in the midst of ideas with which he is perfectly familiar'.[3] The Levellers and the Diggers,[b] however, received short shrift from the leaders of the victorious Parliament and Army. The small and vulnerable Digger community on St George's Hill, Cobham, was easily scattered. The Levellers, stronger and more tenacious, survived longer, and when last we hear of them it is of their negotiations with exiled Royalists in 1658–9. They may have had more to hope for from the King than from Cromwell or the briefly reinstated Rump Parliament.

The causes of the Civil War are classic territory for the battles of modern historians. The evolutionary myth (if myth it be) entails a long retrospection and the principle of something like historical inevitability. In this view the causes of the Civil War are to be sought in the sixteenth century, and explanations in terms of long social and economic change have frequently been propounded: most famously concerning the rise or decline of the gentry. Such hypotheses may be vulnerable to the charge that they attempt 'to explain events which did not happen in terms of a social change for which the evidence remains uncertain' (Conrad Russell on Lawrence Stone's version of the rise of the gentry),[4] though any expansion of the gentry class may be thought to have created a more volatile political public. Certainly it is hard to show how 'deep causes' such as 'the rise of the gentry', the development of ideas concerning resistance to rulers, or even the narrow economic basis of the Tudor and Stuart monarchy, are true causes in the sense that they specifically determined the outbreak of the Civil War. They

[a] The Levellers was the name given by their opponents, particularly the Army leaders, to the radical movement which supported the *Agreement of the People*, Nov. 1647 (given here as an appendix); but not accepted by them. 'We profess therefore that we never had it in our thoughts to Level mens estates', but rather to enable all men 'with as much security as may be to enjoy their propriety' (*A Manifestation*, 14 April 1649, signed by the four Leveller leaders, prisoners in the Tower, Lilburne, Walwyn, Prince and Overton). 'Commonly (though unjustly) styled LEVELLERS' Overton describes those to whom he addressed *The Baiting of the Great Bull of Bashan* (p. 145, below).

[b] The Diggers was the name given by Gerrard Winstanley to the small community of labourers he set up on 1 April 1649, who were to subsist by digging and cultivating the common land on St George's Hill, Cobham. It was adopted by other similar colonies. They also called themselves 'True Levellers'.

are, rather, among the circumstances of the Civil War, contributing to an outcome which was not inevitable, but was prompted by more specific and more recent events. We are on surer ground if we look at the nature of Charles I's reign to see whether there were not there sufficient causes of the Civil War, whatever long-term factors may then have contributed to the trend of events.

It was not a time of general discontent: 'the most serene, quiet and halcion days that could possibly be imagined' were the words of Lord Falkland, one of the King's Parliamentary opponents, who rallied to him on the eve of the Civil War.[5] Clarendon,[a] another opponent who came over, attested to the 'balm' and 'felicity' of the time, as also to its latent 'mutiny, and discontent'; in addition the continuing move to enclose and 'improve' common land caused considerable social unrest.[6] The peace and prosperity, then, though real enough, rested on a precarious foundation. The feel of the times with their celebration of peace and intimations of war is well conveyed from the courtier's point of view by that most accomplished of Caroline poets, Thomas Carew, especially in 'To my Friend G. N. from *Wrest*' and in 'To Aurelian Townshend. In answer of an Elegiacall Letter upon the Death of the King of *Sweden*':

> Then let the Germans feare if *Cæsar* shall,
> Or the United Princes, rise, and fall,
> But let us that in myrtle bowers sit
> Under secure shades, use the benefit
> Of peace and plenty, which the blessed hand
> Of our good King gives this obdurate Land,
> Let us of Revels sing, and let thy breath
> (Which fill'd Fames trumpet with *Gustavus* death . . .

> These harmelesse pastimes let my *Townsend* sing
> To rurall tunes; not that thy Muse wants wing
> To soare a loftier pitch, for she hath made
> A noble flight, and plac'd th'Heroique shade
> Above the reach of our faint flagging ryme;
> But these are subjects proper to our clyme.
> Tourneyes, Masques, Theaters, better become
> Our *Halcyon* dayes; what though the German Drum
> Bellow for freedome and revenge, the noyse
> Concernes not us, nor should divert our joyes;
> Nor ought the thunder of their Carabins

---

[a] Edward Hyde (1609–74), first Earl of Clarendon, Parliamentarian, royal adviser and statesman, managed Charles II's affairs in exile. He was elevated to the peerage and made Lord Chancellor on the King's return in 1660 and helped shape the Restoration Settlement. In 1667 he fell from favour and returned to exile. There he completed his famous *History of the Rebellion and Civil Wars* (published in 1702–4) and also wrote his autobiography.

Introduction

Drowne the sweet Ayres of our tun'd Violins;
Beleeve me friend, if their prevailing powers
Gaine them a calme securitie like ours,
They'le hang their Armes up on the Olive bough,
And dance, and revell then, as we doe now.

(lines 43–50, 89–104)

There was indeed ground for gratitude, if England had so far kept clear of the Thirty Years War on the continent.

But the King's government lacked the resources to do what was expected of it. It lacked the bureaucracy (though that might itself have provoked opposition); above all it lacked the money. If there is one long-term factor which approaches to being a cause of the Civil War, it is the narrowing financial base of the Tudor and Stuart monarchy in a century of severe inflation. Many of the complaints against Charles's government, for example those concerning monopolies, had been complaints against Elizabeth in her last years: monopolies were inevitably unpopular, but they were one of the few ways of raising revenue and controlling trade.

The crown was therefore more dependent on Parliament for funds as time went on. Not only in the event of a foreign war, but even to protect fishing and guard the coast of England from pirates, the Government had either to rely on a vote of supply from Parliament, or levy taxes without Parliamentary consent. In the Ship Money case, seven out of twelve judges decided the tax was legal, but this did not prevent an effective tax strike on the part of some of the gentry. Tax strikes and the threat of tax strikes were to be common during the Interregnum. For the King thus to be forced into the arms of Parliament might have been well enough if his policies had been likely to please Parliament. 'That unwieldy club of landlords'[7] might then have borne some of the unpopularity of the necessary increase in taxes. Charles, however, was unwilling to relinquish the freedoms and responsibilities of his predecessors, 'Our Just, Ancient, Regall power'. It would be wrong to pretend that his policies were entirely sustained and coherent but in so far as they were they did not please Parliament. Parliament wanted an active Protestant foreign policy; Charles, while desirous of helping his exiled Protestant nephew the Elector Palatine, was more interested in alliance with the Catholic powers. Parliament was a predominantly Calvinist body; Charles and Archbishop Laud favoured the newest form of Protestantism, propounded by the Dutchman Arminius, which moved away from predestinarian views of salvation towards an emphasis on individual choice and action,

4

and led to a renewal of concern with ceremony and the sacraments. Parliament did not wish to see the Church of England materially strengthened at the expense of landowners; Charles and Laud did. Parliament did not wish to see itself relegated to a subordinate part of the constitution, as had come to be the case with the French Estates General and *parlements*, and with the Cortes in Spain. Charles was willing to rule for long periods without calling Parliament, if he thought Parliament would not enter into his measures. He called no parliament between 1629 and 1640.

Each side insisted, truly enough, that it was only exercising and defending its traditional rôle in the ancestral constitution. To act within law and historical precedent did not automatically produce co-operation: the parameters of the constitution, enshrined in both Common Law and historical precedent, were too wide. Within these parameters, it is fair to say, a crisis in government was being brought nearer, not because Parliament originally wished to introduce innovations, but because the King did. In so far as this crisis was a clash between old and new, the royal government, anticipating the absolute continental monarchies of the coming century, was the new. Parliament was the old.

Yet the crisis might have been long deferred, and perhaps thereby transformed to a less dangerous kind, had not the forward policy of Charles I and Laud made a major and fatal miscalculation: the twice deferred attempt to impose their ecclesiastical policy on Scotland, a predominantly Presbyterian and deeply Calvinist nation. The Scots rose in arms against the royal revolution. The financial balancing act of rule without Parliament was now at an end, for to put down the Scots required an army, and to raise an army it was necessary to call Parliament to vote supply. Thus the King was at the mercy of a Parliament filled with anger and alarm at the innovations of the last ten years. The King's situation now steadily worsened. The Short Parliament was hostile and was soon dissolved, but another, the Long Parliament, had to be called within months; Laud was imprisoned, and Strafford, the King's most loyal and effective minister, was attainted. While the court made spasmodic attempts to prepare for war, Charles's overt policy was now to concede more or less everything the English Parliament and the Scots Estates demanded. These concessions are recalled by the first tract in the present volume, Parker's extremely influential *Observations* (1642), which well expresses the opinions and mood of the Long Parliament in the last years before the war:

the first phase of the crisis. It is not a position which demands revolution in the modern sense, certainly not civil war, certainly not trial and execution of the King.

Nevertheless by the end of 1641 John Pym's Parliamentary campaign against Charles revealed itself to be disturbingly ambitious. Charles had now conceded everything necessary to put the clock back to James I, perhaps to Elizabeth. Yet Pym still mounted his Grand Remonstrance against the King's government, with what could only now be propagandist motives, aiming at further concessions. More defiant still, he proposed Parliamentary control over the King's appointment of councillors. This was a Parliamentary innovation. It marked the point where Falkland and Clarendon deserted Pym and rallied to the court. Somewhat uncertainly each side allowed itself some aggressive moves: early in January in 1642 the King attempted to arrest in Parliament by force of arms five of his Parliamentary opponents. This was illegal, ill-judged and had disastrous consequences for his cause. Soon after, Parliament put its own man, Sir John Hotham, in charge of the important port and magazine of Hull. Government had now virtually broken down. The King withdrew to the north and when he demanded entry into Hull, Hotham (acting on carefully drafted instructions) refused to admit him. This too was an aggressive and perhaps illegal move. What had never been intended, and foreseen only as something to be feared, had now come about: the nation, as Bulstrode Whitelocke said of Parliament, had now 'insensibly slipped into this beginning of civil war by one unexpected accident after another, as waves of the sea which have brought us thus far, and we scarce know how; but from paper combats by declarations, notes, messages and replies we are now come to the question of raising forces'.[8]

If each side had miscalculated, Parliament had perhaps miscalculated more, for how could it have been predicted that the King, with no army and so little of a party behind him, would attempt to defy them in the field? Parliament's aim had not been to effect a revolution but to compel the Crown to restrict its rôle along the lines to be indicated by Parker in his *Observations*. But Charles, though an unskilful politician, was a determined man who may have believed in his own cause all the more firmly when he considered how little he had gained by making concessions. His raising of his standard at Nottingham on 22 August 1642 slowly brought in support. Parliament too raised its forces. Yet it would be wrong to suppose that Crown and Parliament now polarised the nation, either by region, class or even capital and country. Study of the provinces in the Civil War reveals an irregular and fluid pattern in which one notable feature seems to have been the desire of various areas to avoid real (as opposed to nominal) commitment to either side.[9]

For a time the tide of military success seemed to be flowing in the royalist direction. On 11 November 1642 the King's army engaged with the Parliamentarians at Brentford, eight miles from London. It had the advantage; only heroic efforts by the Leveller John Lilburne enabled the Parliamentary troops to withdraw in good order.[10] The Royalists advanced to Turnham Green, the occasion of Milton's sonnet 'When the assault was intended upon the City', before retiring to Oxford. In 1643, when the advantage may have appeared roughly equal between the two sides, there was published *Queres and Conjectures, Concerning the present state of this Kingdome* (see below), an appeal for peace couched in studiedly neutral terms. But in July 1645 the royal armies were decisively defeated and the King was taken prisoner.

This is the situation in which the remarkable Army Debates at Putney (represented here) took place. The question that dominated the period between the capture of the King and the passing of the ordinance for his trial on 28 December 1648, was that of a settlement. 'If we beat the king ninety and nine times, yet he is king still, and so will his posterity be after him; but if the king beat us once we shall all be hanged': so the Earl of Manchester, Commander-in-Chief of the Eastern Association, is reported to have said in 1644.[11] This sentiment records the continuing importance of the King, and explains why politically speaking a settlement – or his death – had to be secured. Not only did the King and Parliament distrust each other, both Parliament and Army distrusted each other and themselves. The Army Debates were part of an effort by Cromwell to heal a dangerous split in the Parliamentary forces. The sense of crisis at these discussions is extraordinary. It is rare in English history to find military and political leaders of such importance engaged in so deep and urgent a debate. While the formal basis of discussion might be said to be the Leveller document, *An Agreement of the People* (see Appendix) together with Ireton's *Heads of the Proposals* as models for a settlement, and the theoretical conflict that between Natural and Human Law, what comes over most powerfully is the soldier's sense that they themselves who had helped to defeat the Royalists were going to be betrayed by the gentry attitudes of their own commanders in negotiations with the King. The feeling that those whose efforts had won the war had, whether landowners or not, a right to a say in the future strongly contributed to Leveller arguments for a franchise based on something close to manhood suffrage.[12]

This is important because here we have the nearest thing to a revolution in the modern sense that is to be found in the Civil War period. In their documents, *The Case of the Army* and *An Agreement of the People* the Levellers recommended a paramount law establishing biennial single-chamber parliaments, with supreme right to legislate and control public officials. The proposals were backed by an affirmation that power lay in the people, government deriving from their original consent. These ideas, while obviously related to those by which Parker had sought to justify the early actions of the Long Parliament, go far beyond the measures of 'King Pym'. Parker fully accepted the representativeness of Parliament, and although in the Army Debates Ireton favoured a partial extension of the franchise, it may be thought that the principles which fortified that formidable antagonist of the Levellers in these discussions were those of Parker.[13] While it is possible to trace the intellectual origins of the Leveller proposals back to the ancient world, it may well seem that the civil crisis and war had themselves virtually generated the Leveller position. Lilburne, the one Leveller we hear of before the outbreak of hostilities, had not been arrested, interrogated in the Star Chamber and flogged at the cart-tail from the Fleet to Westminster on 18 April 1638 for advocating manhood suffrage and biennial parliaments, but for distributing forbidden pamphlets against episcopacy.[14]

In the end a committee including Cromwell, Ireton, Sexby and Rainborough adopted a scheme closer to *The Heads of the Proposals* than to *An Agreement of the People*. It proposed biennial parliaments, a Council of State which mentioned the King, redistribution of seats in proportion to population, and voting rights for those who had served Parliament in the late war. The question of a wider franchise was referred to the existing Parliament. The whole scheme was to be established by agreement with the captive King and the House of Lords. At this stage Cromwell genuinely wanted an agreement with the King, but Charles believed he could gain more by holding out. He had now made a remarkably favourable agreement with the Scots to invade England on his behalf; there were royalist risings in Kent, Essex and South Wales; and a considerable part of the fleet repudiated their Leveller Vice-Admiral Rainborough and declared for the King. So the Second Civil War was fought. At its height, after Cromwell's victory over the Scots at

Preston and before the surrender of the Royalists at Colchester, was published Walwyn's pamphlet *The Bloody Project* (included in this volume). The quest for a settlement continued after the King's supporters were beaten a second time, and foundered in the end through Charles's refusal to give up the King's veto, or 'negative voice'. The eventual trial and execution of the King were of course illegal: 'first the king can be tried by no court; secondly, no man can be tried by this court', commented the young Republican Algernon Sidney.[15] They were also unpopular. Even the death warrant had to be doctored and some signatures erased.[16] Thus was accomplished the most striking reversal in government of the century. Yet its very violence helped generate its defeat. The King's arguments and bearing at the trial strengthened the cause of the monarchy, as did the publication, the day after the funeral, of John Gauden's *Eikon Basiliké*, perhaps the most successful piece of propaganda of the Civil War period, which used the literary conventions of soliloquy and prayer to dramatise the dead King as a sacred monarch and faulty though penitent man.

Through the several drastic political changes between the death of Charles I and the restoration of Charles II the great question was how to establish a convincing basis for political obligation. Since the monarchy, however defied and circumscribed, was a part of the ancestral constitution, the question of allegiance was more acute than ever after the King's death. The House of Commons, legally summoned by Charles I, had on 6 December 1648 been 'purged' of some forty of its members by the armed force of Colonel Pride. In the end Pride's Purge expelled a hundred and forty members. In addition this House of Commons had already been reduced in numbers by the withdrawal of loyalists early in the Civil War to join the King's Parliament in Oxford – the London Parliament was not the only parliament in this period. Recruiter elections between 1645 and 1648 raised its membership, however; and the Rump of the House of Commons that remained at Westminster retained, in the opinion of many, more legitimacy than any other institution in the nation. Shortly before the execution of the King, this House of Commons declared that 'the people are, under God, the original of all just power' and that the Commons itself comprised Parliament which held 'supreme power in this nation'. In March 1649 monarchy and House of Lords were formally abolished and in May the Commons affirmed that the people of England should be ruled as 'a Commonwealth and free state by the supreme authority of this nation, the representatives of the people in parliament'.[17] Despite these ringing declarations the Rump was a doubtfully representative body which dared not face a general election. Cromwell was to expel it in 1653. Four tracts in the present collection appeared during the first year of the Commonwealth thus established. The first, Milton's *The Tenure of Kings and Magistrates* (?13 February 1649), premises that Charles I was a tyrant and his trial sanctioned by the will of the people. The premise granted, the argument is not unconvincing. The second, *Englands New Chains Discovered* (26 February) by John Lilburne, who opposed Charles's execution, is a bitter accusation of betrayal:

> Behold! in the close of all, we hear and see what gives us fresh and pregnant cause to believe . . . that all those specious pretenses, and high Notions of Liberty, with those extraordinary courses that have of late bin taken (as if of necessity for liberty, and which indeed can never be justified, but deserve the greatest punishments, unless they end in just liberty, and an equal Government) appear to us to have bin done and directed by some secret powerful influences, the more securely and unsuspectedly to attain to an absolute domination over the Common-wealth . . . (p. 106, below)

and backed up its protest by specific criticisms and proposals. For this and the second part of the pamphlet, Lilburne, Walwyn, Overton and Prince were imprisoned on a charge of treason on 28 March 1649. The third tract, Overton's *The Baiting of the Great Bull of Bashan* (July), is more remarkable for its style than its political content. It celebrates with impudent *badinage* and wit the very act of defying, by publication from prison, Cromwell and the Rump. This example of literary action, not argument, is itself politically significant. The fourth pamphlet, Gerrard Winstanley's *A New-Yeers Gift Sent to the Parliament and Armie* (December 1649), gives the view of the tiny and vulnerable Digger community whose significance is no doubt greater from a modern view than it can have been at that time. By comparison with the other writings in this volume, *A New-Yeers Gift* stands out as a sermon. Its language is imaginative, religious and hortatory, and by an easy and bold metaphor it extends the meaning of 'Kingly power which you have made an act to cast out' into most government and all property. The Diggers were closest of all the political sects to the sporadic but repeated outbreaks of the rural poor against enclosures that had occurred through the reigns of Elizabeth, James and Charles. Winstanley presents the most powerful and radical challenge that can be found to the principles of a Charles I, a Parker, an Ireton, a Cromwell, a Harrington or a Milton. In the modern sense of the word 'revolutionary'[18] Winstanley's sermon is without doubt the most revolutionary tract in this collection.

On radical grounds, moral, political and religious, Walwyn, Lilburne, Overton and Winstanley questioned the claims of the Rump – after May 1649 the formally instituted 'Commonwealth and free state' – to command men's allegiance. In this year was published John Dury's *Case of Conscience Resolved*, a tract building upon Calvinist foundations to argue that the Commonwealth had a *de facto* claim to allegiance even if it were regarded as an unlawful government. Dury's pamphlet was first of a series of works to argue along these lines, and the case was slowly shifted and strengthened until, in Thomas Hobbes's *Leviathan* (1651) and several other works independently, it was insisted that any government that confers protection can command allegiance.[19] It will be noted that this argument, though evidently welcome to countless thoughtful, moderate and peaceable men, could be used to justify obedience to any form of government, indeed any government. The Vicar of Bray had behind him some of the most sophisticated political theory in our history. This argument would have been as relevant in enjoining obedience to Charles I in 1642 as to Oliver Cromwell when, on 20 April 1653, he expelled the Rump – an act displaying less respect for the representativeness of Parliament than any act of Charles I. After the eight months' experiment of the nominated 'Barebone's Parliament', which dissolved itself, the Cromwellian Protectorate was established. The Diggers had been dispersed, the Levellers defeated; and Lilburne, with his eye upon Cromwell, said that if England must have a king he would as soon have Charles II as another.[20] In due course the Levellers and the Royalists came to discuss terms, though the notion of alliance can have been of little more than a tactical move against a common enemy.

Because Cromwell was a successful military and political leader the Protectorate appears more stable than it really was. The quest for a proper constitutional settlement went on, but the goal continued to recede. Since taxation was now higher than under Charles I – on a European scale for the first time – disputes between Cromwell and his Parliaments over taxes and levies resembled those of the 1630s. Harmony between the Protector and his Parliaments proved elusive. The future looked uncertain. Some Cromwellians wished Cromwell to become king, for this would both restrict his power and settle the succession.[21] To James Harrington, however, Cromwell's quasi-monarchical rule was the great opportunity for that prince to establish an equal and lasting republic upon the Venetian model but with laws to ensure the adjustment of power and property on a rationalised franchise. To the description of such a republic, together with an account of how it might be introduced, Harrington devoted his romance *Oceana* (1656), with *Leviathan* and Sir Robert Filmer's *Patriarcha* among the greatest political works of the period. After the collapse of the Protectorate under Richard Cromwell the Rump, that vestige of 1640 legitimacy, was recalled, dissolved, and then recalled again. The year 1659 was another great one for political pamphlets. Harrington and the Harringtonians refined his principles and published them in a series of works shorter and plainer than *Oceana*, of which *Valerius and Publicola*, included here, is one of the most engaging. Milton saw the finally recalled Rump as an opportunity to establish a republic on his own more oligarchical and authoritarian principles: he spoke his mind with great courage in *The Readie and Easie Way to Establish A Free Commonwealth* (March–April 1660) (also included below). As new pamphlets streamed from the press, however, the last Rump Government was breaking down. As it collapsed, General Monck was marching south from Scotland, resolved to use his military power to ensure a stable and comprehensive settlement of some kind.

This the Rump showed itself unable to produce. The long-secluded members from Pride's Purge were now allowed back into the Commons, thus creating a majority for dissolving the Long Parliament and calling new elections. It was widely and correctly expected that this would produce a Parliament in favour of bringing back the Stuart monarchy. The election was based on the same franchise that the Levellers had assailed in the Army Debates and which had never been significantly altered. Of the Convention Parliament that resulted it has been said that 'Probably at least ninety per cent . . . hoped that Charles II would be recalled.'[22] No royal or government pressure could be exerted on these elections. Opinions are understandably divided as to whether what now happened is to be admired or deplored. Few today will see it as the 'glorious revolution' that Bevil Higgons, doubtless with deliberate provocation, called it in 1726.[23] Yet so great a change in English government had perhaps never before been decided by an election. For while the Long Parliament in 1640 never intended to destroy the monarchy, this Parliament was elected to bring it back.

Biography

Parliament was fortunate in having the early support of one of the most original and shrewd political thinkers of the century. Henry

Parker (1604–52) was a younger son of Sir Nicholas Parker, a Sussex landowner and successful Elizabethan soldier. His mother, Catherine Temple, of Stowe, Buckinghamshire, came from another landowning family. He took his B.A. from St Edmund Hall, Oxford, in 1625, and was called to the Bar by Lincoln's Inn in 1637. Between 1640 and 1651 he wrote nearly twenty pamphlets on Parliament's behalf, of which the one given here, *Observations Upon Some of His Majesties Late Answers and Expresses*, was the most comprehensive and important. In 1642, shortly after the outbreak of the Civil War, he was appointed Secretary to Essex's Army. Four years later, after acting as Joint-Secretary to a Parliamentary Commission, he went to Hamburg as Secretary to the Merchant Adventurers Company; at the same time he acted there as an agent for the Council of State. In 1649 he was rewarded with the joint registrarship of the Prerogative Office and in August made Secretary to Cromwell's Army in Ireland, where he died late in 1652.

Parker clearly, then, had some administrative capacity; but he was essentially a revolutionary political theorist. Through all his pamphlets, whatever the immediate political crisis, runs his theory of Parliamentary sovereignty. *Observations* argues at length, and with great cogency, for what he passionately believed in: the supremacy of Parliament; the King's responsibility for the War by misusing the Royal Prerogative; the necessity for Parliament to defend both itself and the people's safety, *salus populi*, which is 'paramount to the law itself'. Parker's belief in Parliamentary sovereignty was paralleled by his absolute Erastianism, his conviction (following the tenets of the sixteenth-century German theorist, Erastus) that the State should control religion. He belonged to no religious party and intensely disliked both the Bishops and the Sectarians, especially the Presbyterians. In both his belief in a strong central State and his Erastianism he foreshadows Hobbes's *Leviathan*, to be published nine years later.[24]

The Army Debates, held by the General Council of the Army in Putney Church from 28 October to 11 November 1647, are unique in English history. Called by Cromwell to discuss a revolutionary document, the Army Agitators' *Agreement of the People* (given here), they were at once a response to a political crisis, with the King a captive at nearby Hampton Court and the Army poised to threaten Parliament; and a debate, within a strongly religious context, on the fundamentals of the English constitution, on the first principles and problems of democracy. The Independents, the 'Party of the Centre' (as A. S. P. Woodhouse calls it), were represented by

Cromwell himself and his son-in-law, and second-in-command, Commissary-General Henry Ireton: the 'Grandees', as they were often named. The leading spokesmen of the 'Left' were the Army Agitator, Colonel Thomas Rainborough, and the civilian Leveller, John Wildman; they were supported by more than a dozen officers and at least one private soldier, Edward Sexby (who later rose to high rank), and by another civilian Leveller, Maximilian Petty. The meetings were chaired by Cromwell, who became increasingly impatient with the opposition; and recorded in shorthand by William Clarke, Assistant Secretary to the General Council.

Until the Debates, Henry Ireton (1611–51) had been a brave, but not particularly successful, soldier, who had fought at Edgehill, Marston Moor and Naseby, and was a staunch supporter of Cromwell and the New Model Army. Marriage to Cromwell's daughter Bridget in June 1646 had helped him to high command. The eldest son of a moderately prosperous and strongly Puritan Nottinghamshire family, he was educated, said Lucy Hutchinson in the memoirs of her husband, 'in the strictest way of godlinesse, . . . being a very grave and solid person.'[25] After graduating from Trinity College, Oxford, he became a member of the Middle Temple. The Army Debates showed his true status as a political thinker. Essentially a conservative reformer, he defended the Independent position with skill and tenacity. Although he sympathised with many of the Levellers' practical reforms, such as biennial parliaments, he believed that the State's fundamental purpose was to preserve peace and defend property: 'All the main thing that I speak for, is because I would have an eye to property. I hope we do not come to contend for victory – but let every man consider with himself that he do not go that way to take away all property' (p. 74, below). For Ireton, that could only lead to anarchy. From his belief in property came his insistence on a limited franchise: that the vote must be dependent on a stake in land or trade. And in the last Debate he made it clear that he accepted some veto on the Commons by King and Lords. To the Levellers, therefore, he was 'the cunningest of the Machiavellians'; he was accused of dealing privately with the King; and in 1649 Lilburne demanded that he be cashiered. In fact, by November 1648 he supported bringing the King to trial; he signed the warrant for his execution in January 1649; and, after it, was a vigorous supporter of the Commonwealth.

In August 1649 Ireton joined Cromwell in Ireland, having been promoted Lieutenant-General; took part in the savage sieges of Drogheda and Wexford; and in May 1650, on Cromwell's recall to

England, was appointed acting Commander-in-Chief. In 1651, after various vicissitudes, he took Limerick; but died soon afterwards from fever and overwork. He was buried with great ceremony in Westminster Abbey. Clarendon was not alone in crediting him with political influence over Cromwell; Ireton, he said, 'was often thought by his obstinacy to prevail over Cromwell and to extort his concurrence contrary to his inclinations'.[26] His was certainly the most cogent voice of the Centre in the Army Debates.

Equally certainly, that of Colonel Thomas Rainborough (1610–48) was the clearest and most dramatic voice of the Left. His plea for an extended suffrage is famous: 'the poorest he that is in England hath a life to live, as the greatest he' (p. 70, below). His voice rings out too on behalf of the rank-and-file of the Army: 'I would fain know what the soldier hath fought for all this while? He hath fought to enslave himself, to give power to men of riches, men of estates, to make him a perpetual slave.' (p. 84). His style of speaking has a biting brevity and directness, unlike the tenacious, sustained and sometimes laborious manner of Ireton, which is less dramatic but more subtle. Rainborough had in fact been brought up as a sailor, the son of a naval captain; and he had served with distinction as Vice-Admiral of the Parliament's fleet, during the first year of the War. But in Autumn 1643 he had been commissioned as Colonel; and as commander of an infantry regiment he had had a succession of military successes. By the end of the First Civil War he was M.P. for Droitwich and Governor of Worcester. His first allegiance was to the Army, but just before the Army Debates he was made second-in-command of the navy, under Warwick.[27]

It was Rainborough who, in August 1647, entered the City of London, at the head of four regiments. By then he had made clear his support for the Army's refusal to be disbanded, or sent to Ireland, without settlement of arrears of pay or indemnity for acts committed during the War. The Army Debates show clearly his commitment to the Leveller programme and his hostility to Cromwell and Ireton. It may well be doubted whether Cromwell would have subdued the Army Levellers so easily at Burford in May 1649, had Rainborough still been their leader. But by then he was dead, killed while resisting with his bare hands illegal arrest by two disguised Royalists, during the siege of Pontefract Castle, on 29 October 1648.

At first sight, William Walwyn (1600–80) seems least likely to have played the influential part he undoubtedly did play in the Leveller movement. The younger son of a Worcestershire landowner and grandson of the Bishop of Hereford, he made a prosperous career in the London cloth-trade and the Merchant Adventurers Company; lived for many years a simple family life, bringing up approximately twenty children; and spent much of his time reading widely in both theology and the classics. His son-in-law Dr Humphrey Brooke recorded his 'inward sweetness and calmness of spirit'. His strong radicalism had its roots in his religious convictions. A formal Independent all his life, his passionate belief in freedom of conscience and in toleration turned him more and more against the Presbyterians as well as against the Laudian clergy. By November 1642 he was raising soldiers and arms for Parliament as a Parliamentary committee-man. But it was the religious pamphlets that he published over the next four years, attacking tyranny, defending liberty of conscience, inveighing against poverty, that pointed the way to his revolutionary future. In 1646 he defended Lilburne against the House of Lords; from 1647 on he was active in framing Leveller petitions to Parliament. *The Bloody Project*, 1648 (given here), besides showing his inherent pacifism, brought together all the Levellers' demands for true democracy under one 'Supream Authority', a new and genuinely representative House of Commons. In March 1649 he was one of the four Leveller leaders committed to the Tower by Parliament. *Walwins Wiles*, an attack on him by seven Independent and Baptist ministers, during his imprisonment, shows that they regarded him as the true intellectual leader of the Levellers; Lilburne's tribute, 'as able in parts as any is in England', suggests the same point more positively. With the end of the Levellers in May 1649 and his own release from prison, Walwyn's public political life virtually ended. He almost certainly took the Engagement to the Commonwealth at the end of 1649 and retired into prosperous family life.

John Lilburne (1614-57) stands out as a true revolutionary leader in the modern sense. A prolific and vehement pamphleteer for his own and the people's liberties, he fully earned his nickname of 'Free-born John'. As he himself acknowledged, in *England's Birth-Right Justified* (1645), his political ideas owed much to Parker's *Observations*. His pamphlets virtually created the Leveller party. Imprisoned five times – by Royalists, House of Lords, United Presbyterians and Independents, the Rump and, finally, by the Council of State – he never ceased to be the symbol of the oppressed free Englishman and to proclaim himself as such.

The son of a land-owning family from County Durham – sent to London as an apprentice to the cloth-trade – he early showed his strong Calvinism by distributing an anti-episcopalian pamphlet; and for this he was flogged, pilloried and imprisoned. In the First Civil War he rose to be Lieutenant-Colonel of Dragoons and could claim Cromwell's personal friendship. During 1647, when the Levellers became organised as a party, Lilburne was in prison again, sentenced by the Lords for a pamphlet attack on the Earl of Manchester. But there can be no doubt of the major part he played, both in the embodying in himself of the spirit and the aims of the Levellers in their defence of 'the fundamental laws and liberties of England' and in their attack on Parliament for destroying them; and in inspiring the creation of the party itself. His own pamphlets, the stream of petitions for his release from his supporters, particularly Overton and Walwyn, and the petitions to Parliament for the *Agreement of the People*, the main Leveller manifesto, constantly proclaimed Lilburne's principles. He was immensely popular with the people of London; and, as martyr and military hero, equally so among the soldiers. The Army was 'one Lilburne throughout', one royalist pamphlet put it; 'the soldier hath continually his sword in one hand and one of Lilburne's epistles in the other', declared another.

Released in August 1648, Lilburne spent the rest of the year trying to persuade Parliament and Army to accept the Leveller programme. Failure to do so, and discovery that the Levellers were to be proceeded against, led to the first part of *Englands New Chains Discovered* (given here) in February 1649, followed by *The Second Part* a month later. The issue now was the continuance or abolition of the Council of State itself; and the report of Cromwell's shouting out to the Council 'If you do not break [the Levellers] they will break you' rings true.[28] Lilburne was never broken in spirit; but he spent all but two of his remaining eight years in prison or in banishment; he was twice tried for his life, in 1649 and 1653, and twice acquitted; and he died a Quaker.

Richard Overton, the third of the Leveller leaders, had, during the party's rise and fall, most in common with Lilburne. Like him, he was imprisoned first by the Lords, in 1646; then by the Independents, in March 1649. From July 1646 on, he was Lilburne's most fervent and powerful supporter; a prolific pamphleteer, like Lilburne, he again made the most of his own sufferings in the pamphlets he clearly enjoyed writing. But his background was quite different. Little is known of his early life, except that by 1615 he was a member of an English congregation of Baptists in Amsterdam; that he returned to England on the eve of the Civil War, probably in late 1640; and that he became an unlicensed printer. His Leveller beliefs lie in the idealistic creeds of his early Baptism; particularly in toleration, absolute separation of Church and State, hatred of oppression, succour of the 'poor brethren'.

Overton's first major pamphlet. *Mans Mortalitie*, 1644 – arguing for the mortality of man's soul, as well as his body, until the final Resurrection – was attacked as atheist; but its premises in fact went back to the early sixteenth-century German sect, the Anabaptists. Six satirical pamphlets against the Presbyterians he wrote as 'Martin-Priest' the following year foreshadow his Leveller principles: above all his faith in the people and hatred of persecution. Those principles came to full fruition in the first pamphlet he wrote in Lilburne's support, in July 1646: *A Remonstrance of Many Thousand Citizens*, to give it its short title. This declared his Republicanism; it also made clear his basic political belief, that all power lies in the people. His pamphlets of 1646–7 are considered by Richard Tuck (*Natural Rights Theories. Their Origin and Development* (Cambridge, 1979), p. 149) as 'the best statements of the Leveller case'. By 1647 he had joined Lilburne in attacking Parliament for betraying the people; and he joined him again in 1649 in attacking the Council of State, Cromwell and Ireton in particular, for their tyranny. In March 1649 he, together with Lilburne, Walwyn and Thomas Prince, was arrested and imprisoned. *The Baiting of the Great Bull of Bashan* (given here), was Overton's second attempt within a week to rally the London Levellers to their cause. The few events known in Overton's later life make clear his continued hostility to whatever government was in office. He supported Lilburne at his trial in 1653; two years later he was involved with Colonel Sexby in Flanders in a plot to overthrow Cromwell and restore Charles II. In 1659 he was again imprisoned; and in 1663 he was arrested for printing an attack on the Restoration Government.

Gerrard Winstanley was, for many years, the obscurest of the revolutionary writers represented here; but the tiny colony of Diggers that he and William Everard, formerly a soldier in the New Model Army, established on St George's Hill, near Cobham, Surrey, on 1 April 1649, has caught the imagination of many recent seventeenth-century scholars and students and there are now several editions of his numerous writings. Christopher Hill has claimed him as giving the world 'its first communist political programme' and as being 'the ultimate ancestor of the English labour and Cooperative movements';[29] others have seen in the inner light Winstanley early claimed the true beginning of the Quaker movement. Facts about his life come from his own writings. He was probably born in Wigan, Lancashire, in 1609, the son of a well-to-do Puritan weaver. He was sent to London in 1630 as a clothing apprentice; by 1637 had set up trade as a freeman of the Merchant Taylors Company; and he married in 1640. In 1643 he was bankrupt, 'beaten out of both estate and trade', as he put it,[30] and was herding cows as a hired labourer in or near Cobham, Surrey. After the dispersal of his second Digger colony on Cobham Heath, in April 1650, he was employed as steward of her estate by an eccentric landowner, Lady Eleanor Douglas, of Pirton, Hertfordshire, who claimed to be a prophetess. In 1657 he was back in Cobham, farming his father-in-law's land. He finally returned to London, became a corn-chandler in St Giles-in-the-Fields, and joined the Quakers. He died in 1676.[31]

Winstanley's first three pamphlets, of 1648, were both religious and radical. He had been a Baptist for a short time; but the ideas he puts forward, and the language he clothes them in, are equally unorthodox and strongly anti-clerical. He develops his own allegory: God is Reason and within every man; the Devil is covetousness and the owning of private property; Christ is freedom, 'the man that will turn the world upside down'; the poor will literally inherit God's kingdom on earth; Babylon is the old order which the oppressed must overthrow. 'The old world . . . is running up like parchment in the fire' (*The True Levellers' Standard Advanced*). This radical-religious conviction is the essential background to the Digger colony he set up and to the many later pamphlets, of which one is given here, he wrote in its support. In all of them he claimed that he was obeying a vision: 'Work together; eat bread together', a voice had said; 'the earth shall be made a common treasury of livelihood to whole mankind, without respect of persons'.

'True Levellers', Winstanley's small colony called themselves: the over-violent reaction of frightened surrounding property-owners is perhaps hardly surprising. In 1652 Winstanley published *The Law of Freedom in a Platform*, a constitution for a republic based on Digger ideals. It was dedicated to Cromwell; but no official reaction to it is known.

John Milton (1608–74) and James Harrington (1611–77) are the two most distinguished Republicans of the century; but there is little, if anything, of the revolutionary in Harrington's career. The eldest son of an ancient landed family, he was given a conventional upper-class education: Trinity College, Oxford, where he was a gentleman-commoner and took no degree; probably a brief period at the Middle Temple (perhaps the source of his later dislike of lawyers); extensive travel in Europe, where he came under the important influence of the Venetian Republic. He played no part in the First Civil War; but, after accompanying the Parliamentary Commissioners on their visit to the King in late 1646, he remained in attendance on him, as groom of the bedchamber, from May 1647 until his execution. There is no evidence to support John Aubrey's story that Harrington was with Charles on the scaffold; but it seems certain that he was personally devoted to him and suffered acutely at his death. It seems equally certain that, as J. G. A. Pocock argues,[32] it was the fall of the monarchy that made Harrington – as many others – a Republican.

Harrington published his most famous work, *The Commonwealth of Oceana*, a comprehensive and detailed account of his ideal Republic, dedicated to Cromwell, in 1656. Almost all his other works, mostly defending *Oceana*, were written and published within the next five years; *Valerius and Publicola* followed *Aphorisms Political* in late 1659. All show him a classical Republican, inspired by admiration for ancient Rome, but, like many of his contemporaries, almost equally impressed by contemporary Venice. Shortly before the Restoration, Harrington founded the Rota Club, ostensibly for political discussion. The Restoration Government clearly saw it as a centre of Commonwealth support; and in December 1661 Harrington was arrested and imprisoned, first in the Tower, then in Plymouth. His health deteriorating, he was allowed back to London, where he married. He wrote nothing more.

The Tenure of Kings and Magistrates was the first and most vehemently argued of Milton's three anti-monarchical tracts. Written almost certainly during the last two weeks of Charles's trial, 15–29 January 1649, it attacks a spate of Presbyterian pamphlets that had condemned the Army's action in bringing the King to judgment. But it does not judge Charles himself; rather, tyrannical kingship. It answers the Scripture quoted by the Presbyterians with Scripture; condemns the claim of divine right ('to say Kings are accountable to none but God, is the overturning of all Law and government'); draws on Aristotle's *Ethics* and *Politics* for its key distinction between true kingship and tyranny; and on the more revolutionary followers of Calvin (such as the Englishmen John Ponet and Christopher Goodman) for its central argument that a tyrant may lawfully be deposed and punished by the people, from whom his power is derived. Its ultimate basis is Milton's passionate belief in natural right. Its form is that of rhetorical discourse, working melodiously – and relentlessly – to its conclusions through long Ciceronian periods. Its success led directly to Milton's appointment as Secretary for Foreign Tongues to the new Government's Council of State on 15 March 1649. At the Restoration a copy was publicly burnt by the common hangman.

The Readie and Easie Way to Establish A Free Commonwealth was the last of eight pamphlets Milton published in the final, confused year of the Commonwealth when the Government was frequently changing hands. The second, much enlarged edition, given here, came out in April 1660 – within a few weeks of the Restoration: its publication an act of remarkable courage. It was Milton's last desperate attempt to perpetuate the Commonwealth Parliament, to shore up the *status quo*, however imperfect, against the return of the Stuarts. But however tied to circumstances, it preserves Milton's essential beliefs: above all, in religious liberty as the prerequisite for all other liberties. Politically, he sees the only chance now as an 'aristocratic' Commonwealth, with a supreme Council representing and responsible to the citizens; and for this he draws on many of the institutions used by Harrington in his *Oceana*: the Areopagus of Athens, the Roman Senate, the constitutions of Venice and the Netherlands – as well as *Oceana* itself. But by the end, as Milton envisages the return of monarchy, the betrayal of 'the Good Old Cause', the tone is disillusioned, almost despairing: like Jeremiah, he will have spoken only to trees and stones; and his words will have been (as he very shortly felt they *were*) 'the last words of our expiring libertie' (p. 229, below).

Political thought

The varying political thought of the writers within this volume is best appreciated in relation to the political thought to which it was opposed. It would be wrong to conclude that the ideas of those who were against the Parliamentarian cause were obviously unsatisfactory or obsolete. The political development of Europe in the next century and a half might suggest that royalist thought accorded better with historical realities than the views of a Milton or even a Parker.

The two great connected issues around which controversy circled were the question of the origin and character of monarchy, and the question of the right to resist the monarch. Let us first consider the question of monarchy.

'Political theory in the early seventeenth century was simple, patriarchal and authoritative.'[33] This judgment may be simplified but to a majority of intelligent people it probably made sense that a monarch should rule the State as a father governed his family and the providence of one God swayed the world. Further, since the peaceful accession of the House of Stuart in 1603 the value of a strictly hereditary monarchy, which under Elizabeth might have been questioned, seemed to have been vindicated. What is more, the original impact of the Reformation strengthened the authority of Protestant rulers from a religious point of view. Luther's repudiation of the Roman Church seemed to leave the ruler absolute under God. This concept was rapidly absorbed beyond the frontiers of Protestantism, and it has been memorably said that: 'Had there been no Luther there could never have been a Louis XIV.'[34] The notions of the divine right (that is of the divine commission) of kings, and of passive obedience (that is the duty of the subject not to resist even a ruler who commits ungodly acts), both gained force from Luther's teaching on Saint Paul, Romans XIII: 'Let every soul be subject unto the higher powers. For there is no power but of God: the powers that be are ordained of God. Whosoever therefore resisteth the power, resisteth the ordinance of God.'[35]

At a more theoretical level, the work of Jean Bodin, perhaps the greatest political thinker of the sixteenth century,[a] whose *Six Livres de la République* (*The six books of a Commonweale*) was published in 1576, was well-known.[36] Bodin's attempt to locate the source of sovereignty within the body politic, together with his penetrating survey of the polities of the ancient and modern world, led him to the view that legal hereditary monarchy was the highest form of government. For Bodin, the turning point of history was when Augustus transformed the Roman republic into a *de facto* monarchy.[37] Considerations concerning patriarchal authority, order in the State, and harmonic recurrence within history, strengthened his view. His thought, at first constitutionalist in bias, leaned towards

---

[a] Jean Bodin (?1529–96) might be called the great theorist of monarchy as Machiavelli is of republicanism. His thought has an astonishing range and boldness within and beyond the fields of history and political theory. Aside from his discussion of sovereignty within the State, his writings defend religious toleration, investigate demonology, explore natural science and attack slavery. His works were influential in England which he visited in 1581 with the Duc d'Alençon when the latter sought the Queen's hand in marriage. He discussed political theory with Elizabeth, but later predicted her overthrow, and seems to have known of the Babington Plot on behalf of the imprisoned Mary Queen of Scots. His chief works are: *Methodus ad Facilem Historiarum Cognitionem* (1566), *Six Livres de la République* (1576), *La Démonomanie des Sorciers* (1580), *Universae Naturae Theatrum* (1596) and *Colloquium Heptaplomeres* (1580; not published until 1857 but widely circulated in manuscript, one copy being possessed by Milton).

royal absolutism as the religious wars of sixteenth-century France tore the nation apart and threatened the throne with force of arms and theories of resistance.

In James I and VI England acquired a ruler who was a serious political author. In *The Trew Law of Free Monarchies* (1598) he had argued that the free monarch was God's lieutenant on earth, and that monarchy, as resembling the divinity, was the highest form of government, 'Unity being the perfection of all things'. He stressed the patriarchal care of monarchs over their subjects.[38] The establishment of kingship among the Jews in 1 Samuel VIII which to the modern reader as to Milton in *The Tenure of Kings and Magistrates* reads like a warning against monarchy, is construed by James as a divine injunction of obedience to kings even when they err.

Bodin had distinguished between three kinds of monarch: royal monarchs, lordly monarchs, and tyrants: the first legally inheriting their crown and ruling according to the laws of Nature and Nations; the second gaining their crown by conquest but ruling according to the laws of Nature and Nations; the third wrongfully acquiring their crown and violating the laws of Nature and Nations. Lordly monarchs, according to Bodin, might found royal monarchies. These distinctions bear on the idea of contract between monarch and people, for if it can be shown in the history of a kingdom that a society and laws existed before kingship was established, and if that kingship had not been specifically established by God as in the case of the Jews, then it was possible to argue that sovereignty lay originally in the people, was conferred only conditionally on kings, and could thus be revoked if the king violated the conditions of his authority: what Parker called 'the Tyranny of entrusted magistrates' (p. 45, below). James does not deny that some monarchies may have been contractual in origin, but points out that both the Scottish crown, and the English crown since William I, derive from conquest; thus that the laws which their kings observed were themselves granted by kings, and afforded no historical basis for thinking that the Scottish and English monarchies were contractual. Yet James's stress on the king's duty to rule according to the law of the land and the word of God does admit of a contract in a certain sense: it is entered into by the king at his coronation or accession when he promises 'to discharge honorably and trewly the office giuen him by God ouer them'.[39] But God only can properly judge the violation of this contract, and it is God's prerogative alone to punish the prince that is unfaithful.

If we take Parker as the first important Parliamentarian theoretician, then what originally divided Parliamentarian from Royalist was not Republic *versus* divine-right monarchy as described above. Parker supports a monarchy with a subordinate place in the constitution to that of Parliament. He argues that sovereignty originally resides in the people, and thus that the King of England and Scotland, like all monarchs, is a monarch on a contractual basis alone.[40] This position, challenged by James I in specifically historical terms, was one which several royalist thinkers during the Civil War period sought to deny. In the 1630s Royalist preachers recognised sovereignty in the King himself: while monarch and parliament should co-operate, parliaments were to assist the monarch in the discharge of his office, not to confer rights upon him. In certain circumstances the King would be justified in ruling from his own prerogative. Henry Parker complained that they preached 'an unlimited prerogative'; though they hardly denounced, as with some exaggeration he claimed, 'all law and liberty as injurious to Kings'.[41]

In the early years of the Civil War the defence of the royal cause had two aspects, each of which had had a place in the thought of James I and Bodin. Partly it was legal and historical, the territory of Clarendon, and argued that the monarchy was enshrined in the ancient constitution of the land, no precedent justifying the limitations upon regal power which Parliament had sought to impose between 1640 and 1642. 'Power', as Clarendon argued, 'was irrecoverably committed to His Majesty and his heirs for ever.' Partly the defence was theoretical and philosophical, arguing, as Henry Ferne and Dudley Digges argued,[a] that while in some respects regal prerogative might over the years have yielded to legal and Parliamentary limitation, there was in the King a clear residuum of sovereignty, 'co-ordinate with, and not subordinate to, the legislative power of the king-in-parliament.'[42] Theirs is a concept not of an absolute, nor of a contractual, but a legal divine-right monarchy.

Such arguments rest upon an historical analysis of the British monarchy. Those who argued for a contractual monarchy, as Parker did, or like Milton for a republic, based their case on the more

---

[a] Ferne's *The Resolving of Conscience* (1642) and Sir Dudley Digges's *Answer to a Printed Book* (Nov. 1642) were among the more significant replies to Parker. Haller has called them 'sentimental' and 'rational' respectively, Ferne's image of the King as natural father of his people anticipating the appeal of *Eikon Basiliké*, while Digges's use of the idea of social contract in defence of the Royalists looked forward in some ways to Hobbes's *Leviathan* (1651) (William Haller, ed. *Tracts on Liberty in the Puritan Revolution, 1638–1647*) (3 vols., New York, 1934), I, pp. 27–8).

ambitious Natural Law claim that mankind was originally free and that all government must therefore derive from the people. As Milton put it in *The Tenure of Kings and Magistrates*, 'No man who knows ought, can be so stupid to deny that all men naturally were borne free, being the image and resemblance of God himselfe' (p. 121, below). In the face of such claims arguments from the history of particular kingdoms were of little avail. Another recourse was to argue that the original contract was irrevocable, but it was the achievement of Sir Robert Filmer, the greatest royalist thinker of the Civil War period, to meet this challenge head-on. An incisive mind and master of a concise and direct prose style, Filmer produced his major work, the *Patriarcha*, in the 1630s (though it was not published until 1680) and drew on it for a series of topical tracts, Answers to Milton, Hobbes, Parker and others, published between 1648 and 1652. His last published work, *An Advertisment to the Jurymen of England* (1653), was an attack on the current witch-craze. Filmer met the concept of original natural freedom on the level, not of particular but of universal history, acknowledging, like his opponents, that the Bible was the fount of historical truth. Filmer argued that the Bible acknowledged no pre-contractual state, but spoke of the 'lordship which Adam by creation had over the whole world'. Political society always existed, for Adam was the first patriarch and families the first societies. 'And this subordination of children is the fountain of all regal authority.'[43] Shorn of its seventeenth-century and biblical garb, Filmer's argument is that man is born into obedience just as he finds himself, without consent, in society. The individual no more consents to be part of society than the child consents to be born. Subordination is the natural state, and Filmer challenges his opponents to say *when* and *how* there was ever a general meeting of a whole kingdom for the election of a prince. Nothing less than the consent of every member would do, for what would here be in question is the conscious yielding of an allegedly absolute natural freedom possessed by all.[44]

Filmer's argument against consent and original contract had several merits. It was universal in scope, simple in form, satisfied the demand for biblical authority and historical truth, and involved what must have seemed a plausible description of seventeenth-century society. Universal history and Natural Law were combined in it. Though radical in the sense of going back to first principles it was conservative in that it sought, with one blow, to destroy the chief theoretical foundation for attempts to resist the King or limit his authority.

Introduction

A consideration of the different concepts of monarchy has brought to the fore the chief basis upon which it was argued that subjects might resist their King: violation of original contract by the King and reassertion of inherent sovereignty by the people. This myth, or absolute presupposition, was doubtless literally believed in, as the urgency of what men wished to do, or found themselves doing, demanded rationalisation. The analogous myth of English liberty before the imposition of the Norman Yoke in 1066, which is both asserted and denied in the Army Debates (see below, p. 70), shows how much men longed to ground the justifying myth in historical fact – and this in turn may explain why Locke, in the *Two Treatises of Government* (1690) was reduced to attacking Filmer by ridicule. This justification for resistance was not, however, generated by the conflict between King and Parliament in the 1640s, nor was it the only ground. All the theories of resistance deployed in the English Civil War were developed in the religious wars of sixteenth-century Germany and France. It is to these that we must finally turn.

Though in *The Tenure of Kings and Magistrates* Milton cited Luther and Calvin as defenders of tyrannicide (pp. 116, 134, below), neither was originally concerned with the evolution of theories of resistance: quite the contrary. The major emphasis of their political thought is rather upon passive obedience. Nevertheless both great reformers, and their followers, moved towards justification of resistance as resurgent Roman Catholicism threatened war in Northern Europe. Two defences were worked out for the Protestant princes of Germany as the Emperor prepared to move against them: a constitutionalist argument, and a private law argument. In the following account we are much in debt to Quentin Skinner, *The Foundations of Modern Political Thought* (volume 2) Chapters 7 and 9. The first argued that Paul's reference to 'the powers that be' was not only to supreme powers, such as the Emperor, but also to subordinate powers, such as princes of the Empire, inferior magistrates, and others in public office, whose responsibility might itself sometimes entail an obligation to resist. The second argued that just as a private subject might in certain circumstances have recourse against an unjust judge, so the judicial capacity of the ruler might, if abused, occasion legitimate resistance. This argument was adopted by Luther in 1530.[45] Versions of these arguments were adopted by Calvinists in France; in England by John Ponet in *A Short Treatise of Politic Power* (1556) and Christopher Goodman in *How Superior Powers Ought to be Obeyed* (1558); in Scotland by John Knox in his

History of the Reformation in Scotland (first published in part, 1584). Without invoking notions of original contract or sovereignty of the people, each of these arguments rests on the recognition that the superior magistrate may possibly abuse his office, persecute his subjects and behave as a tyrant. The religious wars of later sixteenth-century France developed further arguments and the Huguenots soon advanced a more powerful and influential justification of resistance.

This was the Natural Law argument based on the assumption of the original freedom and sovereignty of the people which was so common in seventeenth-century England, and which Parker, Milton and the Levellers all used. It was deployed by Theodore Beza in his *The Right of Magistrates* (1574) and by Philippe Du Plessis Mornay in his *Defence of Liberty Against Tyrants* (1579). The argument is in fact Roman Catholic and medieval, and goes back to William of Occam, Jacques Almain, and the Conciliar Movement of the fourteenth century,[a] as was recognised by John Maxwell in *The Sacred and Royal Prerogative of Christian Kings* (1644). Filmer summarised its history in his usual trenchant fashion: 'This tenet was first hatched in the Schools for good Divinity, and hath been fostered by succeeding Papists. The Divines of the Reformed Churches have entertained it, and the common people everywhere embrace it as being most plausible to flesh and blood, for that it prodigally distributes a portion of liberty to the meanest of the multitude.'[46] Filmer's words from the *Patriarcha* recognised the latest development of the argument, for while the Huguenots, anxious not to afford any kind of justification for popular revolt, often combined the argument with that concerning the duties of subordinate magistrates, the Scottish Calvinist George Buchanan and the Spanish Jesuit Juan de Mariana cast the argument into forms more readily available to sanction social revolution. Buchanan turned to Cicero's *De Inventione* for a formulation of man's pre-contractual freedom, and in his *Right of the Kingdom in Scotland* (1579; written 1567–8) and *History of Scotland* (1582) argued that the people have the right to resist the government they have originally established, even individuals having the right to overthrow a tyrant. In *The King and the Education of the King* (1599)

---

[a] The Conciliar Movement of the twelfth and fourteenth centuries sought to subordinate the power of the Papacy to Councils of the Church. William of Occam (d.?1349), the great medieval schoolman, defended conciliar positions in his *Breviloquium de Potestate* (c. 1341) and *De Imperatorum Pontificum Potestate* (a late work), as did Jacques Almain (c. 1480–1515) in his *Libellus de Auctoritate Ecclesiae* (1512).

Mariana also argued that the people, and even an individual, had in the last analysis the right of tyrannicide.[47]

It is clear that Parker's *Observations* draws equally on the Huguenot Natural Law argument concerning the sovereignty of the people, and on the constitutionalist argument originally propounded by the Lutherans. His concern with the rôle of the subordinate magistrate comes out in his discussion of 'Ephors, Tribunes, Curatores' and it is clear that in Parker's view Parliament itself is the duly constituted 'inferior' power which has the duty to resist a superior power that has betrayed its trust.

Milton, in *The Tenure of Kings and Magistrates*, defending the actual execution of the King, immediately avails himself of all the most recent and powerful arguments for resistance when in his full title and opening paragraph he designates Charles a tyrant. It is not at all surprising to find him citing Knox and Buchanan, especially in connection with the deposition by the Scots of Mary 'thir lawful and hereditary Queen' (p. 134, below). Whether Charles I was a tyrant in a contemporary sense of the term it is perhaps hopeless to debate. Aristotle, while insisting that tyranny combined the vices of oligarchy and democracy, most tyrants beginning as demagogues, allowed that some tyrannies 'had their origin in the ambition of kings', who transgressed traditional limitations (*Politics*, v, x). *His Majesties Answer to the nineteen Propositions* said that 'The Ill of absolute Monarchy is Tyrannic.' Sixteenth-century justifications of resistance took their rise from religious conflict, and Luther was at one point persuaded to see the Emperor Charles V as a tyrant.[48] Beza and Du Plessis Mornay chiefly wished to justify resistance to idolatrous princes. If a prince who seeks to impose on his subjects an alien form of Christianity is a tyrant, then the Arminian Charles I was perhaps a tyrant in the eyes of some of his Calvinist subjects. A prince who makes war on his subjects seems to be a tyrant, though of course he appears in a different light if he is considered as attempting to put down a rebellion. Charles I was no tyrant according to Bodin's precise definition, but Parker spoke of the 'Tyranny of entrusted magistrates' and the general concept of tyranny is perhaps merely partisan. In 1642 Clarendon considered it tyrannous of Parliament to legislate without the royal consent: 'What is Tyrannie but to admit no Rule to Govern by, but their own wills.' Cromwell, who availed himself of Buchanan's and Mariana's justification of tyrannicide,[49] seemed a tyrant to some. As William Walwyn said in *The Bloody Project* (1648):—'all the quarell we have at this day in the Kingdome, is no other then a quarrel of

Interests, and Partyes, a pulling down of one Tyrant, to set up another, and instead of Liberty, heaping upon ourselves a greater slavery then that we fought against' – (p. 94, below).

Style

Most of the writers represented in this volume were writing political pamphlets, or debating crucial political issues, with an urgent purpose: to defend themselves and to attack their adversaries. The questions at issue were questions literally of life and death. Their concern was with the here-and-now; their hope, persuasion and instant action; their aim (in Marvell's words on Cromwell) to 'cast the Kingdom old / Into another mold.'[50] But they have, in addition, a remarkable literary self-consciousness, an absolute belief in the power of the written or spoken word.[51] Such self-consciousness creates a highly individual, at times unforgettable, style.

The three Levellers represented here, Walwyn, Lilburne and Overton, share an immediate political purpose, to wrest power from the Long Parliament and the Army and to give it to the people; their pamphlets have a common source in the coarse and railing pamphlets of the late sixteenth-century Puritan controversialist, 'Martin Marprelate'; but their styles work in very different ways. Walwyn is the least railing of the three; his argument for the ending of the War on the Levellers' terms is self-evident to himself, and should be to all men; he need only appeal to first principles, religious and ethical. His style mirrors that conviction: 'Besides, where is the man that would fight against the supream Authority, and a just Cause? and certainly there is none of you (whether Royalists, Presbyterians or Independents) so wicked as to desire to kill men without exceeding just grounds and upon the greatest necessity, it being the saddest work in the world' (p. 97, below).

Lilburne's style has been well examined by Joan Webber in *The Eloquent 'I'*.[52] In his frequently autobiographical pamphlets he is dramatic, often histrionic: the account of his trial in 1649, *The Trial of Lieut. Collonel John Lilburne*, reads like a dramatic performance. He is a natural rhetorician: 'I will set my hand to whatever I doe, and seale it with my blood.' He is also a patriot, a martyr, the oppressed leader with whom the people will identify themselves; the defender of 'the right, freedome, safety, and well-being of every particular man, woman, and child in England'. *Englands New Chains* is stating the Leveller case and therefore more argumentative; but the style, especially when he lashes the Council of State, is still concrete, physical, immediate. Words are the only weapons he has; and he uses them, his metaphors especially, with great effect: 'And thus after these fair blossoms of hopefull liberty, breaks forth this bitter fruit, of the vilest and basest bondage that ever English men groan'd under' (p. 110, below).

Overton's style may not be as overtly dramatic as Lilburne's; but his zest, energy, vituperation and sardonic wit make his best pamphlets still highly readable. He combines endless biblical allusions with a coarsely comic language that, as Margot Heinemann has suggested,[53] may well have had its roots in Jacobean city comedy. At times, indeed, he goes too far even for his Leveller readers; and in the pamphlet given here he tries to justify the language he had used of Cromwell as a bull baited by Leveller dogs in his previous pamphlet: 'Hold, hold, he hath caught him by the Gennitals, stave him off, give the Bull fair play. – A pox – they have burnt my Dog's mouth' (p. 257, below). He can also strike out a phrase that rings as true as anything in these passionate *credos* of the times: here, of his belief in the Leveller Cause: 'for truly to me it is as the life of my life; without it I'm nothing, with it I live'.

Milton, of course, is the most self-conscious, as well as much the greatest, of the writers represented here. The two pamphlets given have their own immediate political purposes, just as much as do those of the three Levellers. But comparison stops there. Throughout both of them, in both the argument and the style that handles it, we are constantly aware of the great poet making himself ready.

If Men within themselves would be govern'd by reason, and not generally give up their understanding to a double tyrannie, of custome from without, and blind affections within, they would discerne better what it is to favour and uphold the Tyrant of a Nation.

Thus much I should perhaps have said though I were sure I should have spoken only to trees and stones; and had none to cry to, but with the Prophet, *O earth, earth, earth!* to tell the very soil it self, what her perverse inhabitants are deaf to. (pp. 117 and 229, below)

The careful balancing of phrase and syntax within each of these passages – the first, the beginning of *The Tenure*, the second, the end of *The Readie and Easie Way* – the resonance of the periods, the quick establishment of a range of mood from barely concealed contempt to bitter despair, are all qualities that will come to ultimate fruition in *Paradise Lost*. Milton's rhetoric is consummately apt for the immediate subject of each of these pamphlets; it is also serving a more personal, complex and important purpose of Milton's own.

Winstanley stands rather apart. His pamphlets are essentially sermons, and they owe a great deal to Latimer and to the popular pulpit of the Reformation. The use of a highly personal allegory is the hallmark of his style; it is strengthened by the familiarity with the Bible he shared with the 'mechanick preachers', by his dramatic directness, and, above all, by his vehement sense of social injustice.

England is a Prison; the variety of subtilties in the Laws preserved by the Sword, are bolts, bars, and doors of the prison; the Lawyers are the Jaylors, and poor men are the prisoners; for let a man fall into the hand of any from the Bailiffe to the Judge, and he is either undone, or wearie of his life. (p. 163, below)

Here is Bunyan:

Then were these two poor men brought before their Examiners again, and there charged as being guilty of the late Hubbub that had been in the *fair*. So they beat them pitifully, and hanged Irons upon them, and led them in Chains up and down the *fair*, for an example and a terror to others. (*The Pilgrims Progress*)

Bunyan's vivid narrative has taken Winstanley's analogy several stages further; but the ring of Winstanley's prose – its mixture of simple speech and confident use of similitude – clearly points forward to the power of the much greater writer.

Parker's style is, as we should expect, that of a strongly secular lawyer: closely-argued, scrupulous, pragmatic, sometimes sardonic. His prose is largely in the modern, brief style, predominantly practical but gaining power as the war goes on. His scathing judgment of the King in 1642: 'this was the foolish sinne of *Rehoboam*, who having deserted and rejected out of an intolerable insolence, the strength of ten tribes, ridiculously sought to reduce them againe with the strength of two' (*Observations*, p. 39, below) is succeeded by the plainer indictment and fine sarcasm of: 'At this time the threed of the King's Counsels was exceeding finely spun, the more zealous He seemed against the *Irish* openly, the more zeal he attested to them privately' (*Scotland's Holy War* (1651), p. 4). The prose of this work is not only shaped and telling; its narrative of the First Civil War is imaginative and dramatic: 'Hitherto the King keeps from open defiance with the Parliament of *England*: but now Gods flaming Minister of Warre begins to brandish his sword against this Nation: now the King is returned from *Scotland*: and now begins the year 1642' (*ibid.*). The contemplation of sovereignty, the mystery of power and the nature of law always make his prose memorable. Sovereignty is, he says, 'as the mayne Ocean; of its vast abundance it feeds all, and is fed by all, as it is the fountain to enrich others, so it is the Cisterne to receive and require back againe all the riches of others'.[54] That is from an early pamphlet. Yet perhaps there is nothing in Parker to match the simplicity and compassion with which he writes about law in one of the central passages of the *Observations*:

Man being depraved by the fall of *Adam* grew so untame and uncivil a creature, that the Law of God written in his breast was not sufficient to restrain him from mischief . . . Without society men could not live, and without laws men could not be sociable, and without authority somewhere invested, to judge according to Law, and execute according to judgement, Law was a vain and void thing. (p. 45, below)

Harrington's admiration for Athens undoubtedly played a part in his choice of the Platonic dialogue for *Valerius and Publicola*; but he was attracted too by the comparative simplicity the form offered: 'There is nothing in this world, next the favour of God, I so much desire as to be familiarly understood', says Publicola (Harrington himself). The style of *Valerius and Publicola* is considerably simpler than that of *Oceana*: both its pointedness and its engaging clarity owe much to the dialogue form. This use of a new genre points again to the literary self-consciousness of these writers; and to the variety of forms in which their very different kinds of radicalism found full expression.

Letter from Cromwell to his brother-in-law, Colonel Valentine Walton, 5 July 1644

Written two days after the Battle of Marston Moor, to tell his brother-in-law of Parliament's victory; but principally to break the news of the death of his son Valentine and to condole with him. The letter is rightly famous for what it shows of Cromwell's directness and human sympathy as well as the fervent religious context in which he saw the Civil War.

Our text is that of W. C. Abbott, ed., *The Writings and Speeches of Oliver Cromwell* (Cambridge, Mass., 1937), I, pp. 287–8.

To Colonel Valentine Walton[a]

DEAR SIR,

It's our duty to sympathise in all mercies; that we may praise the Lord together in chastisements or trials, that so we may sorrow together.

Truly England and the Church of God hath had a great favour from the Lord, in this great victory given unto us, such as the like never was since this war began. It had all the evidences of an absolute victory obtained by the Lord's blessing upon the godly party principally. We never charged but we routed the enemy. The left wing, which I commanded, being our own horse, saving a few Scots in our rear,[b] beat all the Prince's[c] horse. God made them as stubble to our swords, we charged their regiments of foot with our horse, routed all we charged. The particulars I cannot relate now, but I believe, of twenty-thousand the Prince hath not four-thousand left.[d] Give glory, all the glory, to God.

Sir, God hath taken away your eldest son by a cannon-shot. It brake his leg. We were necessitated to have it cut off, whereof he died.

Sir, you know my trials this way;[e] but the Lord supported me

---

[a] Of Great Staughton, near Huntingdon; married to Cromwell's sister, Margaret.

[b] Cromwell has been accused of deliberately minimising the part played by David Leslie and his Scottish cavalry; but to describe the battle was not the true purpose of his letter.

[c] Prince Rupert. [d] Over 4,000 Royalists were killed, and at least 1,500 taken prisoner.

[e] Cromwell had lost two sons: Robert, his eldest, who had died as a schoolboy of 17 at Felsted; and Oliver, who had died of smallpox that spring, aged 21, at Newport Pagnell, while serving in the Army.

with this: that the Lord took him into the happiness we all pant after and live for. There is your precious child full of glory, to know sin nor sorrow any more. He was a gallant young man, exceeding gracious. God give you His comfort. Before his death he was so full of comfort that to Frank Russel[a] and myself he could not express it, it was so great above his pain. This he said to us. Indeed it was admirable. A little after, he said one thing lay upon his spirit. I asked him what it was. He told me that it was, that God had not suffered him to be no more the executioner of His enemies. At his fall, his horse being killed with the bullet, and as I am informed three horses more, I am told he bid them open to the right and left, that he might see the rogues run. Truly he was exceedingly beloved in the Army, of all that knew him. But few knew him, for he was a precious young man, fit for God. You have cause to bless the Lord. He is a glorious saint in Heaven, wherein you ought exceedingly to rejoice. Let this drink up your sorrow; seeing these are not feigned words to comfort you, but the thing is so real and undoubted a truth. You may do all things by the strength of Christ.[b] Seek that, and you shall easily bear your trial. Let this public mercy to the Church of God make you to forget your private sorrow. The Lord be your strength; so prays

Your truly faithful and loving brother,

July 5th, 1644.   OLIVER CROMWELL.

[P.S.] My love to your daughter, and to my Cousin Percevall, Sister Desbrowe[c] and all friends with you.

---

[a] Colonel Francis Russell, of Chippenham Hall, near Cambridge. Cromwell's son Henry later married his daughter Elizabeth.

[b] Cf. Philippians IV, 13.

[c] Jane Cromwell, married to John Desborough, now Cromwell's Quartermaster.

1. Henry Parker, 'Observations Upon Some of His Majesties Late Answers and Expresses', 1642

(second edition, corrected)

The first edition of Parker's tract was purchased by George Thomason the bookseller on 2 July 1642. A second edition appeared in the same year.

Parker's *Observations* reflects more fully than the other tracts in this volume the conflict between Crown and Parliament in the years before the Civil War. It was written to justify the Parliamentary position as it appeared to a supporter during that ominous period between the King's withdrawal from London to travel north, and the setting up of the royal standard in Nottingham which formally marked the outbreak of war. The *Observations* has its place in the prolonged 'contestation' of declarations and replies by which each side attempted to win the support of the political nation. The royal documents to which Parker chiefly refers are: *His Majesties Answer to a Book* (i.e. Parliament's Declaration of 19 May 1642); *His Majesties Answer, to a printed Book, intituled, A Remonstrance* ... (i.e. Parliament's Declaration of 26 May 1642); and *His Majesties Answer to the nineteen Propositions*. The last was drafted by Lord Falkland and Culpeper; the first two were written by Clarendon (*The Life of Clarendon ... Written by Himself*, Part II; B. H. G. Wormald, *Clarendon: Politics, History and Religion, 1640–1660* (Cambridge, 1951), pp. 111–12). Parker may thus be seen as in dialogue with the group of up-to-date intellectuals centred on Falkland's house at Great Tew, as well as with the King. The *Observations* has great importance in framing a theory of Parliamentary sovereignty; it lies behind the Army Debates and especially perhaps the contributions of Ireton; and it rapidly drew royalist attack. It has been described as 'perhaps the most influential pamphlet of the entire civil war' (Tuck, *Natural Rights Theories*, p. 146).

Parker reaches his bold conclusion that Parliament 'is indeed the State itself' (p. 56) by first arguing that 'Power is originally inherent in the people.' When fallen man found that 'the Law of God written in his brest was not sufficient to restrain him from mischief' his social existence could be upheld only by reasonable laws entrusted to a magistrate 'for the preventing of common injuries between subject and subject'. A contractual theory of government is thus grounded in the very existence of law, and 'God confirms that Law'. This enables Parker to argue that, at times of political crisis or breakdown, self-preservation and reason direct allegiance to that institution which most expresses *salus populi*.

Parker has no doubt that Parliament is this institution. He is quite untroubled by doubts as to its representativeness such as were to arise in the Army Debates five years later. While he makes heavy use of the age-old tactic of attacking the King's evil councillors, and goes on record as being 'as zealously addicted to Monarchy, as any man can, without dotage', he certainly supports a limited monarchy with a subordinate place in the constitution. In pressing his view Parker does not admit that

Parliament has introduced any innovation: in his view it is the King who in attempting innovation has betrayed the ancestral constitution. In consequence, Parker may expect civil war, but the last thing he wishes to do is to advocate it. Parliament, in his view, is on the defensive.

Our text is taken from the copy of the corrected second edition in the Cambridge University Library, compared with the facsimile reproduced by William Haller in *Tracts on Liberty in the Puritan Revolution*, I, pp. 165–213. In editing this relatively unfamiliar work, we have thought it right to modernise the spelling. Punctuation has been silently amended in a few cases where the sense demanded. Capitals have been retained save where they had no possible expressive significance. Four passages have been omitted and replaced by summaries.

In this contestation[a] between Regal and Parliamentary power, for method's sake it is requisite to consider first of Regal, then of Parliamentary Power, and in both to consider the efficient, and final causes, and the means by which they are supported. *The King attributeth the original of his royalty to God, and the Law, making no mention of the grant, consent, or trust of man therein,*[1] but the truth is, God is no more the author of Regal, than of Aristocratical power, nor of supreme, than of subordinate command; nay, that dominion which is usurped, and not just, yet whilst it remains dominion, and till it be legally again divested, refers to God, as to its Author and donor, as much as that which is hereditary. *And that Law which the King mentioneth, is not to be understood to be any special ordinance sent from heaven by the ministry of Angels or Prophets, (as amongst the Jews it sometimes was).* It can be nothing else amongst Christians but the Pactions[b] and agreements of such and such politic corporations. Power is originally inherent in the people,[2] and it is nothing else but that might and vigour which such and such a society of men contains in itself, and when by such or such a Law of common consent and agreement it is derived into such and such hands, God confirms that Law: and so man is the free and voluntary Author, the Law is the Instrument, and God is the establisher of both. And we see, not that Prince which is the most potent over his subjects, but that Prince which is most Potent in his subjects, is indeed most truly potent, for a King of one small City, if he be entrusted with a large Prerogative, may be said to be more Potent over his subjects, than a King of many great Regions, whose prerogative is more limited; and yet in true reality of power, that King is most great and glorious, which hath the most and strongest subjects, and not he which tramples upon the most contemptible vassals. This is there-

[a] A contest chiefly of public argument and military preparation. King Charles had not yet raised his standard, the legally recognised way of opening formal hostilities. This he did on 22 Aug. 1642.
[b] Bargains.

fore a great and fond error in some Princes to strive more to be great over their people, than in their people, and to eclipse themselves by impoverishing, rather than to magnify themselves by enfranchising their Subjects. This we see in France at this day,[3] for were the Peasants there more free, they would be more rich and magnanimous, and were they so, their King were more puissant; but now by affecting an aldulterate power over his Subjects, the King there loses a true power in his Subjects, embracing a cloud instead of *Juno*.[4] But thus we see that power is but secondary and derivative in Princes, the fountain and efficient cause is the people, and from hence the inference is just, the King, though he be *singulis Major*,[a] yet he is *universis minor*,[b] for if the people be the true efficient cause of power, it is a rule in nature *quicquid efficit tale, est magis tale*.[c] And hence it appears that at the founding of authorities, when the consent of societies conveys rule into such and such hands, it may ordain what conditions, and prefix what bounds it pleases, and that no dissolution ought to be thereof, but by the same power by which it had its constitution.

As for the final cause of Regal Authority, I do not find anything in the King's papers denying, that the same people is the final, which is the efficient cause of it, and indeed it were strange if the people in subjecting itself to command, should aim at anything but its own good in the first and last place. 'Tis true according to Machiavelli's politics,[6] *Princes ought to aim at greatness, not in, but over their Subjects, and for the achieving of the same, they ought to propose to themselves, no greater good than the spoiling and breaking the spirits of their Subjects, nor no greater mischief, than common freedom, neither ought they to promote and cherish any servants but such as are most fit for rapine and oppression, nor depress and prosecute any as enemies, but such as are gracious with the populace for noble and gallant Acts.*

To be *deliciae humani generis*[d] is grown sordid with Princes, to be public torments and carnificines,[e] and to plot against those Subjects whom by nature they ought to protect, is held *Caesar*-like, and therefore bloody *Borgias* by mere cruelty and treachery hath gotten room in the Calendar of witty, and of spirited Heroes.[7] And our English Court of late years has drunk too much of this State poison, for either we have seen favourites raised to poll the people, and razed again to pacify the people;[8] or else (which is worse for King and people too) we have seen engines or mischief preserved against the

---

[a] Greater than each single man.   [b] Less than the collective body.
[c] Whatever has produced something is greater than that thing.[5]
[d] The delights of the human race.   [e] Executioners.

people, and upheld against Law, merely that mischief might not
want encouragement. *But our King here, doth acknowledge it the great
business of his coronation oath to protect us*:[9] And I hope under this
word *protect*, he intends not only to shield us from all kind of evil,
but to promote us also to all kind of Political happiness according to
his utmost devoir,[a] and I hope he holds himself bound thereunto,
not only by his oath, but also by his very Office, and by the end of
his sovereign dignity. And though all single persons ought to look
upon the late Bills[10] passed by the King as matters of Grace with all
thankfulness and humility, yet the King himself looking upon the
whole State, ought to acknowledge that he cannot merit of it, and
that whatsoever he hath granted, if it be for the prosperity of his
people (but much more for their ease) it hath proceeded but from
his mere duty. If Ship money, if the Star Chamber, if the High
Commission, if the Votes of Bishops and Popish Lords in the upper
House,[11] be inconsistent with the welfare of the Kingdom, not only
honour but justice itself challenges that they be abolished; the King
ought not to account that a profit or strength to him, which is a loss
and wasting to the people, nor ought he to think that perished to
him which is gained to the people: The word grace sounds better in
the people's mouths than in his, his dignity was erected to preserve
the Commonalty, the Commonalty was not created for his service:
and that which is the end is far more honourable and valuable in
nature and policy, than that which is the means. This directs us then
to the transcendent ἀκμή of all Politics,[b] to the Paramount Law that
shall give Law to all human Laws whatsoever, and that is *Salus
Populi*:[c] The Law of Prerogative[d] itself, it is subservient to this Law,
and were it not conducing thereunto, it were not necessary nor
expedient. Neither can the right of conquest[13] be pleaded to acquit
Princes of that which is due to the people as the Authors, or ends of
all power, for mere force cannot alter the course of nature, or
frustrate the tenor of Law, and if it could, there were more reason,
why the people might justify force to regain due liberty, than the
Prince might to subvert the same. And 'tis a shameful stupidity in
any man to think that our Ancestors did not fight more nobly for
their free customs and Laws, of which the conqueror and his
successors had in part disinherited them[14] by violence and perjury,
than they which put them to such conflicts, for it seems unnatural to
me that any nation should be bound to contribute its own inherent
puissance, merely to abet Tyranny, and support slavery: and to

---

[a] Duty.   [b] High point, essence of politics.   [c] The well-being of the people.[12]
[d] I.e. the Royal Prerogative.

make that which is more excellent, a prey to that which is of less worth. And questionless a native Prince, if mere Force be right, may disfranchise his Subjects as well as a stranger, if he can frame a sufficient party, and yet we see this was the foolish sin of *Rehoboam*,[15] who having deserted and rejected out of an intolerable insolence, the strength of ten tribes, ridiculously sought to reduce them again with the strength of two. I come now from the cause, which conveys Royalty, and that for which it is conveyed, to the nature of the conveyance. The word *Trust* is frequent in the King's Papers, and therefore I conceive the King does admit that his interest in the Crown is not absolute, or by a mere donation of the people, but in part conditionate and fiduciary. And indeed all good Princes without any express contract betwixt them and their Subjects, have acknowledged that there did lie a great and high trust upon them; nay Heathen Princes that have been absolute, have acknowledged themselves servants to the public, and born for that service, and professed that they would manage the public weal, as being well satisfied *populi Rem esse, non suam*.[a] And we cannot imagine in the fury of war, (when laws have the least vigour) that any *Generalissimo* can be so uncircumscribed in power, but that if he should turn his Canons upon his own Soldiers, they were *ipso facto* absolved of all obedience, and of all oaths and ties of allegiance whatsoever for that time, and bound by higher duty, to seek their own preservation by resistance and defence: wherefore if there be such tacit trusts and reservations in all public commands, though of the most absolute nature, that can be supposed, we cannot but admit, that in all well formed monarchies, where kingly Prerogative has any limits set, this must needs be one necessary condition, that the subject shall live both safe and free. The Charter of nature entitles all Subjects of all Countries whatsoever to safety by its Supreme Law. But freedom indeed has diverse degrees of latitude, and all Countries therein do not participate alike, but positive Laws must everywhere assign those degrees.

The great Charter of England[16] is not strait in Privileges to us, neither is the King's oath of small strength to that Charter for that though it be more precise in the care of Canonical Privileges,[b] and of Bishops and Clergymen (as having been penned by Popish Bishops) than of the Commonalty, yet it confirms all Laws and rightful customs, amongst which we most highly esteem Parliamentary Privileges; and as for the word *Eligerit*,[c] whether it be

---

[a] To belong to the people rather than being autonomous.   [b] I.e. pertaining to the Church.
[c] It has chosen/will choose: a crucial word from the Coronation Oath, referring in a debatable way to the will of the people.[17]

future, or past, it skills not much; for if by this oath, Law, Justice and discretion be executed amongst us in all judgements (as well in, as out of Parliament) and if peace and godly agreement be entirely kept amongst us all, and if the King defend and uphold all our laws and customs, we need not fear but the King is bound to consent to new Laws if they be necessary, as well as defend old: for both being of the same necessity, the public trust must needs equally extend to both; and we conceive it one Parliamentary right and custom, that nothing necessary ought to be denied. And the word *Eligerit*, if it be in the *perfect tense*, yet shows that the people's election had been the ground of ancient Laws and customs, and why the people's election in Parliament should not be now of as great moment as ever, I cannot discover.

That which results then from hence, is, if our Kings receive all royalty from the people and for the behoof of the people, and that by a special trust of safety and liberty expressly by the people limited, and by their own grants and oaths ratified, then our Kings cannot be said to have so unconditionate and high a propriety in all our lives, liberties and possessions, or in anything else to the Crown appertaining, as we have in their dignity, or in ourselves, and indeed if they had, they were not born for the people, but merely for themselves, neither were it lawful or natural for them to expose their lives and fortunes for their Country, as they have been hitherto bound to do, according to that of our Saviour, *Bonus Pastor ponit vitam pro ovibus.*[a] But now of Parliaments: Parliaments have the same efficient cause as monarchies, if not higher, for in the truth, the whole Kingdom is not so properly the Author as the essence itself of Parliaments, and by the former rule 'tis *magis tale*,[b] because we see *ipsum quid quod efficit tale.*[c] And it is I think beyond all controversy, that God and the Law operate as the same causes, both in Kings and Parliaments, for God favours both, and the Law establishes both, and the act of men still concurs in the sustentation of both. And not to stay longer upon this, Parliaments have also the same final cause as Monarchies, if not greater, for indeed public safety and liberty could not be so effectually provided for by Monarchs till Parliaments were constituted, for the supplying of all defects in that Government.[18]

[In the next four paragraphs, here omitted, Parker argues that Parliaments have been 'lessened and injured' during the course of

[a] The good shepherd cares for the life of his sheep.   [b] The more so.
[c] This it is which creates something.

English history, and considers Edward I and Elizabeth in this connection.]

And though all Monarchies are not subject to the same conditions, yet there scarce is any Monarchy but is subject to some conditions, and I think to the most absolute Empire in the world this condition is most natural and necessary, That the safety of the people is to be valued above any right of his, as much as the end is to be preferred before the means; it is not just nor possible for any nation so to enslave itself, and to resign its own interest to the will of one Lord, as that that Lord may destroy it without injury, and yet to have no right to preserve itself: For since all natural power is in those which obey, they which contract to obey to their own ruin, or having so contracted, they which esteem such a contract before their own preservation are felonious to themselves, and rebellious to nature.[19]

The people then having entrusted their protection into the King's hands irrevocably, yet have not left that trust without all manner of limits, some things they have reserved to themselves out of Parliament, and something in Parliament, and this reservation is not at all inconsistent with the Prince's trust, though he desire to violate the same; but on the contrary, it is very aiding and strengthening to that trust, so far as the Prince seeks to perform it, for the people's good; but it is objected, that a temporary power ought not to be greater than that which is lasting and unalterable, if this were so, the Romans had done unpoliticly, in creating Dictators, when any great extremity assailed them, and yet we know it was very prosperous to them, sometimes to change the form of government; neither always living under circumscribed Consuls, nor yet under uncircumscribed Dictators: but it is further objected, that if we allow the Lords and Commons *to be more than Counsellors, we make them Commanders and Controllers, and this is not suitable to Royalty.*[20] We say here, that to consent is more than to counsel, and yet not always so much as to command and control; for in inferior Courts,[a] the Judges are so Counsellors for the King, as that the King may not countermand their judgements, and yet it were an harsh thing to say, that they are therefore Guardians and Controllers of the King: and in Parliament, where the Lords and Commons represent the whole Kingdom, (to whom so great a Majesty is due) and sit in a far higher capacity than inferior Judges do, being vested with a right both to counsel and consent, the case is far stronger; and as we ought not to conceive, that they will either counsel or consent to anything, but what is

---

[a] Ordinary lawcourts, considered as subordinate to the supreme court of Parliament itself.

publicly advantageous; so by such Counsel and consent, we cannot imagine the King limited or lessened: for if it was by so known a Law, and so wisely established in *Edward* the first's days, the right of the people to be summoned at *tractandum, ordinandum, faciendum, approbandum*,ᵃ in all things appertaining to the people, and this as then was not prejudicial to the King, why should the King's Writ now abbreviate or annul the same? If the King himself be disable for many high matters, till consent in Parliament add vigour to him, it cannot be supposed that he comes thither merely to hear Counsel, or that when he is more than counselled, that it is any derogation, but rather a supply of virtue to him. A fourth thing alleged to the derogation of Parliaments is, *That whatsoever the right of Parliaments is to assemble or treat in all cases of a public nature, yet without the King's concurrence and consent,*[22] *they are lifeless conventions without all virtue and power, the very name of Parliament is not due to them.* This allegation at one blow confounds all Parliaments, and subjects us to as unbounded a regiment of the King's mere will, as any Nation under Heaven ever suffered under. For by the same reason, that Parliaments are thus virtueless and void Courts, upon the King's desertion of them, other Courts must needs be the like, and then what remains, but that our laws, rights, and liberties, be either nowhere at all determinable, or else only in the King's breast? We contend not merely about the name Parliament, for the same thing was before that name, and therefore the intent is, that the great Assembly of the Lords and Commons do not represent and appear in the right of the whole Kingdom, or else that there is no honour, nor power, nor judicature, residing in that great and Majestical Body, than which, scarce anything can be more unnatural. But these divisions between the King and Parliament, and betwixt the Parliament and Kingdom, seeming more uncouth, 'tis attempted to divide further between part and part in Parliament, so making the major part not fully concluding, and in the major part, between a faction misleading, and a party misled. Such excellent Masters of division has *Machiavel's* rule[23] (*divide and impera*) made since the 3 of *November* 1640.[24] 'Tis a wonderful thing, that the King's Papers being freighted scarce with anything else but such doctrines of division, tending all to the subversion of our ancient fundamental constitutions which support all our ancient liberties, and to the erection of arbitrary rule, should find such applause in the world: but we say further, that there is manifest difference

---

ᵃ Drawing up, ordering, making and approving.[21]

between deserting, and being deserted: if the wife leave her husband's bed, and become an adulteress, 'tis good reason that she lose her dowry, and the reputation of a wife; but if the husband will causelessly reject her, 'tis great injustice that she should suffer any detriment thereby, or be dismissed of any privilege whatsoever. So if the King have parted from his Parliament,[25] merely because they sought His oppression, and he had no other means to withstand their tyranny, let this proclaim them a void Assembly: but if ill Counsel have withdrawn him, for this wicked end merely, that they might defeat this Parliament, and derogate from the fundamental rights of all Parliaments (as His Papers seem to express) under colour of charging some few factious persons in this Parliament, (God forbid) that this should disable them from saving themselves and the whole state, or from seeking justice against their enemies. So much of the Subjects' right in Parliament.

Now of that right which the Parliament may do the King by Counsel; if the King could be more wisely or faithfully advised by any other Court, or if His single judgement were to be preferred before all advice whatsoever, 'twere not only vain, but extremely inconvenient, that the whole Kingdom should be troubled to make Elections, and that the parties elected should attend the public business; but little need to be said, I think every man's heart tells him, that in public Consultations, the many eyes of so many choice Gentlemen out of all parts, see more than fewer, and the great interest the Parliament has in common justice and tranquillity, and the few private ends they can have to deprave them, must needs render their Counsel more faithful, impartial, and religious, than any other. That dislike which the Court has ever conceived against Parliaments, without all dispute is a most pregnant proof of the integrity, and salubrity of that public advice, and is no disparagement thereof; for we have ever found enmity and antipathy betwixt the Court and the country, but never any till now betwixt the Representatives, and the Body, of the Kingdom represented. And were we not now, those dregs of human race upon whom the unhappy ends of the world are fallen, Calumny and Envy herself would never have attempted, to obtrude upon us such impossible charges of Treason and Rebellion against our most sacred Counsel, from the mouths of Popish, Prelatical, and Military Courtiers.

The King says; *'Tis improbable and impossible that His Cabinet Counsellors, or his Bishops or soldiers, who must have so great a share in the misery, should take such pains in the procuring thereof, and spend so much time, and run so many hazards to make themselves slaves, and to ruin the freedom of this Nation*: how strange is this? We have had almost 40 years experience, that the Court way of preferment has been by doing public ill Offices, and we can nominate what Dukes, what Earls, what Lords, what Knights, have been made great and rich by base disservices to the State: and except Master *Hollis* his rich Widow,[26] I never heard that promotion came to any man by serving in Parliament: but I have heard of trouble and imprisonment. But now see the traverse of fortune; The Court is now turned honest, my Lord of *Strafford's* death[27] has wrought a sudden conversion amongst them, and there is no other fear now, but that a few Hypocrites in Parliament will beguile the major part there, and to usurp over King, Kingdom, and Parliament for ever; sure this is next to a prodigy, if it be not one: but let us consider the Lords and Commons as mere Counsellors without any power or right of Counselling or consenting, yet we shall see if they be not less knowing and faithful than other men, they ought not to be deserted, unless we will allow that the King may choose whither he will admit of any counsel at all or no, in the disposing of our lives, lands, and liberties. But the King says, *that he is not bound to renounce his own understanding, or to contradict his own conscience for any Counsellor's sake whatsoever*. 'Tis granted in things visible and certain, that judge which is a sole judge and has competent power to see his own judgement executed, ought not to determine against the light of nature, or evidence of fact.

The sin of *Pilate* was, that when he might have saved our Saviour from an unjust death, yet upon accusations contradictory in themselves, contrary to strange Revelations from Heaven, he would suffer Innocence to fall, and pass sentence of death, merely to satisfy a blood-thirsty multitude. But otherwise it was in my Lord of *Strafford's* case, for there the King was not sole Judge, nay, he was incapable of sitting as judge at all, and the delinquent was legally condemned,[28] and such heinous matters had been proved against him, that his greatest friends were ashamed to justify them, and all impartial men of three whole Kingdoms conceived them mortal; and therefore the King might therein, with a clear conscience have signed a warrant for his death, though he had dissented from the judgement. So if one judge on the same bench, dissent from three, or one juror at the bar from an eleven, they may submit to the major number, though perhaps less skilful then themselves without imputation of guilt: and if it be thus in matters of Law, *a fortiore*, 'tis so in matters of State, where the very satisfying of a multitude sometimes in things not otherwise expedient, may prove not only expedient, but necessary for the settling of peace, and ceasing of strife. For example: It was the request of the whole Kingdom in the Parliament to the King, to entrust the *Militia*, and the Magazine of *Hull*,[29] etc. into such hands as were in the people's good esteem. Conscience and understanding could plead nothing against this, and if it could have been averred (as it could not, for the contrary was true) that this would have bred disturbance, and have been the occasion of greater danger, yet where the people by public authority will seek any inconvenience to themselves, and the King is not so much intressed[a] in it as themselves, 'tis more inconvenience and injustice to deny than grant it: what blame is it then in Princes when they will pretend reluctance of conscience and reason in things behoveful for the people? and will use their fiduciary power in denying just things, as if they might lawfully do whatsoever they have power to do, when the contrary is the truth, and they have no power to do but what is lawful and fit to be done. So much for the ends of Parliamentary power. I come now to the true nature of it, public consent: we see consent as well as counsel is requisite and due in Parliament and that being the proper foundation of all power (for *omnis Potestas fundata est in voluntate*[b]) we cannot imagine that public consent should be anywhere more vigorous or more orderly than it is in Parliament. Man being depraved by the fall of *Adam* grew so untame and uncivil a creature, that the Law of God written in his breast was not sufficient to restrain him from mischief, or to make him sociable, and therefore without some magistracy to provide new orders, and to judge of old, and to execute according to justice, no society could be upheld. Without society men could not live,[30] and without laws men could not be sociable, and without authority somewhere invested, to judge according to Law, and execute according to judgement, Law was a vain and void thing. It was soon therefore provided that laws agreeable to the dictates of reason should be ratified by common consent, and that the execution and interpretation of those Laws should be entrusted to some magistrate, for the preventing of common injuries betwixt Subject and Subject, but when it after appeared that man was yet subject to unnatural destruction, by the Tyranny of entrusted magistrates, a mischief almost as fatal as to be without all magistracy, how to provide a wholesome remedy therefore, was not so easy to be invented. 'Twas not difficult to invent Laws, for the limiting of supreme governors, but to invent how those Laws should be

[a] Concerned.   [b] All power is founded on will.

executed or by whom interpreted, was almost impossible, *nam quis custodiat ipsos custodes*;[a] To place a superior above a supreme, was held unnatural, yet what a lifeless fond thing would Law be, without any judge to determine it, or power to enforce it; and how could human consociation be preserved, without some such Law? Besides, if it be agreed upon, that limits should be prefixed to Princes, and judges appointed to decree according to those limits, yet another great inconvenience will presently affront us; for we cannot restrain Princes too far, but we shall disable them from some good, as well as inhibit them from some evil, and to be disabled from doing good in some things, may be as mischievous, as to be enabled for all evils at mere discretion. Long it was ere the world could extricate itself out of all these extremities, or find out an orderly means whereby to avoid the danger of unbounded prerogative on this hand, and too excessive liberty on the other: and scarce has long experience yet fully satisfied the minds of all men in it. In the infancy of the world, when man was not so artificial and obdurate in cruelty and oppression as now, and when policy was more rude, most Nations did choose rather to submit themselves to the mere discretion of their Lords, than to rely upon any limits: and to be ruled by Arbitrary edicts, than written Statutes. But since, Tyranny being grown more exquisite, and policy more perfect, (especially in Countries where Learning and Religion flourish) few Nations will endure that thraldom which uses to accompany unbounded and unconditionate royalty. Yet long it was ere the bounds and conditions of supreme Lords were so wisely determined or quietly conserved as now they are, for at first when *Ephori, Tribuni, Curatores etc.*[b] were erected to poise against the scale of Sovereignty, much blood was shed about them, and, states were put into new broils by them, and in some places the remedy proved worse than the disease. In all great distresses the body of the people was ever constrained to rise, and by the force of a Major party to put an end to all intestine strifes, and make a redress of all public grievances, but many times calamities grew to a strange height, before so cumbersome a body could be raised; and when it was raised, the motions of it were so distracted and irregular, that after much spoil and effusion of blood, sometimes only one Tyranny was exchanged for another: till some way was invented to regulate the motions of the people's moliminous[c] body, I think arbitrary rule was most safe for the world, but now since most Countries have

---

[a] For who should govern the governors?[31] [b] Magistrates and guardians of the state.[32]
[c] Striving with difficulty, cumbersome.

found out an Art and peaceable Order for Public Assemblies, whereby the people may assume its own power to do itself right without disturbance to itself, or injury to Princes, he is very unjust that will oppose this Art and order. That Princes may not be now beyond all limits and Laws, nor yet left to be tried upon those limits and Laws by any private parties, the whole community in its underived Majesty shall convene to do justice, and that this convention may not be without intelligence, certain times and places and forms shall be appointed for its reglement, and that the vastness of its own bulk may not breed confusion: by virtue of election and representation, a few shall act for many, the wise shall consent for the simple, the virtue of all shall redound to some, and the prudence of some shall redound to all. And sure, as this admirably composed Court which is now called a Parliament, is more regularly and orderly formed, then when it was called the mickle Synod, or Witenagenot,[a] or when this real body of the people did throng together at it: so it is not yet perhaps without some defects, which by art and policy might receive further amendment, some divisions have been sprung of late between both Houses, and some between the King and both Houses, by reason of the uncertainty of jurisdiction; and some Lawyers doubt how far the Parliament is able to create new forms and precedents; and has a jurisdiction over itself. All these doubts would be solemnly solved. But in the first place, the true Privileges of Parliaments, not only belonging to the being and efficacy of it, but to the honour also and complement of it, would be clearly declared: for the very naming of Privileges of Parliament, as if they were Chimeras to the ignoranter sort, and utterly unknown to the learned, hath been entertained with scorn since the beginning of this Parliament.[33] The virtue of representation hath been denied to the Commons, and a severance has been made betwixt the parties chosen and the parties choosing, and so that great Privilege of all Privileges, that unmoveable Basis of all honour and power, whereby the House of Commons claims the entire right of all the Gentry and Commonalty of *England*, has been attempted to be shaken and disturbed. Most of our late distempers and obstructions in Parliament have proceeded from this: that the people upon causeless defamation and unproved accusations have been so prone to withdraw themselves from their representatives, and yet there can be nothing under Heaven, next to renouncing God, which can be more perfidious and more pernicious in the people than this.

[a] National council or assembly.

Having now premised these things, I come to the main difficulties lying at this time in dispute before us. It is left unquestioned that the legislative power of this Kingdom is partly in the King, and partly in the Kingdom, and that in ordinary cases, when it concerns not the saving of the people from some great danger or inconvenience, neither the King can make a general binding Law or Ordinance without the Parliament, or the Parliament without the King, and this is by a known Maxim, *Non recurrendum est ad extraordinaria etc.*[a]

It ought to be also as unquestioned, that where this ordinary course cannot be taken for the preventing of public mischiefs, any extraordinary course that is for that purpose the most effectual, may justly be taken and executed by the most transcendent over-ruling *Primum Mobile* of all human Laws; if the King will not join with the people, the people may without disloyalty save themselves, and if the people should be so unnatural as to oppose their own preservation, the King might use all possible means for their safety. Yet this seems to be denied by the King, *for he sets forth Proclamations and cites Statutes in them to prove, that the power of levying arms and forces is solely in him,*[34] and he presses them indefinitely, not leaving to the Subject any right at all of rising in arms, though for their own necessary defence, except he joins his consent and Authority: In the same manner also, he so assumes to himself a share in the legislative power, as without his concurrence the Lords and Commons have no right at all to make any temporary orders putting the Kingdom into a posture of defence, in what public distress soever: And therefore in Sir *John Hotham's* case, he doth not only charge him of Treason, for observing the Parliament's instructions and Commissions in a pretended danger, but he pronounceth the mere act Treason, let the circumstances be what they will. Let the world judge whether this be not contrary to the clearest beams of human reason, and the strongest inclinations of nature, for every private man may defend himself by force, if assaulted, though by the force of a Magistrate or his own father,[35] and though he be not without all confidence by flight, etc. yet here whole nations being exposed to enmity and hazard, being utterly uncapable of flight, must yield their throats and submit to Assassinates, if their King will not allow them defence.

See if this be not contrary to the original, end, and trust of all power and Law, and whether it do not open a gap to as vast and arbitrary a prerogative as the Grand Signor[36] has, and whether this be not the main ground of all those bitter invectives almost which are

[a] Not reverting to the exceptional case.

iterated and enforced with so much eloquence in all the King's late papers. See if we are not left as a prey to the same bloody hands as have done such diabolical exploits in *Ireland*,[37] or to any others which can persuade the King that the Parliament is not well affected to him, if we may not take up arms for our own safety, or if it be possible for us to take up arms, without some Votes or ordinances to regulate the *Militia*, or to make our defence manly, and not bestial and void of all Counsel; the name of a King is great I confess, and worthy of great honour, but it not the name of people greater? Let not mere terms deceive us, let us weigh names and things together, admit that God sheds here some rays of Majesty upon his vicegerents on earth,[38] yet except we think he doth this out of particular love to Princes themselves, and not to communities of men, we must not hence invert the course of nature, and make nations subordinate in end to Princes. My Lord of *Strafford* says that the Law of Prerogative is like that of the first Table,[a] but the Law of Common safety and utility like that of the second, and hence concludes, that precedence is to be given to that which is more sacred, (that is) Regal Prerogative. Upon this ground all Parasites build when they seek to hoodwink Princes for their own advantages, and when they assay to draw that esteem to themselves, which they withdraw from the people: and this doctrine is common, because 'tis so acceptable: for as nothing is more pleasant to Princes than to be deified, so nothing is more gainful to Courtiers than so to please. But to look into terms a little more narrower, and dispel umbrages; *Princes are called Gods, Fathers, Husbands, Lords, Heads, etc.*[39] *and this implies them to be of more worth and more unsubordinate in end, than their Subjects are, who by the same relation must stand as Creatures, Children, Wives, Servants, Members, etc.* I answer, these terms do illustrate some excellency in Princes by way of similitude, but must not in all things be applied, and they are most truly applied to Subjects, taken *divisim*, but not *conjunctim*:[b] Kings are Gods to particular men, *secundum quid*,[c] and are sanctified with some of God's royalty; but it is not for themselves, it is for an extrinsical end, and that is the prosperity of God's people, and that end is more sacred than the means; as to themselves they are most unlike God, for God cannot be obliged by any thing extrinsical, no created thing whatsoever can be of sufficient value or excellency to impose any duty or tie upon God, as Subjects upon Princes: therefore granting Prerogative to be but mediate, and the Weal

---

[a] I.e. the First Table of the Law. [b] Separately but not collectively.
[c] A second thing.

Public to be final, we must rank the Laws of liberty in the first Table, and Prerogative in the second, as Nature doth require; and not after a kind of blasphemy ascribe that unsubordination to Princes, which is only due to God; so the King is a Father to his People, taken singly, but not universally; for the father is more worthy than the son in nature, and the son is wholly a debtor to the father, and can by no merit transcend his duty, nor challenge any thing as due from his father; for the father doth all his offices meritoriously, freely, and unexactedly. Yet this holds not in the relation betwixt King and Subject, for it's more due in policy, and more strictly to be challenged, that the King should make happy the People, than the People make glorious the King. This same reason is also in relation of Husband, Lord, etc. for the wife is inferior in nature, and was created for the assistance of man, and servants are hired for their Lord's mere attendance; but it is otherwise in the State betwixt man and man, for that civil difference which is for civil ends, and those ends are, that wrong and violence may be repressed by one for the good of all, not that servility and drudgery may be imposed upon all, for the pomp of one. So the head naturally doth not more depend upon the body,[40] than that does upon the head, both head and members must live and die together; but it is otherwise with the Head Political, for that receives more subsistence from the body than it gives, and being subservient to that, it has no being when that is dissolved, and that may be preserved after its dissolution.

[In the following paragraph, here omitted, Parker trenchantly repeats the above conclusions, and once again links the concept of monarchy which he is denouncing with Machiavelli: 'the Florentines wretched Politics'.]

I will now suppose the danger of the Commonwealth uncertain: the King says; the Parliament denies; the King commands, the Parliament forbids: The King says the Parliament is seduced by a traitorous faction; the Parliament says the King is seduced by a Malignant Party: the King says the Parliament tramples upon his crown; the Parliament says the King intends War upon them: to whether now is the Subject bound to adhere? I will not insist much upon general presumptions, though they are of moment in this case: for without all question 'tis more likely, that Princes may err and have sinister ends, than such general conventions of the Nobility, Gentry, and Commonalty so instituted, and regulated as ours are in England. The King does highly admire *the ancient, equal, happy, well poised and never enough commended constitution of this Government, which hath made this Kingdom, so many years both famous and happy, to a great degree of envy, and amongst the rest, our Courts of Parliament: and therein more especially, that power which is legally placed in both Houses, more than sufficient* (as he says) *to prevent and restrain the power of Tyranny;*[41] But how can this be? If the King may at His pleasure take away the being of Parliament merely by dissent, if they can do nothing but what pleases Him, or some Clandestine Counsellors, and if upon any attempt to do anything else, they shall be called Traitors, and without further arraignment, or legal proceeding, be deserted by the Kingdom whose representations they are, what is there remaining to Parliaments? Are they not more servile than other inferior Courts; nay, are they not in a worse condition than the meanest Subject out of Parliament? And how shall they restrain tyranny, when they have no subsistence at all themselves; nay, nor no benefit of Justice, but arbitrary. Surely if these principles hold, they will be made the very Engines and Scaffolds whereby to erect a government more tyrannical than ever was known in any other Kingdom, we have long groaned for them, but we are likely now to groan under them: but you will say, the King *hath a power of dissent, he may use it at his pleasure, if he have none, then he is a mere Cypher, and the Parliament may tyrannise at pleasure: either the one or the other must be predominant, or else by a mutual opposition all must perish; and why not the King predominant rather than the Parliament?* We had a maxim, and it was grounded upon Nature, and never till this Parliament withstood, that a community can have no private ends to mislead it, and make it injurious to itself, and no age will furnish us with one story of any Parliament freely elected, and held, that ever did injure a whole Kingdom, or exercise any tyranny, nor is there any possibility how it should. The King may safely leave his highest rights to Parliaments, for none knows better, or affects more the sweetness of this so well-balanced a Monarchy than they do, and it hath been often in their power under great provocations to load that rule with greater fetters and clogs, but they would not. Let us mark but the nature, the right, the power, the wisdom, the justice, of Parliaments, and we shall find no cause to suspect them, of such unmatchable treasons and conspiracies as are this day, and never was before charged upon them; for our Chronicles makes it apparent, that there is scarce any other Nation wherein Monarchy has been more abused by rash inconsiderate Princes, than in this, nor none at all wherein it hath been more inviolably adored, and loyally preserved from all diminution, I wish it were not some incitement to those execrable Instruments, which steal the King's heart from us, that they think the Religion of Protestants too tame, and the Nation of the English too insensible of injuries; but I hope God will the more tenderly resent these things. The composition of Parliaments, I say, takes away all jealousies, for it is so equally, and geometrically proportionable, and all the States do so orderly contribute their due parts therein, that no one can be of any extreme predominance,[42] the multitude loves Monarchy better than Aristocracy, and the Nobility and Gentry prefer it as much beyond Democracy, and we see the multitude hath only a representative influence, so that they are not likely to sway, and yet some influence they have, and that enough to preserve themselves from being overswayed. We also in England have not a Nobility and Gentry so independent and potent as in France, Germany, Denmark, etc. Nor as they were here immediately after the Conquest, by reason of their great Feoffes,[a] whereby to give Laws either to the Crown, or the people; but they stand at such fair and comely distances between the King and people, and also between themselves, *that they serve for an excellent Screen and bank* (as the King's words are) *to assist both King and people against the encroachments of each other.*[43] And as the middle Region of the air treats loving offices betwixt heaven and earth, restraining the fumes and exhalations of Sea and Land, that they ascend not too high, and at the same instant, allaying that restless Planet's scorching flames, which else might prove insufferable to the lower Elements: So doth both Houses of Parliament, as peaceably and sweetly arbitrate betwixt the Prince and his poorest Vassals, and declining Tyranny on the one side, and Ochlocracy[b] on the other, preserving entire to the King the honour of His Sceptre, and to the people the patrimony of freedom. Let us not then seek to corrupt this purity of composition, or conceive that both Gentry and Nobility can combine against the King, when they have no power but derivative, the one more depending upon the King, and the other upon the people, but both most excellently to affect the good of the whole, and to prevent the exorbitance of any one part. Next, the right of all the Lords and Commons in this State is so great, that no change of government can be advantage to them in that temporary capacity, except they could each one obtain an hereditary Crown, which is a thing utterly impossible. Next, their power is merely derivative, so that except we will conceive that both

[a] Freehold estate in land granted in trust. [b] Mob rule.

King and people will be consenting to the usurpation, nothing can be done; and if we conceive that they may by fraud gain their consent, nothing can withstand them. Lastly, their wisdom hath been ever held unquestionable, and their justice inviolable, no Prince that ever cast himself thereupon was defrauded, no Prince that ever declined the same, proved prosperous. In sum, Parliamentary government being used as Physic, not diet by the intermission of due spaces of time, has in it all that is excellent in all forms of Government whatsoever. If the King be an affector of true liberty, he has in Parliament a power as extensive as ever the Roman Dictator's was, for the preventing of all public distresses. If the King be apt to intrude upon the common liberties, the people have hereby many Democratical advantages to preserve themselves. If War be, here is the Unitive virtue of Monarchy to encounter it, here is the admirable Counsel of Aristocracy to manage it. If Peace be, here is the industry and courage of democracy to improve it. Let us now see how Kings usually govern without Parliaments, especially such as are ruled by Counsel averse from Parliaments. I need not speak of France, and other Countries, where together with these general Assemblies, all liberty is fallen to the ground;[44] I need not travel further then our stories, nay, I need not pass beyond our own Times, my discourse will be endless if I do.

[Having brought his central argument to its climax Parker embarks, in sections here omitted, upon an aggressive analysis of the present political situation, distinguishing the nature of the resistance to the King shown by the Scottish Covenanters in 1638–9, the Irish Rebellion in 1641, and the actions of Sir John Hotham at Hull in 1642. 'Let not all resistance to Princes be under one notion confounded', he declares, and draws an extended comparison between Charles I and Richard II in order to show that those who seem to oppose the King may be doing so in the King's and the nation's best interest. The public advice of Parliament is always wiser and more loyal than the private advice of special counsellors.]

The main body of the difference being thus stated, I come now to the observations of some other several objections against this Parliament, and exceptions taken against arbitrary power in all Paliaments, and I shall observe no order, but consider them as I find them, either dispersed or recollected in the King's late Expresses.

The Parliament being complained against for undutiful usage to the King above all former Parliaments, hath said, *that if they should make the highest precedents of other Parliaments their pattern, there would be no cause to complain of want of modesty and duty.*

The King, because some Parliaments formerly have deposed Kings, applies these words to those Precedents, but it may justly be denied that free Parliaments did ever truly consent to the dethroning of any King of England, for that Act whereby *Richard* the second was deposed, was rather the Act of *Henry* the fourth, and his victorious Army, than of the whole Kingdom.

The Parliament is taxed of reproaching this King's government, to render him odious to his subjects, whereas indeed all the miscarriages and grievous oppressions of former times are solely imputed to the ill Ministers and Counsellors of the King, *And all the misfortunes of these times since November, 1640*[45] *are imputed to the blame of the Parliament*: the King's words to the Parliament are, *That the condition of his Subjects when it was at worst under his government was by many degrees more pleasant and happy than this to which the Parliament's furious pretence of reformation hath brought them to.* In this case the Parliament being accused of so heinous crimes, did unjustly betray themselves, if they should not lay the blame upon the King's evil Counsellors, the only enemies and interrupters of Parliaments. Nevertheless the King takes this as a way of the Parliament to let them into their frank expressions of him and his actions, and takes all things spoken against his ministers, as spoken against himself; how miserable here is the condition of the Parliament, either they must sink under unjust charges, or be censured for the reproachers of their king, nay they are undutiful, if they tell not the King himself, that he ought not to onerate himself[a] with the blame of his Counsellors.

The Parliament, because it could obtain no equal Justice from the Court-Cavaliers, who are conceived to be the first movers of those stirs and tumults[46] which happened at *Westminster*, did reserve the hearing of some of the contrary side itself; upon this it is objected, *that the Parliament incited those seditious; and protected the actors in it*, whereas they desire Justice yet, and that both sides may be brought fairly to an equal hearing, and before such hearing they desire that no parties may be condemned.

And whereas the Parliament, upon those rude commotions, are condemned as unheard, and of that which is unproved, and never can be proved, *That they levied War upon the King, and drove him away*, yet they desire that the mere imputation may not draw any

---

[a] Burden himself, take on the responsibility.

further opposition to their proceedings, and the necessities of the State; for if the King could not stay at *London* with safety, yet being now at *York* in safety, he may concur with the advice of his Parliament; the distance of the place needs not cause any distance of affection, since the King conceives *He hath so few enemies, and assures himself of so many friends in Parliament.*

The Parliament says, *That none of its Members may be apprehended in case of suspicion, where no information or witnesses appear, to make good the Prosecution, without acquainting the Parliament, if leave may be conveniently obtained.* In opposition to this a case is put, *Of a Parliament-man that rides from* York *to* London, *and takes a purse by the way,*[47] the Parliament doth not privilege Robberies so done; for though no such thing be likely ever to be done, yet if it be, in that case, the evidence of the fact in that instant, allows not only the apprehending, but the causal killing of such a Robber: Who sees not many differences betwixt such a case, and that of the five Members of the lower House,[48] where neither Witnesses, nor Informers, nor Relaters, nor any particularity of crime could be produced? And yet by the same act the whole House might have been surprised: And all the world knows, that the impeached Members still suffer by the Charge, and yet can obtain no right against any Informers, though it be now converted to their disadvantage.

The Parliament does not deny the King a true real Interest in any thing held by him, either *in jure Coronae, or in jure Personae,*[a] yet merely[b] it affirms, That in the same thing the State hath an Interest Paramount in cases of public extremity; by virtue of which it may justly seize, and use the same for its own necessary preservation. Hereupon, the King replies, *That this utterly abolishes His Interest in all things, so that by this device, He is made incapable, either of suffering wrong, or receiving right*: a strange violented wrested conclusion; and yet the King's Interest in *Hull*, and in the lives of his subjects, is not such an Interest as in other moveables, neither is the King's Interest taken away from him; the same things are still reserved for him, in better hands than he would have put them. The Parliament maintains its own Counsel to be of honour and power above all other, and when it is unjustly rejected, by a King seduced, and abused by private flatterers, to the danger of the Commonwealth, it assumes a right to judge of that danger, and to prevent it: the King

---

[a] By right of the crown or by right of the person.
[b] Our text reads: 'merely because', thus making incomplete sense. The omission of the word may serve to clarify Parker's broad argument.

says, *That this gives them an arbitrary unlimitable power to unsettle the security of all men's estates, and that they are seduceable, and may abuse this power, nay they have abused it*; and he cites the Anabaptists in *Germany*,[49] and the 30 Tyrants at *Athens*.[50] That there is an Arbitrary power in every State somewhere 'tis true, 'tis necessary, and no inconvenience follows upon it; every man has an absolute power over himself; but because no man can hate himself, this power is not dangerous, nor need to be restrained: So every State has an Arbitrary power over itself, and there is no danger in it for the same reason. If the State entrusts this to one man, or few, there may be danger in it; but the Parliament is neither one nor few, it is indeed the State itself;[51] it is no good consequence, though the King makes so much use of it, that the Parliament doth abuse power, because it may: The King would think it hard that we should conclude so against him, and yet the King challenges a greater power than Parliaments: and indeed if the Parliament may not save the Kingdom without the King, the King may destroy the Kingdom in despite of the Parliament; and who[a] then challenges that which is most Arbitrary, and of most danger? But the King says, *This Parliament has abused their power.* (I wish Kings had never abused theirs more.) And the Parliament answers, *That this is but his nude averment,*[b] *and in controversies that ought not to condemn private men; much less ought Parliaments to fall under it.* And as for *Mr Hooker*,[52] he does not say, that the Anabaptists in *Germany* did deceive Parliaments with their hypocrisy, and therefore infer that Parliaments ought no further to be trusted: the stirs of the Anabaptists in *Germany* conclude no more against Parliaments, than the impostures of *Mahomet* in *Arabia* do. *And as for the 30 Tyrants of Athens*, we know they were not so chosen by the people, as our Knights, Citizens, and Burgesses are, nor created or called by any King's Writ, as our Peers are; nor did they so merely depend upon their own good abearing, and the good liking both of King and State, as our Lords and Commons now do; neither had they so many equals and Rivals as both our Houses contain; we know their power was not founded upon the consent of the Citizens, but the strength of their Soldiers; neither were their Soldiers such as our Train Bands, but mere mercenaries of desperate, or perhaps no Fortunes, whose Revenue was rapine, whose Trade was murder: I fear they were more like our Cavaliers at *York*, than the *Militia* at *London*: Were our

---

[a] Our text reads 'whether'. We have conjecturally amended to 'who' in the hope of restoring Parker's sense.
[b] Unsupported statement.

new *Militia* any other than our old Train Bands, or our new Lieutenants, and Deputies, any other than the same Lords and Gentlemen, with very little variation, which before were very well reputed of, both by King and Commons, and not yet by either excepted against, or did the whole fate of the kingdom depend merely upon the new *Militia*, this new device of an *Aristocracy*[a] might seem the more plausible; but as things now stand, this new *Aristocratical* Fabric cannot seem to any impartial man, but as empty a shadow, and airy a dream as ever man's fancy abused itself withal.

[Parker now proceeds, in further omitted sections, to meet other royalist objections: 'May anything be taken from a man, because he is trusted with it?'; 'Is the Law itself subject to your Votes?'; 'a case is put of the Irish Rebels, making themselves a major part in Parliament, and so voting against the true Religion'; that the King cannot perform his oaths of protecting his people if he abandon his power of appointing the great officers of State: 'That should he pass this, He should retain nothing but the Ceremonious Ensigns of Royalty . . . the outside, the picture, the sign of a King.' To all these objections Parker argues that 'the *Venetians* live more happily under their conditionate Duke, than the *Turks* do under their most absolute Emperors' and instances the success of the United Provinces against Spain under 'a General much limited' (i.e. the Prince of Orange).]

I speak not this in favour of any alteration in *England*, I am as zealously addicted to Monarchy, as any man can, without dotage: but I know there are several degrees of Prerogatives Royal, some whereof have greater power of protection, and less of oppression; and such I desire to be most studious of: In some things I know 'tis dangerous to circumscribe Princes, but in others there may be great danger in leaving them to their pleasure, and scarce any hope at all of benefit; and amongst other things, the choice of public Officers, if the State have (at least) some share therein with the King, what considerable inconvenience can happen thereby to the State or King, is not in me to foresee: but if it have no share, experience sufficient teacheth us what great disasters may happen. And so for the diffusing and dissolving of Parliaments; if the Parliament divide some part of that power with the King, I see great good, but no harm at all that can ensue, either to weaken the Crown, or disturb

---

[a] By implementing the Militia Bill without royal assent Parliament seemed to be ignoring the ancient constitution of the State as a kingdom, and assuming (if then Parliament were the State itself) an Aristocracy.

the subject thereby. But it will be said in the next place, *If this disables not the King from protecting the Subject, yet it diminishes his own Right, and leaves him but the shadow of Royalty.* This is grounded upon a great mistake; for some men think it a glorious thing to be able to kill, as well as to save, and to have a kind of a Creator's power over Subjects: but the truth is, such power procures much danger to ill Princes, and little good to any; for it begets not so much love as fear in the subject, though it be not abused; and the fear of the subject does not give so perfect a Dominion as love. Were *Hannibal*,[53] *Scipio*,[54] etc. the less honoured or beloved because they were not independent? Surely no, they were the less feared, and for the same cause the more honoured and beloved. Or were *Alexander*,[55] *Pyrrhus*,[56] etc. the more honoured or beloved, because they were independent? I believe the contrary, and that they had lived more gloriously, and died less violently, if a more moderate power had rendered them less insolent in their own thoughts, and less feared in other men's. Was *Caesar* the private man less successful in his Wars, or less dear in all his soldiers' eyes, or less powerful in his Country-men's affections, than *Caesar* the perpetual Dictator? No, if the Imperial Throne of the World added anything to *Caesar*, 'twas not excellence, nor true glory, 'twas but the external complements of pomp and ostentation, and that might perhaps blow up his mind with vanity, and fill the people with jealousy; it could not make *Caesar* a nobler, gallanter, greater *Caesar* than he was. I expect no less than to be laughed at at Court, and to be held the author of a strange paradox, by those men which stick not to say, that our King is now no more King of *Scotland*,[57] than he is King of *France*, because his mere pleasure there, is not so predominant in all cases of good and evil whatsoever: but I regard not those fond things which cannot see in human nature what is depraved in it, and what not, and what proceeds from vain, and what from true glory; and wherein the natural perfection of power and honour, differs from the painted rays of spurious Majesty and Magnificence. To me the Policy of *Scotland* seems more exquisite in point of prerogative, than any other in *Europe*, except ours: And if the splendour, and puissance of a Prince consist in commanding religious, wise, magnanimous, warlike subjects, I think the King of *Scotland* is more to be admired than the King of *France*; and that he is so, to the mere ingenuity of Government, I ascribe it. But some will allow, *That to follow the pattern of* Antoninus[58] *freely, and voluntarily, as he did, is not dishonourable in a Prince; but to be under any Obligation or Law to do so, is ignoble.* And this is as much as to say, that Law, though Good, yet *quatenus*ᵃ Law is burdenous to man's nature; and though it be so but to corrupted nature, inasmuch as it restrains from nothing, but that which nature in its purity would itself restrain from; yet corrupted nature itself is to be soothed and observed. I have done with this point: 'twas spoken in honour of *Henry 7* that he governed his subjects by his Laws, his Laws, by his Lawyers, and (it might have been added) his subjects, Laws and Lawyers by advice of Parliament, by the regulation of that Court which gave life and birth to all Laws. In this Policy is comprised the whole art of Sovereignty; for where the people are subject to the Law of the Land and not to the will of the Prince, and where the Law is left to the interpretation of sworn upright Judges, and not violated by power; and where Parliaments superintend all, and in all extraordinary cases, especially betwixt the King and Kingdom, do the faithful Offices of Umpirage, all things remain in such harmony, as I shall recommend to all good Princes.

The Parliament conceives that the King cannot apprehend any just fear from Sir *John Hotham*, or interpret the mere shutting of *Hull* gates, and the sending away of Arms and Ammunition in obedience to both Houses, to be any preparation for War and Invasion against him at *York*, and therefore they resolve to raise Forces against those Forces which the King raises to secure himself from Sir *John Hotham*. *The King hereupon charges the Parliament of levying War against Him, under pretence of His levying War against them.*⁵⁹ This is matter of fact and the World must judge whether the King's preparations in the North be only suitable to the danger of Sir *John Hothan* or no; and whether the Parliament be in danger of the King's strength there or no: Or whether is more probable at this time, that the King is incensed against the Parliament, or the Parliament against the King: or that the King is more intentive to assail the Parliament, or the Parliament the King. 'Tis true, the King abjures any intention of making War against his Parliament; but what he intends against the malignant party in or out of Parliament, is not expressed: and the King abjures invasive War against them; but whether he thinks not himself first invaded already, is not expressed; and the specifying of a faction in Parliament of some few malignants, secures none; for none can plead force, and none ought to plead folly in Treasons of this nature, and the major part of the Houses can neither plead absence or dissent; and those which can, must not be their own purgators. Besides, the act of Sir *John*

ᵃ To the extent that.

Hotham is disputable; the King adjudges it Treason, the Parliament adjudge it no Treason; and the King has not declared whether he will refer this to the trial of the sword only, or to some other trial; and if so, to what kind of trial the judgement of a Parliament shall be submitted: If we call another Parliament to judge of this, so we may appeal in *infinitum*; and why another should be clearer than this, we cannot imagine: If we could constitute a higher Court for this appeal, so we might do in *infinitum* also; but we know no higher can be imagined: and if we appeal to a lower, that were to invert the course of nature: and to confound all Parliaments for ever; if we call all the Kingdom to judge of this, we do the same thing as to proclaim Civil War, and to blow the Trumpet of general confusion: And if we allow the King to be the sole, supreme competent Judge in this case, we resign all into his hands, we give lives, liberties, Laws, Parliaments, all to be held at mere discretion? For there is in the interpretation of Law upon the last appeal, the same supremacy of power requisite, as is in making it; and therefore grant the King supreme interpreter, and 'tis all one, as if we granted him to be supreme maker of Law; and grant him this, and we grant him to be above all limits, all conditions, all human bonds whatsoever. In this Intricacy therefore, where the King and Parliament disagree, and judgement must be supreme, either in the one or other, we must retire to ordinary justice, and there we see, if the King consent not with the ordinary Judge, the Law thinks it fit, that the King subscribe, rather than the Judge.

And if this satisfy not, we must retire to the principles of Nature, and there search, whether the King or Kingdom be to be looked upon as the efficient, and final cause, and as the proper Subject of all power. Neither is the oath of supremacy endangered hereby; for he that ascribes more to the whole universality, than to King; yet ascribes to the King a true supremacy of power, and honour above all particulars: Nor is our allegiance temerated,[a] for when the Judge on the Bench delivers Law contrary to the King's command; this is not the same thing, as to proceed against the King's person, upon any judgement given against him. The King as to His own person, is not to be forcibly repelled in any ill doing, nor is He accountable for ill done, Law has only a directive, but no coactive force upon his person; but in all irregular acts where no personal force is, Kings may be disobeyed, their unjust commands may be neglected, not only by communities, but also by single men sometimes. Those men therefore that maintain, that all Kings are in all things and com-

[a] Brought into contempt.

mands (as well where personal resistance accompanies, as not) to be obeyed, as being like Gods, unlimitable, and as well in evil, as in good unquestionable, are sordid flatterers. And those which allow no limits but directive only, and those no other but divine and natural; and so make all Princes as vast in power as the Turk,[60] (for He is subject to the directive force of God, and nature's Laws); and so allow subjects a dry right without all remedy, are almost as stupid as the former. And those lastly, that allow human Laws to oblige Kings more than directively, in all cases where personal violence is absence, and yet allow no Judges of those Laws, but the King Himself, run into absurdities as gross as the former.

I come now to those seven doctrines, and positions, which the King by way of recapitulation lays open as so offensive – And they run thus:

1. *That the Parliament has an absolute indisputable power of declaring Law, so that all the right of the King and people, depends upon their pleasure.* It has been answered, That this power must rest in them, or in the King, or in some inferior Court, or else all suits must be endless, and it can nowhere rest more safely than in Parliament.

2. *That Parliaments are bound to no precedents.* Statutes are not binding to them, why then should precedents? Yet there is no obligation stronger than the Justice and Honour of a Parliament.

3. *That they are Parliaments, and may judge of public necessity without the King, and dispose of anything.* They may not desert the King, but being deserted by the King, when the Kingdome is in distress, They may judge of that distress, and relieve it, and are to be accounted by the virtue of representation, as the whole body of the State.

4. *That no Member of Parliament ought to be troubled for treason, etc. without leave.* This is intended of suspicions only, and when leave may be seasonably had, and when competent accusers appear not in the impeachment.

5. *That the Sovereign power resides in both Houses of Parliament, the King having no negative voice.*[61] This power is not claimed as ordinary; nor to any purpose, But to save the Kingdom from ruin, and in case where the King is so seduced, as that He prefers dangerous men, and prosecutes His loyal Subjects.

6. *That levying forces against the personal commands of the King, (though accompanied with his presence) is not levying war against the King: But war against His authority, though not person, is war against the King?* If this were not so, the Parliament seeing a seduced King, ruining Himself and the Kingdom, could not save both, but must stand and look on.

7. *That according to some Parliaments, they may depose the King?*
'Tis denied, That any King was deposed by a free Parliament fairly
elected.

To stand in comparison with these, I shall recite some such
positions as the King's papers offer to us; And they follow thus.

1. *That regal power is so derived from God and the Law, as that it has
no dependence upon the trust, and consent of man; and the King is
accountable therefore to God and His other Kingdoms, not to this; and it
is above the determination of Parliaments, and by consequence bound-
lesss.*

2. *That the King is supreme indefinitely,* viz. *as well* universis, *as*
singulis.[a]

3. *That the King has such a propriety[b] in His Subjects, Towns, Forts,
etc. as is above the propriety of the State, and not to be seized by the
Parliament, though for the public safety.*

4. *That so far as the King is trusted, He is not accountable how He
performs,* **So that in all cases the Subject is remediless.**

5. *That the being of Parliaments is merely of grace, so that the King
might justly have discontinued them, and being summoned, they are
limited by the writ, and that* ad consilium[c] *only, and that but in*
quibusdam arduis,[d] *And if they pass the limits of the Writ, they may be
imprisoned. That if the King desert them, they are a void assembly, and
no honour due to them, nor power to save the Kingdom; That Parliamentary privileges are nowhere to be read of, and so their representation of this whole Kingdom is no privilege, nor adds no Majesty, nor
authority to them. That the major part in Parliament is not considerable,
when so many are absent, or dissent. That the major part is no major
part, because the fraud, and forces of some few overrules them. That
Parliaments may do dishonourable things, nay treasonable: Nay, That
this hath been so blinded by some few malignants, That they have abetted
treason in Sir* John Hotham, *trampled upon all Law, and the King's
prerogative, And sought to enslave the whole Kingdom under the
Tyranny of Some few, And sought the betraying of Church, and State,
And to effect the same erected an upstart Authority in the New* Militia,
*and levied war upon the King, under pretence that He levies war upon
them. That Parliaments cannot declare Law, but in such and such
particular cases legally brought before them. That Parliaments are
questionable, and tryable elsewhere.*

These things, we all see, tend not only to the desolation of this
Parliament, but to the confusion of all other, and to the advancing

---

[a] As much over everything as particular things.   [b] I.e. property.   [c] For advice.
[d] In whatever is difficult.[62]

of the King to a higher power over Parliaments, than ever He had before over inferior Courts. Parliaments have hitherto been Sanctuaries to the people, and banks against Arbitrary tyranny; but now the mere breath of the King, blasts them in an instant; and how shall they hereafter secure us, when they cannot now secure themselves? Or how can we expect justice, when the mere imputation of treason, without hearing, trial, or judgment, shall sweep away a whole Parliament; nay all Parliaments for ever? And yet this is not yet the depth of our misery, for that private Counsel which the King now adheres to, and prefers before Parliaments, will still enforce upon our understandings, That all these doctrines, and positions tend to the perfection of Parliaments; and all the King's forces in the North, to the protection of Law and liberty. I find my Reason already captivated, I cannot further –

FINIS

2. *Extracts from the Army Debates, October 1647*

In June and July 1645 the royal armies were defeated by Cromwell at Naseby and Langport. Soon after, the Presbyterian royalist Montrose was beaten at Philiphaugh. The King gave himself up to the Scots who, finding they could come to no agreement with him, handed him over to the English Parliament. They too failed to secure a settlement from the defeated but determined monarch. Meanwhile distrust between Parliament and Army, and between the Army leaders and its more radical officers, was growing. The regiments began to elect their own representatives, named Agents or Agitators, in March 1647, and in June a General Council of the Army was formed to attempt to contain them and prevent a split in the Parliamentary forces. The Agitators were included, but balanced by two officers from each regiment, and by the Army leadership. Both the leadership and the Agitators may have been behind the capture of the King by the Army in the same month. Cromwell and Ireton now attempted to reach a settlement with the King based on *The Heads of the Proposals*, a document drawn up by Ireton. This approach was endorsed by the Army Council on 16 September in Putney, despite fierce attack from Colonel Rainborough, an eloquent and highly placed defender of Leveller views. Growing alarm in the Army caused the election of new Agitators who issued a manifesto, *The Case of the Army truly stated*. These are the events in the immediate background of the Army Debates held in Putney Parish Church on 28, 29 October and 1 November 1647, which were another attempt to keep the Army united. (Further Army Debates of which record has survived, ostensibly on religious issues, were held at Whitehall on 14 December 1648 and 13 January 1649. These are not represented in the present volume.)

The text of the following extracts is derived from the Clarke MSS. in Worcester College, Oxford. They were not printed until 1891–1901. They have been helpfully edited, with a wealth of comparative material, by A. S. P. Woodhouse in *Puritanism and Liberty, Being the Army Debates (1647–49)*. His text (with his expansions of the recorder's many abbreviations) is used here.

The debate was opened by Cromwell on 28 October. The Agitator Sexby said that Cromwell had desired to know 'the bottom' of the Agitators' desires. In response he had come to present *The Case of the Army*. 'We have been by providence put upon strange things, such as the ancientest here doth scarce remember. The Army acting to these ends, Providence hath been with us, and yet we have found little fruit of our endeavours.'

Cromwell: I hope we know God better than to make appearances of religious meetings covers for designs or for insinuation amongst you.[1] I desire that God, that hath given us some sincerity, will own us according to his own goodness and that sincerity that he hath given us. I dare be confident to speak it, that design that hath been amongst us hitherto is to seek the guidance of God, and to recover that presence of God that seems to withdraw from us. And to accomplish that work which may be for the good of the kingdom is our end. But it seems as much to us in this as anything, we are not all of a mind. And for our parts we do not desire or offer you to be with us in our seeking of God further than your own satisfactions lead you, but only that against to-morrow in the afternoon (which will be designed for the consideration of these businesses with you) you will do what you may to have so many as you shall think fit, to see what God will direct you to say to us, that whilst we are going one way, and you another, we be not both destroyed. This requires guidance from the Spirit. It may be too soon to say it, yet 'tis my present apprehension: I had rather we should devolve our strength to you than that the kingdom for our division should suffer loss. For that's in all our hearts, to profess above anything that's worldly, the public good of the people; and if that be in our hearts truly and nakedly, I am confident it is a principle that will stand. Perhaps God may unite us and carry us both one way. And therefore I do desire you, that against to-morrow in the afternoon, if you judge it meet, you will come to us to the Quartermaster-General's quarters – where you will find us at prayer if you will come timely to join with us; at your liberty, if afterwards to speak with us. There you will find us.

Wildman:[2] I desire to return a little to the business in hand, that was the occasion of these other motions. I could not but take some notice of something that did reflect upon the Agents of the five regiments, in which I could not but give a little satisfaction as to them; and I shall desire to prosecute a motion or two that hath been already made. I observed that it was said, that these gentlemen do insist upon engagements in *The Case of the Army*,[3] and therefore it was said to be contrary to the principles of the Agents, that an engagement which was unjust could lawfully be broken. I shall only observe this: that though an unjust engagement, when it appears unjust, may be broken; yet when two parties engage each that the other party may have satisfaction, because they are mutually engaged each to other one party that apprehends they are broken is justified to complain of them; and so it may be their case, with which, I confess, I made my concurrence.

The other thing I would mention is a principle much spreading, and much to my trouble, and that is this: that when persons once be engaged, though the engagement appear to be unjust, yet the person must sit down and suffer under it; and that therefore, in case a Parliament, as a true Parliament, doth anything unjustly, if we be engaged to submit to the laws that they shall make, though they make an unjust law, though they make an unrighteous law, yet we must swear obedience. I confess, to me this principle is very dangerous, and I speak it the rather because I see it spreading abroad in the Army again – whereas it is contrary to what the Army first declared: that they stood upon such principles of right and freedom, and the Laws of Nature and Nations, whereby men were to preserve themselves though the persons to whom authority belonged should fail in it; and they urged the example of the Scots, and argued that the general that would destroy the army, they might hold his hands; and therefore if anything tends to the destruction of a people, because the thing is absolutely unjust that tends to their destruction, they may preserve themselves by opposing it[4] I could not but speak a word to that.

The motion that I should make upon that account is this. That whereas it is said there must be a meeting to examine differences and promote union, I could not find but that they were desirous to give all satisfaction, and they desire nothing but the union of the Army. Thus far it is their sense. But they apprehend that the necessity of the kingdom is such for present actings, that two or three days may lose the kingdom. I desire in the sight of God to speak – I mean plainly: there may be an agreement between the King and the Parliament by propositions, with a power to hinder the making of any laws that are good, and the tendering of any good laws. And therefore, because none of the people's grievances are redressed, they do apprehend that thus a few days may be the loss of the kingdom. I know it is their sense: that they desire to be excused, that it might not be thought any arrogancy in them, but they are clearly satisfied that the way they proceed in is just, and they desire to be excused if they go on in it; and yet, notwithstanding, they will give all satisfaction. And whereas it is desired that engagements may be considered, I shall desire that only the justice of the thing that is proposed may be considered. I would know whether the chief thing in the Agreement,[5] the intent of it, be not this, to secure the rights of the people in their Parliaments, which was declared by this Army, in the declaration of the fourteenth of June, to be absolutely insisted on. I shall make that motion to be the thing considered: Whether the thing be just, or the people's due? And then there can be no engagement to bind from it.

Ireton: Truly, sir, by what Lieutenant-Colonel Goffe moved,[6] I confess, I was so taken off from all other thoughts in this business that I did not think of speaking anything more. But what this gentleman hath last said hath renewed the occasion, and indeed if I did think all that he hath delivered to be truth and innocence – nay, If I did not think that it hath venom and poison in it. – I would not speak it.

First, I cannot but speak something unto the two particulars that he holds forth as dangerous things – indeed he hath clearly yoked them together, when before I was sensible of those principles and how far they would run together; that is that principle of not being obliged, by not regarding what engagements men have entered into, if in their future apprehensions the things they engaged to are unjust;. and that principle, on the other hand, of not submitting passively to that authority we have engaged to for peace' sake. For he does hold forth his opinion in those two points to clear their way; and I must crave leave on my part to declare that my opinion of that distinction doth lie on the other way.

I am far from holding that if a man have engaged himself to a thing that is not just – to a thing that is evil, that is sin if he do it – that that man is still bound to perform what he hath promised; I am far from apprehending that. But when we talk of just, it is not so much of what is sinful before God (which, depends upon many circumstances of indignation to that man and the like), but it intends of that which is just according to the foundation of justice between man and man. And for my part I account that the great foundation of justice, that we should keep covenant one with another; without which I know nothing of justice betwixt man and man – in particular matters I mean, nothing in particular things that can come under human engagement one way or other. There is no other foundation of right I know, of right to any one thing from another man, no foundation of that particular justice or that particular righteousness, but this general justice, and this general ground of righteousness, that we should keep covenant one with another. Covenants freely made, freely entered into, must be kept one with another. Take away that, I do not know what ground there is of anything you can call any man's right. I would very fain know what you gentlemen, or any other, do account the right you have to anything in England – anything of estate, land or goods, that you have, what ground, what right you have to it. What right hath any man to anything if you lay not down that principle, that we are to keep covenant? If you will resort only to the Law of Nature,[7] by the Law of Nature you have no more right to this land, or anything else, than I have. I have as much right to take hold of anything that

is for my sustenance, to take hold of anything that I have a desire to
for my satisfaction, as you. But here comes the foundation of all
right that I understand to be betwixt men, as to the enjoying of one
thing or not enjoying of it: we are under a contract, we are under an
agreement, and that agreement is what a man has for matter of land
that he hath received by a traduction from his ancestors,[8] which
according to the law does fall upon him to be his right. That
agreement is that he shall enjoy, he shall have the property of, the
use of, the disposing of the land, with submission to that general
authority which is agreed upon amongst us for the preserving of
peace, and for the supporting of his law. This I take to be the
foundation of all right for matter of land. For matter of goods, that
which does fence me from that right which another man may claim
by the Law of Nature, of taking my goods, that which makes it mine
really and civilly, is the law. That which makes it unlawful originally
and radically is only this: because that man is in covenant with me to
live together in peace one with another, and not to meddle with that
which another is possessed of, but that each of us should enjoy, and
make use of, and dispose of, that which by the course of law is in his
possession, and another shall not by violence take it away from him.
This is the foundation of all the right any man has to anything but
to his own person. This is the general thing: that we must keep
covenant one with another when we have contracted one with
another. And if any difference arise among us, it shall be thus and
thus: that I shall not go with violence to prejudice another, but with
submission to this way. And therefore when I hear men speak of
laying aside all engagements to consider only that wild or vast
notion of what in every man's conception is just or unjust, I am
afraid and do tremble at the boundless and endless consequences of
it. What are the principles you apply to this paper? You say, 'If these
things in this paper, in this engagement, be just, then' – say
you – 'never talk of any prior engagement, for if anything in that
engagement be against this, your engagement was unlawful; consider singly this paper, whether it be just.' In what sense do you
think this is just? There is a great deal of equivocation as to what is
just and unjust.

Wildman: I suppose you take away the substance of the question.
Our sense was, that an unjust engagement is rather to be broken
than kept. The Agents think that to delay is to dispose their enemy
into such a capacity as he may destroy them. I make a question
whether any engagement can be binding to an unjust thing. If a man
may promise to do that which is never so much unjust, a man may

promise to break all engagements and duties. But I say this: we must lay aside the consideration of engagements, so as not to take in that as one ground of what is just or unjust amongst men in this case. I do apply this to the case in hand: that it might be considered whether it be unjust to bring in the King in such a way as he may be in a capacity to destroy the people. This paper may be applied to the solution of it.

Ireton: You come to it more particularly than that paper leads. There is a great deal of equivocation (and that I am bound to declare) in the point of justice.

Audley:[9] Mr. Wildman says, if we tarry long, if we stay but three days before you satisfy one another, the King will come and say who will be hanged first.

[After this clash between Wildman and Ireton, Rainborough intervened to enlarge upon the question of engagements, siding with Wildman over the non-binding nature of unjust engagements, but skilfully urging that the Army had engaged 'for Parliament and for the liberties of the people of England'. He ended on a conciliatory note, and soon after Cromwell and Goffe managed to wind up the meeting.

On the next day, 29 October, the morning was devoted to the prayer-meeting, as arranged, and in the afternoon the debate was resumed. Much time was spent on preliminaries and procedure; the serious debate began with a long discourse by Ireton, turning on the nature of the original engagement of the Army. During its course he says: 'If God saw it good to destroy, not only King and Lords, but all distinctions of degrees – nay if it go further, to destroy all property . . . that there be nothing at all of civil constitution left in the kingdom – if I see the hand of God in it I hope I shall with quietness acquiesce . . .']

Major William Rainborough:[10] I desire we may come to that end we all strive after. I humbly desire you will fall upon that which is the engagement of all, which is the rights and freedoms of the people, and let us see how far we have made sure to them a right and freedom, and if anything be tendered as to that in this paper. And when that engagement is gone through, then, let us consider of those things only that are of greater weight.

(*The paper called the Agreement*[11] *read. Afterwards the first article read by itself.*)

Ireton: The exception that lies in it is this. It is said, they are to be distributed according to the number of the inhabitants: 'The people of England,' &c. And this doth make me think that the meaning is, that every man that is an inhabitant is to be equally considered, and to have an equal voice in the election of those representers, the persons that are for the general Representative; and if that be the meaning, then I have something to say against it. But if it be only that those people that by the civil constitution of this kingdom, which is original and fundamental, and beyond which I am sure no memory of record does go –

Cowling [interrupting]:[12] Not before the Conquest.[13]

Ireton: But before the Conquest it was so. If it be intended that those that by that constitution that was before the Conquest, that hath been beyond memory, such person that have been before by that constitution the electors, should be still the electors, I have no more to say against it.

Colonel Rainborough objected: That others might have given their hands to it.

Captain Denne[14] denied that those that were set of their regiment were their hands.

Ireton asked: Whether those men whose hands are to it, or those that brought it, do know so much of the matter as to know whether they mean that all that had a former right of election are to be electors, or that those that had no right before are to come in.

Cowling: In the time before the Conquest. Since the Conquest the greatest part of the kingdom was in vassalage.

Petty:[15] We judge that all inhabitants that have not lost their birthright should have an equal voice in elections.

Rainborough: I desired that those that had engaged in it might be included. For really I think that the poorest he that is in England hath a life to live, as the greatest he; and therefore truly, sir, I think it's clear, that every man that is to live under a government ought first by his own consent to put himself under that government; and I do think that the poorest man in England is not at all bound in a strict sense to that government that he hath not had a voice to put himself under; and I am confident that, when I have heard the reasons against it, something will be said to answer those reasons, insomuch that I should doubt whether he was an Englishmen or no, that should doubt of these things.

Ireton: That's the meaning of this, 'according to the number of the inhabitants'?

Give me leave to tell you, that if you make this the rule I think you must fly for refuge to an absolute natural right, and you must deny all civil right; and I am sure it will come to that in the consequence. This, I perceive, is pressed as that which is so essential and due: the right of the people of this kingdom, and as they are the people of this kingdom, distinct and divided from other people, and that we must for this right lay aside all other considerations; this is so just, this is so due, this is so right to them. And that those that they do thus choose must have such a power of binding all, and loosing all, according to those limitations, this is pressed as so due, and so just, as it is argued, that it is an engagement paramount to all others: and you must for it lay aside all others; if you have engaged any otherwise, you must break it. We must so look upon these as thus held out to us; so it was held out by the gentleman that brought it yesterday. For my part, I think it is no right at all. I think that no person hath a right to an interest or share in the disposing of the affairs of the kingdom, and in determining or choosing those that shall determine what laws we shall be ruled by here – no person hath a right to this, that hath not a permanent fixed interest in this kingdom, and those persons together are properly the represented of this kingdom, and consequently are also to make up the representers of this kingdom, who taken together do comprehend whatsoever is of real or permanent interest in the kingdom. And I am sure otherwise I cannot tell what any man can say why a foreigner coming in amongst us – or as many as will coming in amongst us, or by force or otherwise settling themselves here, or at least by our permission having a being here – why they should not as well lay claim to it as any other. We talk of birthright. Truly by birthright there is thus much claim. Men may justly have by birthright, by their very being born in England, that we should not seclude them out of England, that we should not refuse to give them air and place and ground, and the freedom of the highways and other things, to live amongst us – not any man that is born here, though by his birth there come nothing at all (that is part of the permanent interest of this kingdom) to him. That I think is due to a man by birth. But that by a man's being born here he shall have a share in that power that shall dispose of the lands here, and of all things here, I do not think it a sufficient ground. I am sure if we look upon that which is the utmost (within any man's view) of what was originally the constitution of this kingdom, upon that which is most radical and fundamental, and which if you take away, there is no man hath any land, any goods, or any civil interest, that is this: that those that choose the representers for the making of laws by which this state and kingdom are to be governed, are the persons who, taken together, do comprehend the local interest of this kingdom; that is, the persons in whom all land lies, and those in corporations in whom all trading lies. This is the most fundamental constitution of this kingdom and that which if you do not allow, you allow none at all. This constitution hath limited and determined it that only those shall have voices in elections. It is true, as was said by a gentleman near me, the meanest man in England ought to have a voice in the election of the government he lives under – but only if he has some local interest. I say this: that those that have the meanest local interest – that man that hath but forty shillings a year, he *hath* as great voice in the election of a knight for the shire as he that hath ten thousand a year, or more if he had never so much; and therefore there is that regard had to it. But this local interest, still the constitution of this government hath had an eye to (and what other government hath not an eye to this?). It doth not relate to the interest of the kingdom if it do not lay the foundation of the power that's given to the representers, in those who have a permanent and a local interest in the kingdom, and who taken all together do comprehend the whole interest of the kingdom. There is all the reason and justice that can be, in this: if I will come to live in a kingdom, being a foreigner to it, or live in a kingdom, having no permanent interest in it, and if I will desire as a stranger, or claim as one freeborn here, the air, the free passage of highways, the protection of laws, and all such things – if I will either desire them or claim them, then I (if I have no permanent interest in that kingdom) must submit to those laws and those rules which they shall choose, who, taken together, do comprehend the whole interest of the kingdom. And if we shall go to take away this, we shall plainly go to take away all property and interest that any man hath either in land by inheritance, or in estate by possession, or anything else – I say, if you take away this fundamental part of the civil constitution.

Rainborough: Truly, sir, I am of the same opinion I was, and am resolved to keep it till I know reason why I should not. I confess my memory is bad, and therefore I am fain to make use of my pen. I remember that, in a former speech which this gentleman brought before this meeting, he was saying that in some cases he should not value whether there were a king or no king, whether lords or no lords, whether a property or no property. For my part I differ in that. I do very much care whether there be a king or no king, lords or no lords, property or no property; and I think, if we do not all take care, we shall all have none of these very shortly. But as to this present business. I do hear nothing at all that can convince me, why any man that is born in England ought not to have his voice in election of burgesses.[16] It is said that if a man have not a permanent interest, he can have no claim; and that we must be no freer than the laws will let us be, and that there is no law in any chronicle will let us be freer than that we now enjoy. Something was said to this yesterday. I do think that the main cause why Almighty God gave men reason, it was that they should make use of that reason, and that they should improve it for that end and purpose that God gave it them. And truly, I think that half a loaf is better than none if a man be anhungry: this gift of reason without other property may seem a small thing, yet I think there is nothing that God hath given a man that any one else can take from him. And therefore I say, that either it must be the Law of God or the law of man that must prohibit the meanest man in the kingdom to have this benefit as well as the greatest. I do not find anything in the Law of God, that a lord shall choose twenty burgesses, and a gentleman but two, or a poor man shall choose none: I find no such thing in the Law of Nature, nor in the Law of Nations. But I do find that all Englishmen must be subject to English laws, and I do verily believe that there is no man but will say that the foundation of all law lies in the people, and if it lie in the people, I am to seek for this exemption.

And truly I have thought something else: in what a miserable distressed condition would many a man that hath fought for the Parliament in this quarrel, be! I will be bound to say that many a man whose zeal and affection to God and this kingdom hath carried him forth in this cause, hath so spent his estate that, in the way the state and the Army are going, he shall not hold up his head, if when his estate is lost, and not worth forty shillings a year, a man shall not have any interest. And there are many other ways by which the estates men have (if that be the rule which God in his providence does use) do fall to decay. A man, when he hath an estate, hath an interest in making laws, but when he hath none, he hath no power in it; so that a man cannot lose that which he hath for the maintenance of his family but he must also lose that which God and nature hath given him! And therefore I do think, and am still of the same opinion, that every man born in England cannot, ought not, neither by the Law of God nor the Law of Nature, to be exempted from the choice of those who are to make laws for him to live under, and for him, for aught I know, to lose his life under. And therefore I think there can be no great stick in this.

Truly I think that there is not this day reigning in England a greater fruit or effect of tyranny than this very thing would produce. Truly I know nothing free but only the knight of the shire, nor do I know anything in a parliamentary way that is clear from the height and fulness of tyranny, but only that. As for this of corporations which you also mentioned, it is as contrary to freedom as may be. For, sir, what is it? The King he grants a patent under the Broad Seal of England to such a corporation to send burgesses, he grants to such a city to send burgesses. When a poor base corporation from the King's grant shall send two burgesses, when five hundred men of estate shall not send one, when those that are to make their laws are called by the King, or cannot act but by such a call, truly I think that the people of England have little freedom.

Ireton: I think there was nothing that I said to give you occasion to think that I did contend for this, that such a corporation as that should have the electing of a man to the Parliament. I think I agreed to this matter, that all should be equally distributed. But the question is, whether it should be distributed to all persons, or whether the same persons that are the electors now should be the electors still, and it be equally distributed amongst *them*. I do not see anybody else that makes this objection; and if nobody else be sensible of it I shall soon have done. Only I shall a little crave your leave to represent the consequences of it, and clear myself from one thing that was misrepresented by the gentleman that sat next me. I think, if the gentleman remember himself, he cannot but remember that what I said was to this effect: that if I saw the hand of God leading so far as to destroy King, and destroy Lords, and destroy property, and leave no such thing at all amongst us, I should acquiesce in it; and so I did not care, if no king, no lords, or no property should be, in comparison of the tender care that I have of the honour of God, and of the people of God, whose good name is so much concerned in this Army. This I did deliver so, and not absolutely.

All the main thing that I speak for, is because I would have an eye to property. I hope we do not come to contend for victory – but let every man consider with himself that he do not go that way to take away all property. For here is the case of the most fundamental part of the constitution of the kingdom, which if you take away, you take away all by that. Here men of this and this quality are determined to be the electors of men to the Parliament, and they are all those who have any permanent interest in the kingdom, and who, taken together, do comprehend the whole permanent, local interest of the kingdom. I mean by permanent and local, that it is not able to be removed anywhere else. As for instance, he that hath a freehold, and that freehold cannot be removed out of the kingdom; and so there's a freeman of a corporation, a place which hath the privilege of a market and trading, which if you should allow to all places equally,

I do not see how you could preserve any peace in the kingdom, and that is the reason why in the constitution we have but some few market towns. Now those people that have free-holds and those that are the freemen of corporations, were looked upon by the former constitution to comprehend the permanent interest of the kingdom. For first he that hath his livelihood by his trade, and by his freedom of trading in such a corporation, which he cannot exercise in another, he is tied to that place, for his livelihood depends upon it. And secondly, that man hath an interest, hath a permanent interest there, upon which he may live, and live a freeman without dependence. These things the constitution of this kingdom hath looked at. Now I wish we may all consider of what right you will challenge that all the people should have right to elections. Is it by the right of nature? If you will hold forth that as your ground, then I think you must deny all property too, and this is my reason. For thus: by that same right of nature (whatever it be) that you pretend, by which you can say, one man hath an equal right with another to the choosing of him that shall govern him – by the same right of nature, he hath the same equal right in any goods he sees – meat, drink, clothes – to take and use them for his sustenance. He hath a freedom to the land, to take the ground, to exercise it, till it; he hath the same freedom to anything that any one doth account himself to have any propriety in. Why now I say then, if you, against the most fundamental part of the civil constitution (which I have now declared), will plead the Law of Nature, that a man should (paramount to this, and contrary to this) have a power of choosing those men that shall determine what shall be law in this state, though he himself have no permanent interest in the state, but whatever interest he hath he may carry about with him – if this be allowed, because by the right of nature we are free, we are equal, one man must have as much voice as another, then show me what step or difference there is, why I may not by the same right take your property, though not of necessity to sustain nature. It is for my better being, and the better settlement of the kingdom? Possibly not for it, neither: possibly I may not have so real a regard to the peace of the kingdom as that man who hath a permanent interest in it. He that is here to-day, and gone to-morrow, I do not see that he hath such a permanent interest. Since you cannot plead to it by anything but the Law of Nature, or for anything but for the end of better being, and since that better being is not certain, and what is more, destructive to another; upon these grounds, if you do, paramount to all constitutions, hold up this Law of Nature, I would fain have any man show me their bounds, where you will end, and why you should not take away all property.

Rainborough: I shall now be a little more free and open with you than I was before. I wish we were all true-hearted, and that we did all carry ourselves with integrity. If I did mistrust you I would not use such asseverations. I think it doth go on mistrust, and things are thought too readily matters of reflection, that were never intended. For my part, as I think, *you* forgot something that was in *my* speech, and you do not only yourselves believe that some men are inclining to anarchy, but you would make all men believe that. And, sir, to say because a man pleads that every man hath a voice by right of nature, that therefore it destroys by the same argument all property – this is to forget the Law of God. That there's a property, the Law of God says it; else why hath God made that law, *Thou shalt not steal?*[17] I am a poor man, therefore I must be oppressed: if I have no interest in the kingdom, I must suffer by all their laws be they right or wrong. Nay thus: a gentleman lives in a country and hath three or four lordships, as some men have (God knows how they got them); and when a Parliament is called he must be a Parliament-man; and it may be he sees some poor men, they live near this man, he can crush them – I have known an invasion to make sure he hath turned the poor men out of doors; and I would fain know whether the potency of rich men do not this, and so keep them under the greatest tyranny that was ever thought of in the world. And therefore I think that to that it is fully answered: God hath set down that thing as to propriety with this law of his, *Thou shalt not steal.* And for my part I am against any such thought, and, as for yourselves, I wish you would not make the world believe that we are for anarchy.

Cromwell: I know nothing but this, that they that are the most yielding have the greatest wisdom; but really, sir, this is not right as it should be. No man says that you have a mind to anarchy, but that the consequence of this rule tends to anarchy, must end in anarchy; for where is there any bound or limit set if you take away this limit, that men that have no interest but the interest of breathing shall have no voice in elections? Therefore I am confident on't, we should not be so hot one with another.[18]

Rainborough: I know that some particular men we debate with believe we are for anarchy.

Ireton: I profess I must clear myself as to that point. I would not desire, I cannot allow myself, to lay the least scandal upon anybody. And truly, for that gentleman that did take so much offence, I do not know why he should take it so. We speak to the paper – not to persons – and to the matter of the paper. And I hope that no man is so much engaged to the matter of the paper – I hope that our persons, and our hearts and judgments, are not so pinned to papers but that we are ready to hear what good or ill consequence will flow from it.

I have, with as much plainness and clearness of reason as I could, showed you how I did conceive the doing of this that the paper advocates takes away that which is the most original, the most fundamental civil constitution of this kingdom, and which is, above all, that constitution by which I have any property. If you will take away that and set up, as a thing paramount, whatever a man may claim by the Law of Nature, though it be not a thing of necessity to him for the sustenance of nature; if you do make this your rule, I desire clearly to understand where then remains property.

Now then – I would misrepresent nothing – the answer which had anything of matter in it, the great and main answer upon which that which hath been said against this objection rests, seemed to be that it will not make a breach of property, for this reason: that there is a law, *Thou shalt not steal*. But the same law says, *Honour thy father and thy mother*, and that law doth likewise hold out that it doth extend to all that (in that place where we are in) are our governors; so that by that there is a forbidding of breaking a civil law when we may live quietly under it, and that by a divine law. Again it is said – indeed was said before – that there is no law, no divine law, that tells us that such a corporation must have the election of burgesses, such a shire of knights, or the like. Divine law extends not to particular things. And so, on the other side, if a man were to demonstrate his right to property by divine law, it would be very remote. Our right to property descends from other things, as well as our right of sending burgesses. That divine law doth not determine particulars but generals in relation to man and man, and to property, and all things else: and we should be as far to seek if we should go to prove a property in a thing by divine law, as to prove that I have an interest in choosing burgesses of the Parliament by divine law. And truly, under favour, I refer it to all, whether there be anything of solution to that objection that I made, if it be understood – I submit it to any man's judgment.

Rainborough: To the thing itself – property in the franchise. I would fain know how it comes to be the property of some men, and not of others. As for estates and those kind of things, and other things that belong to men, it will be granted that they are property; but I deny that that is a property, to a lord, to a gentleman, to any man more than another in the kingdom of England. If it be a property, it is a property by a law – neither do I think that there is very little property in this thing by the law of the land, because I think that the law of the land in that thing is the most tyrannical law under heaven. And I would fain know what we have fought for. For our laws and liberties? And this is the old law of England – and that which enslaves the people of England – that they should be bound by laws in which they have no voice at all! With respect to the divine law which says *Honour thy father and thy mother* the great dispute is, who is a right father and a right mother? I am bound to know who is my father and mother; and – I take it in the same sense you do – I would have a distinction, a character whereby God commands me to honour them. And for my part I look upon the people of England so, that wherein they have not voices in the choosing of their governors – their civil fathers and mothers – they are not bound to that commandment.

Petty: I desire to add one word concerning the word *property*. It is for something that anarchy is so much talked of. For my own part I cannot believe in the least that it can be clearly derived from that paper. 'Tis true, that somewhat may be derived in the paper against the King, the power of the King, and somewhat against the power of the Lords; and the truth is when I shall see God going about to throw down King and Lords and property, then I shall be contented. But I hope that they may live to see the power of the King and the Lords thrown down, that yet may live to see property preserved. And for this of changing the Representative of the nation, of changing those that choose the Representative, making of them more full, taking more into the number than formerly, I had verily thought we had all agreed in it that more should have chosen – all that had desired a more equal representation than we now have. For now those only choose who have forty shillings freehold. A man may have a lease for one hundred pounds a year, a man may have a lease for three lives, but he has no voice. But as for this argument, that it destroys all right to property that every Englishman that is an inhabitant of England should choose and have a voice in the representatives, I suppose it is, on the contrary, the only means to preserve all property. For I judge every man is naturally free; and I judge the reason why men chose representatives when they were in so great numbers that every man could not give his voice directly, was that they who were chosen might preserve property for all; and therefore men agreed to come into some form of government that they might preserve property, and I would fain know, if we were to begin a government, whether you would say, 'You have not forty shillings a year, therefore you shall not have a voice.' Whereas before there was a government every man had such a voice, and afterwards, and for this very cause, they did choose representatives, and put themselves into forms of government that they may preserve property, and therefore it is not to destroy it, to give every man a voice.

[Speeches by Ireton, Colonel Nathaniel Rich, and an interjection by Rainborough have here been omitted. Ireton now addresses himself to a question by Rich – one which crucially underlies all the foregoing disagreements over engagements, Civil Law and the Law of Nature:]

Ireton: Let the question be so: Whether a man can be bound to any law that he doth not consent to? And I shall tell you, that he may and ought to be bound to a law that he doth not give a consent to, nor doth not choose any to consent to; and I will make it clear. If a foreigner come within this kingdom, if that stranger will have liberty to dwell here who hath no local interest here, he, as a man, it's true, hath air, the passage of highways, the protection of laws, and all that by nature; we must not expel him our coasts, give him no being amongst us, nor kill him because he comes upon our land, comes up our stream, arrives at our shore. It is a piece of hospitality, of humanity, to receive that man amongst us. But if that man be received to a being amongst us, I think that man may very well be content to submit himself to the law of the land; that is, the law that is made by those people that have a property, a fixed property, in the land. I think, if any man will receive protection from this people though neither he nor his ancestors, not any betwixt him and Adam, did ever give concurrence to this constitution, I think this man ought to be subject to those laws, and to be bound by those laws, so long as he continues amongst them.[19] That is my opinion. A man ought to be subject to a law, that did not give his consent, but with this reservation, that if this man do think himself unsatisfied to be subject to this law he may go into another kingdom. And so the same reason doth extend, in my understanding, to that man that hath no permanent interest in the kingdom. If he hath money, his money is as good in another place as here; he hath nothing that doth locally fix him to this kingdom. If that man will live in this kingdom, or trade amongst us, that man ought to subject himself to the law made by the people who have the interest of this kingdom in them. And yet I do acknowledge that which you take to be so general a maxim, that in every kingdom, within every land, the original of power of making laws, of determining what shall be law in the land, does lie in the people – but by the people is meant those that are possessed of the permanent interest in the land. But whoever is extraneous to this, that is, as good a man in another land, that man ought to give such a respect to the property of men that live in the land. They do not determine that I shall live in this land. Why should I have any interest in determining what shall be the law of this land?

Major William Rainborough: I think if it can be made to appear that it is a just and reasonable thing, and that it is for the preservation of all the native freeborn men, that they should have an equal voice in election – I think it ought to be made good unto them. And the reason is: that the chief end of this government is to preserve persons as well as estates, and if any law shall take hold of my person it is more dear than my estate.

Colonel Rainborough: I do very well remember that the gentleman in the window[20] said that, if it were so, there were no propriety to be had, because five parts of the nation, the poor people, are now excluded and would then come in. So one on the other side said that, if it were otherwise, then rich men only shall be chosen. Then, I say, the one part shall make hewers of wood and drawers of water of the other five, and so the greatest part of the nation be enslaved. Truly I think we are still where we were; and I do not hear any argument given but only that it is the present law of the kingdom. I say still, what shall become of those many men that have laid out themselves for the Parliament of England in this present war, that have ruined themselves by fighting, by hazarding all they had? They are Englishmen. They have now nothing to say for themselves.

Rich: I should be very sorry to speak anything here that should give offence, or that may occasion personal reflections that we spoke against just now. I did not urge anything so far as was represented, and I did not at all urge that there should be a consideration had of rich men, and that a man that is poor shall be without consideration, or that he deserves to be made poorer and not to live in independence at all. But all that I urged was this: that I think it worthy consideration, whether they should have an equality in their interest. However, I think we have been a great while upon this point, and if we be as long upon all the rest, it were well if there were no greater difference than this.

Mr. Hugh Peter:[21] I think that this matter of the franchise may be easily agreed on – that is, there may be a way thought of. I think you would do well to set up all night if thereby you could effect it, but I think that three or four might be thought of in this company to form a committee. You will be forced only to put characters upon electors or elected; therefore I do suppose that if there be any here that can make up a Representative to your mind, the thing is gained. But I would fain know whether that will answer the work of your meeting. The question is, whether you can state any one question for removing the present danger of the kingdom, whether any one question or no will dispatch the work.

Sir, I desire, if it be possible, that some question may be stated to finish the present work, to cement us in the points wherein lies the distance; and if the thoughts be of the commonwealth and the people's freedom, I think that's soon cured. I desire that all manner of plainness may be used, that we may not go on with the lapwing and carry one another off the nest. There is something else that must cement us where the awkwardness of our spirits lies.

Rainborough: For my part, I think we cannot engage one way or other in the Army if we do not think of the people's liberties. If we can agree where the liberty and freedom of the people lies, that will do all.

Ireton: I cannot consent so far. As I said before: when I see the hand of God destroying King, and Lords, and Commons too, or any foundation of human constitution, when I see God hath done it, I shall, I hope, comfortably acquiesce in it. But first, I cannot give my consent to it, because it is not good. And secondly, as I desire that this Army should have regard to engagements wherever they are lawful, so I would have them have regard to this as well: that they should not bring that scandal upon the name of God and the Saints, that those that call themselves by that name, those whom God hath owned and appeared with – that we should represent ourselves to the world as men so far from being of that peaceable spirit which is suitable to the Gospel, as we should have bought peace of the world upon such terms – as we would not have peace in the world but upon such terms – as should destroy all property. If the principle upon which you move this alteration, or the ground upon which you press that we should make this alteration, do destroy all kind of property or whatsoever a man hath by human constitution, I cannot consent to it. The Law of God doth not give me property, nor the Law of Nature, but property is of human constitution. I have a property and this I shall enjoy. Constitution founds property. If either the thing itself that you press or the consequence of that you press do destroy property, though I shall acquiesce in having no property, yet I cannot give my heart or hand to it; because it is a thing evil in itself and scandalous to the world, and I desire this Army may be free from both.

Sexby: I see that though liberty were our end, there is a degeneration from it. We have engaged in this kingdom and ventured our lives, and it was all for this: to recover our birthrights and privileges as Englishmen; and by the arguments urged there is none. There are many thousands of us soldiers that have ventured our lives; we have had little propriety in the kingdom as to our estates, yet we have had a birthright. But it seems now, except a man hath a fixed estate in this kingdom, he hath no right in this kingdom. I wonder we were so much deceived. If we had not a right to the kingdom, we were mere mercenary soldiers. There are many in my condition, that have as good a condition as I have; it may be little estate they have at present, and yet they have as much a birth right as those two[22] who are their law-givers, as any in this place. I shall tell you in a word my resolution. I am resolved to give my birthright to none. Whatsoever may come in the way, and whatsoever may be thought, I will give it to none. If this thing be denied the poor, that with so much pressing after they have sought, it will be the greatest scandal. There was one thing spoken to this effect: that if the poor and those in low condition were given their birthright it would be the destruction of this kingdom. I think this was but a distrust of Providence. I do think the poor and meaner of this kingdom – I speak as in relation to the condition of soldiers, in which we are – have been the means of the preservation of this kingdom. I say, in their stations, and really I think to their utmost possibility; and their lives have not been held dear for purchasing the good of the kingdom. And now they demand the birthright for which they fought. Those that act to this end are as free from anarchy or confusion as those that oppose it, and they have the Law of God and the law of their conscience with them. But truly I shall only sum up in this. I desire that we may not spend so much time upon these things. We must be plain. When men come to understand these things, they will not lose that which they have contended for. That which I shall beseech you is to come to a determination of this question.

Ireton: I am very sorry we are come to this point, that from reasoning one to another we should come to express our resolutions. I profess for my part, what I see is good for the kingdom, and becoming a Christian to contend for, I hope through God I shall have strength and resolution to do my part towards it. And yet I will profess direct contrary in some kind to what that gentleman said. For my part, rather than I will make a disturbance to a good constitution of a kingdom wherein I may live in godliness and honesty, and peace and quietness, I will part with a great deal of my birthright. I will part with my own property rather than I will be the man that shall make a disturbance in the kingdom for my property; and therefore if all the people in this kingdom, or the representatives of them all together, should meet and should give away my property I would submit to it, I would give it away. But that gentleman, and I think every Christian, ought to bear that spirit, to carry that in him, that he will not make a public disturbance upon a private prejudice.

Now let us consider where our difference lies. We all agree that you should have a Representative[a] to govern, and this Representative to be as equal as you can make it. But the question is, whether this distribution can be made to all persons equally, or whether only amongst those equals that have the interest of England in them. That which I have declared is my opinion still. I think we ought to keep to that constitution which we have now, both because it is a civil constitution – it is the most fundamental constitution that we have – and because there is so much justice and reason and prudence in it – as I dare confidently undertake to demonstrate – that there are many more evils that will follow in case you do alter it than there can be in the standing of it. But I say but this in the general, that I do wish that they that talk of birthrights – we any of us when we talk of birthrights – would consider what really our birthright is.

If a man mean by birthright, whatsoever I can challenge by the Law of Nature (suppose there were no constitution at all, no civil law and no civil constitution), and that *that* I am to contend for against constitution; then you leave no property, nor no foundation for any man to enjoy anything. But if you call that your birthright which is the most fundamental part of your constitution, then let him perish that goes about to hinder you or any man of the least part of your birthright, or will desire to do it. But if you will lay aside the most fundamental constitution, which is as good, for aught you can discern, as anything you can propose – at least it is a constitution, and I will give you consequence for consequence of

[a] I.e. the body of elected representatives.

good upon that constitution as you can give upon your birthright without it – and if you merely upon pretence of a birthright, of the right of nature, which is only true as for your being, and not for your better being; if you will upon that ground pretend that this constitution, the most fundamental constitution, the thing that hath reason and equity in it, shall not stand in your way, it is the same principle to me, say I, as if but for your better satisfaction you shall take hold of anything that another man calls his own.

Rainborough: Sir, I see that it is impossible to have liberty but all property must be taken away. If it be laid down for a rule, and if you will say it, it must be so. But I would fain know what the soldier hath fought for all this while? He hath fought to enslave himself, to give power to men of riches, men of estates, to make him a perpetual slave. We do find in all presses that go forth none must be pressed that are freehold men. When these gentlemen fall out among themselves they shall press the poor scrubs to come and kill one another for them.

Ireton: I confess I see so much right in the business that I am not easily satisfied with flourishes. If you will not lay the stress of the business upon the consideration of reason, or right relating to anything of human constitution, or anything of that nature, but will put it upon consequences, I will show you greater ill consequences – I see enough to say that, to my apprehensions, I can show you greater ill consequences to follow upon that alteration which you would have, by extending voices to all that have a being in this kingdom, than any that can come by this present constitution, a great deal. That that you urge of the present constitution is a particular ill consequence. This that I object against your proposal is a general ill consequence, and this is as great as that or any ill consequence else whatsoever, though I think you will see that the validity of that argument must be that for one ill that lies upon that which now is, I can show you a thousand upon this that you propose.

Give me leave to say but this one word. I will tell you what the soldier of the kingdom hath fought for. First, the danger that we stood in was that one man's will must be a law. The people of the kingdom must have this right at least, that they should not be concluded but by the Representative of those that had the interest of the kingdom. Some men fought in this, because they were immediately concerned and engaged in it. Other men who had no other interest in the kingdom but this, that they should have the benefit of those laws made by the Representative, yet fought that they should have the benefit of this Representative. They thought it was better to be concluded by the common consent of those that were fixed men, and settled men, that had the interest of this kingdom in them. 'And from that way,' said they, 'I shall know a law and have a certainty.' Every man that was born in the country, that is a denizen in it, that hath a freedom, he was capable of trading to get money, to get estates by; and therefore this man, I think, had a great deal of reason to build up such a foundation of interest to himself: that is, that the will of one man should not be a law, but that the law of this kingdom should be by a choice of persons to represent, and that choice to be made by, the generality of the kingdom. Here was a right that induced men to fight, and those men that had this interest, though this be not the utmost interest that other men have, yet they had *some* interest. Now tell me why we should go to plead whatsoever we can challenge by the right of nature against whatsoever any man can challenge by constitution. I do not see where that man will stop, as to point of property, so that he shall not use against other property that right he hath claimed by the Law of Nature against that constitution. I desire any man to show me where there is a difference. I have been answered, 'Now we see liberty cannot stand without destroying property.' Liberty may be had and property not be destroyed. First, the liberty of all those that have the permanent interest in the kingdom, *that* is provided for by the constitution. And secondly, by an appeal to the Law of Nature liberty cannot be provided for in a general sense, if property be preserved. For if property be preserved by acknowledging a natural right in the possessor, so that I am not to meddle with such a man's estate, his meat, his drink, his apparel, or other goods, then the right of nature destroys liberty. By the right of nature I am to have sustenance rather than perish; yet property destroys it for a man to have this by the right of nature, even suppose there be no human constitution.

[By this stage in the second day's debate, it may be thought, the main arguments had been brought forward – Rainborough was soon to complain that 'there is not an objection made but that it hath been answered; but the speeches are so long'. It may also be felt that Ireton, in his continually substantial contributions, began to lay more stress on the inherent merits of the present constitution and franchise, and less upon the impossibility of innovating without anarchy. Before the debate ended Rainborough gave notice of a motion that the Army might be called to a new rendezvous, 'and things settled as promised in its printed engagements'.

The debate on 1 November was more specifically concerned than the others with the future rôle of King, Lords and Commons. A brief extract is given here.]

Rainborough: I observe that the Commissary-General[a] is willing to lay that of constitution aside, and that of custom aside,[23] and I think it well for us to consider the equality and reasonableness of the thing, and not to stand upon a constitution which we have broken again and again. I do not find in all the reading that I have done – I do not know that ever the Commons made war with the King till now, though the Barons did. Yet, besides the oath he found, I would add that one of the main articles against Richard the Second was that he did not concur with, and agree upon, those wholesome laws which were offered him by the Commons for the safety of the people.[24] If that were so great a right as did depose him, it is in the kingdom still, and therefore let us go to the justice of the thing. That justice and reason doth not give to the major part—

Ireton: You would have us lay aside arguments of constitution, and yet you have brought the strongest that may be. I have seen the Articles of Richard the Second, and it is strange that the Parliament should not insist upon that.

Rainborough: That is not the thing that I would consider of.

Ireton: I suppose no man will make a question that that may be justice and equity upon no constitution, which is not justice and equity upon a constitution. As for instance in the matter of a common, &c.

I wish but this, that we may have a regard to safety – safety to our persons, safety to our estates, safety to our liberty. Let's have that as the law paramount, and then let us regard the positive constitution as far as it can stand with safety to these. Now therefore – thus for my part I confess it – if I should have ever given a consent in my heart to propound anything that did not consist with this, with regard to any constitution whatsoever, I revoke it; but for my part I cannot see that anything but safety is provided for. Mr. Wildman says that many godly men would not be satisfied with this that we have read,[25] which amounts to this: that the Commons have power to make laws for all the Commons of England, and that only the person of the King and the persons of the Lords as persons, with their estates, are freed from them. If this be so, I do not see that they are satisfied with anything without having a power over other men's liberties.

[a] I.e. Ireton.

Wildman: Whereas you are pleased to say I produced no other evidence, Colonel Rainborough brought another.[26] Because you did confess the Lords had no other power in making laws –

Ireton [interrupting]: I never confessed it in my life, otherwise than by the recitation of that oath: 'which the people shall choose.'

Wildman: I could wish we should have recourse to principles and maxims of just government, instead of arguments of safety which are as loose as can be.[27] By these principles, government by King and Lords is seen to be unjust.

Ireton: The government of Kings, or of Lords, is as just as any in the world, is the justest government in the world. *Volenti non fit injuria*. Men cannot wrong themselves willingly, and if they will agree to make a King, and his heirs, their ruler, there's no injustice. They may either make it hereditary or elective. They may give him an absolute power or a limited power. Here hath been agreements of the people that have agreed with this. There hath been such an agreement when the people have fought for their liberty, and have established the King again.

Wildman: 'Twas their superstition, to have such an opinion of a great man.

Ireton: Any man that makes a bargain, and does find afterwards 'tis for the worse, yet is bound to stand to it.

Wildman: They were cozened, as we are like to be.

Ireton: I would not have you talk of principles of just government when you hold that all governments that are set up by consent are just. Argue instead that such or such a way, *that* can consist with the liberty of the people. Then we shall go to clear reason. That's one maxim, that all government must be for the safety of the people.

Tichborne: Let us keep to that business of safety. 'Tis upon the matter of safety that the real power of making laws is vested solely in the people by what hath been proposed. In that I give King and Lords no more than an opportunity to do me a courtesy if they will—

Wildman [interrupting]: No courtesy.

Tichborne: It is only an opportunity – and to show themselves as willing as the Commons. Let us not fight with shadows.

Wildman: We do not know what opportunity God will give us.

Ireton: If God will destroy King or Lords he can do it without our or your wrong-doing. If you not only take away all power from them, which this clearly does, but do also take away all kind of distinction of them from other men, then you do them wrong. Their having such a distinction from other men cannot do us wrong. That you can do to the utmost for their safety is this: that a Lord or King may preserve his own person or estate free from the Commons. Now I would know whether this can be destructive to the Commons, that so few men should be distinct from a law made by the Commons, especially when we have laws made as to the preserving of the peace of the kingdom and preserving every man in his right. The King and Lords are suable, impleadable, in any court. The King may be sued, and tried by a jury, and a Lord may be sued, and tried *per pares* only, as a knight by esquires. What needs more, where there are such laws already that the King and Lords are so bound?

Wildman: I conceive that the difference does not lie here, but whether the King shall so come in that the Parliament must make their addresses themselves unto him for the confirmation of everything they pass. Whether it be a shadow or no, I think it is a substance when nothing shall be made but by address to the King. This will be very shameful in future chronicles, that after so much blood there should be no better an issue for the Commons.[28]

3. *William Walwyn,* *'The Bloody Project', August 1648*

There is a copy of the pamphlet in the Thomason Collection, British Museum. Its attribution to Walwyn by the *Discoverer* (1649), an attack on the Levellers, was not denied, and is supported by argument and style. Thomason dated his copy 21 August 1648, at the climax of the Second Civil War, a week before the Royalists' surrender at Colchester.

The pamphlet carries on the Levellers' demands for true democracy against military rule, now in the context of the new war. It demands individual liberty, equality of all before the law, freedom in religion (denied by the Presbyterians), the ending of poverty, and the right to individual enterprise. As an immediate constitutional reform, it demands the dissolution of the Long Parliament and annual general elections. To carry on the war without granting such fundamental liberties would, argues Walwyn, turn the people into slaves and murderers.

Our text is taken from W. Haller and G. Davies, eds., *The Leveller Tracts 1647–1653* (Gloucester, Mass., 1964).

The Bloody Project. or New design in the present War discovered

In all undertakings, which may occasion war or bloodshed, men have great need to be sure that their cause be right, both in respect of themselves and others: for if they kill men themselves, or cause others to kill, without a just cause, and upon the extreamest necessity, they not only disturbe the peace of men, and familyes, and bring misery and poverty upon a Nation, but are indeed absolute murtherers.

Nor will it in any measure satisfy the Conscience, or Gods justice, to go on in uncertainties, for in doubtfull cases men ought to stand still, and consider, untill certainty do appear, especially when killing and sleying of men (the most horrid worke to Nature and Scripture) is in question.

Far be it from any man hastily to engage in any undertaking, which may occasion a War, before the cause he is to fight for, be rightly, and plainly stated, well considered, and throughly understood to be just, and of absolute necessity to be maintained; nothing being more abominable in the sight of God or good men, then such persons who runne but to shed blood for money, or to support this or the other Interest, but neither consider the cause for which they engage, nor ought else, but pay, interest, honour, &c. such are they who so eagerly endeavour to support the interest of a King, by the destruction of the Peoples Interest, the Interest of the Scots against the Interest of the English, the Interest of the Independents,[a] by the ruine of the Presbyterians: and because it best consists with their present honour, profit or humours, make it their busines to pick quarrels, and encrease divisions, and jealousies, that so they may fish in the waters which they themselves have troubled.

But let such know, who ever they be, that though they may and do for a while brave it out, and flourish, yet a time is comming and draweth on apace, when for all the murthers they have caused, and mischiefs they have committed, they shall come to judgement, and then their Consciences will be as a thousand witnesses against them.

But especially let men pretending conscience take heed how they either engage themselves, or perswade others to engage to fight and kill men, for a cause not rightly stated, or not throughly understood to be just, and of necessity to be maintained; for it is one of the most unreasonable, unchristian, and unnaturall things that can enter into the mind of man, though it be to be feared that more than a few that have of late both in the Citie and Country [been], (and at present are) active to engage in killing and sleying of men cannot acquit themselves of this abomination.

I beseech you, (you that are so forward and active to engage in the defence of the Kings, Presbyterian, or Independent interest, and yet know no just cause for either) consider, was it sufficient that the King at first invited you in generall termes to joyn with him, for the defence of the true Protestant Religion, his own just Prerogatives, the Priviledges of Parliament, and the Liberty of the Subject; but never declared in particular what that Protestant Religion was he would have defended, or what Prerogative would please him, what priviledges he would allow the Parliament, or what Freedoms the People?

Or was it sufficient thinke you now, that the Parliament invited you at first upon generall termes, to fight for the maintenance of the true Protestant Religion, the Libertyes of the People, and Priviledges of Parliament; when neither themselves knew, for ought is yet seen, nor you, nor any body else, what they meant by the true Protestant Religion, or what the Liberties of the People were, or what those Priviledges of Parliament were, for which yet neverthe-

---

[a] The party of the Independent churches.

lesse thousands of man have been slain, and thousands of Familyes destroyed?

It is very like that some of you that joyned with the King upon his invitation, thought, that though the King had formerly countenanced Popery, and Superstition, had stretcht his Prerogative to the oppression and destruction of his People, by Pattents, Projects[a] &c. yet for the future he would have been more zealous for the truth, and more tender of his People, and not have persisted (notwithstanding his new Protestations) to maintain his old Principles.

And so likewise many of you that joyned with the Parliament, who had formerly seen, felt, or considered the persecution of godly conscientious people by the Bishops and their Cleargy, with the reproaches cast upon them, and their grievous and destructive imprisonment, did beleeve the Parliament under the notion of Religion, intended to free the Nation from all compulsion in matters of Religion, and from molestation, or persecution for opinions, or non-conformity; and that all Lawes or Statutes tending thereunto should have been repealed: But since you find (by killing and destroying their opposers) you have enabled them to performe all things that might concern your freedome, or be conducible to the peace of the Kingdome. But do you now find that they do mean that, or the contrary? And will your consciences give you leave any longer to fight or engage in the cause of Religion, when already you see what fruits you and your friends reap thereby.

And no doubt many of you understood by the Liberties of the People, that they intended to free the Commons in Parliament the peoples Representative, from a Negative voyce, in King, or Lords, and would have declared themselves the highest Authority, and so would have proceeded to have removed the grievances of the Common-wealth: And when you had seen Pattents, Projects, and Shipmoney taken away, the High Commission, and Starchamber abolished,[b] did you ever imagine to have seen men and women examined upon Interrogatories, and questions against themselves, and imprisoned for refusing to answer? Or to have seen Commoners frequently sentenced and imprisoned by the Lords? Did you ever dream that the oppressions of Committees would have exceeded those of the Councel-table; or that in the place of Pattents and Projects, you should have seen an Excise established, ten fold surpassing all those, and Shipmoney together? You thought rather that Tythes would have been esteem'd an oppression, and that

---

[a] The granting of monopolies to individuals.
[b] All abolished by the Long Parliament in 1641.

Trade would have been made perfectly free, and that Customs if continued, would have been abated, and not raysed, for the support of domineering factions, and enrichment of foure or five great men, as they have been of late times, to the sorrow and astonishment of all honest men, and the great prejudice of the Trade of the Nation.

Doubtlesse you hoped that both Lawes and Lawyers, and the proceeding in all Courts should have been abreviated, and corrected, and that you should never more have seen a Begger in England.

You have seen the Common-wealth enslaved for want of Parliaments, and also by their sudden dissolution, and you rejoyced that this Parliament was not to be dissolved by the King; but did you conceive it would have sat seavn yeares to so little purpose, or that it should ever have come to passe, to be esteemed a crime to move for the ending thereof? Was the perpetuating of this Parliament, and the oppressions they have brought upon you and yours, a part of that Liberty of the People you fought for? Or was it for such a Priviledge of Parliament, that they only might have liberty to oppresse at their pleasure, without any hope of remedy? If all these put together make not up the cause for which you fought, what was the Cause? What have ye obtained to the People, but these Libertyes, for they must not be called oppressions? These are the fruits of all those vast disbursements, and those thousands of lives that have been spent and destroyed in the late War.

And though the Army seemed to be sensible of these grosse juglings, and declared, and engaged against them, and professed that they tooke not paines as a mercenary Army, hired to fight for the Arbitrary ends of a State, but in judgement and conscience, for the preservation of their own, and the Peoples just Rights and Libertyes: Yet when they had prevailed against those their particular opposers, and accomplished the ends by them aymed at, all these things were forgotten, and those persons that appeared for the Peoples Freedoms, by them esteemed and proceeded against as Mutineers, or Incendiaries.

In like manner, the present Ruling Party of Presbyterians make a great shew of their apprehensions of the great slavery and servitude brought upon the People, by the exercise of an Arbitrary power in the Parliament, and by the jurisdiction of the Sword in the hands of the Army: They tell us that by this meanes the Trade of the Nation is destroyed, and that without the removall of these things, the peace of the Nation cannot be secured: And it is exceeding true: But I beseech you consider, whether they do not revive the same Play, and drive the same Designe, which was acted by the Parliament at first, and by the Army the last Summer.[a]

First, they cry out against the exercise of an arbitrary power in the Parliament, and yet labour to invest it in the King, nay challenge the exercise of it by themselves: for what greater arbitrary power can there be in the world, then that a Priest or two, and a few Lay Elders, under the name of a Presbytery, should have power to bind or loose, bring in, or cast out, save or destroy at their pleasure, and enforce all persons within the limits of their jurisdiction, to beleeve as they beleeve, and submit to whatever they command, or else to be by them delivered over to Sathan.

Nay if you looke into those of that party of the Magistracy of this City, that are the great promoters of the present worke: do there any men in the world exercise a more arbitrary power? Do not many of them act only by the Rule of will and pleasure, and have they not openly professed themselves to be obliged to observe no other Rule then Discretion.

And though they decry against the power of the Sword in the hands of the Independents, yet do they not with all their might, labour to get it into the hands of the Presbyterians? and being there, will they not do that themselves, which they complain of in others? will they not say that there are gain-sayers whose mouthes must be stopt, and with the Sword, rather then faile,[b] and though Royalists or Independents may not use the Sword to enforce their Principles, yet Presbyterians may, as if all knowledge of the truth were centred in a Presbytery, consisting of halfe Scotch, halfe English, part Puritan, part Cavalier, luke-warm christianity, neither hot nor cold, zealous for the truth which they know not, only by hearesay, and only because they love not Independency, that being too pure, nor Episcopacy, that being too prophane, they will be between both, (but not in a golden Meane, for that were well) but more zealous then either in outward performances, but for the power of godlines. – I cease to judge, but we say we may know the tree by the fruit, and certain I am that Thistles never bore Figgs.

But if you shall examine what grounds of freedome they propose in all their Papers; what equall Rules of justice they offer to be insisted on as a sure foundation for a lasting peace? Surely if you looke but seriously into the bottom of their design, you will find that the peace they aime at is only their own; not the Nations, and that their own ease, honour and dominion, is the only thing they

---

[a] Four regiments of the Army had entered the City of London in August 1647.
[b] I.e. rather than they fail themselves.

pursue, and so they could enjoy ease and plenty, and stretch themselves upon Beds of Down, they would never care what the poor Country should suffer.

To be short, all the quarrell we have at this day in the King-dome, is no other then a quarrel of Interests, and Partyes, a pulling down of one Tyrant, to set up another, and instead of Liberty, heaping upon our selves a greater slavery then that we fought against: certainly this is the Liberty that is so much strove for, and for which there are such fresh endeavours to engage men; but if you have not killed and destroyed men enough for this, go on and destroy, kill and sley, till your consciences are swoln so full with the blood of the People, that they burst agen, and upon your death-beds may you see your selves the most horrid Murtherers that ever lived, since the time that Cain kild his brother without a just Cause; for where, or what is your cause? Beleeve it yee have a heavy reeckoning to make, and must undergo a sad repentance, or it will go ill with you at the great day, when all the sophistry of your great Reformers will serve you to little purpose, every man for himselfe being to give an account for the things which he hath done in the body, whether they be good or evill: Then it will serve you to little purpose to say, the King, Parliament, Army, Independents, Presbyterians, such an Officer, Magistrate, or Minister deluded me; no more then it did Adam, to say the woman whom thou gavest, &c. It being thus decreed in heaven, the soule which sinneth shall surely dye.

And though what is past cannot be recalled, yet it must be repented of, and speciall care taken for the future, that you sin no more in this kind, and either stand still or go right for the Future, to which end, let these following directions be your guide.

You are to know, that a People living under a Government, as this Nation hath done, and doth, cannot lawfully put themselves into Arms, or engage in War, to kill and sley men, but upon a lawfull call and invitation from the Supream Authority, or Law-making power.

Now if the Supream Authority of this Nation were never yet so plainly declared, as that you understand certainly where it is, and who are invested therewith, you have then had no Warrant for what you have done, nor have any Plea in Law for your Indempn-ity, as some of all Parties have lately found to their costs.

And that this point of Supream Authority was ever certainly stated, is absolutely denyed; for according to the common suppo-sition, it is 3 Estates, which till within these few yeares were ever taken to be 1. Lords Spirituall. 2. Lords Temporall. 3. The Commons in Parliament assembled.

Now if these three were essentiall and equall, as all former Times seem to allow; How could the Lords Temporall and the Commons, cast out the Lords Spirituall? For by the same rule, the Lords Spirituall, and Lords Temporall, might have cast out the Commons, but the casting out the Bishops hath both answered the question, and ended the controversie.

Since when the supream Authority is pretended to rest in the King, Lords and Commons; and if so, when did the King assent to your Proceedings in this War, which all the art in the world will not perswade him to be for him, but against him, and to ruine him and his? Or when did the Parliament assent to the proceedings of you that joyned with the King in the late war pretendedly raised for the defence of Religion, the priviledges of Parliament, and Liberty of the Subject; and if the supream power reside in all three, King, Lords and Commons, how can the King justly do anything without the consent of the Lords and Commons, or the Lords and Commons without the King? May not the King and Lords as justly proceed to make Laws, War or Peace, without the Commons as they without the King? If they are not equal, which of them are supream, and declared and proved by convincing reason so to be? If any, that you are to observe? If none, what have you done? what can you lawfully do?

That there should be either three or two distinct Estates equally supream is an absurd nullity in government, for admit two of them agree, and not the third, then there can be no proceedings or determination, and if there be but two, as is now pretended, in Lords and Commons, whose Ordinances have served (how justly judge you) to make War and confiscate mens estates: admit they agree not, then also nothing can be done, which in Government is ridiculous to imagine, besides it is now a known case that their Ordinances are not pleadable against the Laws, and give no Indempnity, which were they the known supream Authority, could not but be effectual. That the King single and alone is the supream Authority himself never pretended to it, claiming only a negative voyce in the Law-making Power, by which rule nothing can be done without him, then which nothing is more un-reasonable: The Lords also never pretended to more then an equal share with the Commons, which in effect is a negative voyce and as unreasonable as in the King: And when the Commons have been by Petitioners stiled the supream authority, they have punished the Petitioners, and disclaimed the supream Authority; and as two years since, so very lately they have voted that the Kingdom shall be governed by King, Lords and Commons; which is a riddle that no man understands; for who knoweth what appertains to the King, what to the Lords, or what to the House of Commons? It is all out as uncertain as at first; and if the trumpet give an uncertain sound, who shall prepare himself for the battel? If by all your endeavors you cannot prevail to have the supream Authority declared and proved, how can you lawfully fight, or upon what grounds with a good conscience can you engage your selves, or perswade others to engage in killing and slaying of men?

And if you should have the supream Authority rationally proved and declared to be in the Commons distinct from any other, as being the sole Representative of the people; you must note that you are a free people, and are not to be pressed or enforced to serve in Wars like horses and bruit beasts, but are to use the understanding God hath given you, in judging of the Cause, for defence whereof they desire you to fight, for it is not sufficient to fight by lawful authority, but you must be sure to fight for what is just: Lawful authority being sometimes mistaken, and many times so perverted and corrupted, as to command the killing and imprisoning men for doing that which is just and commendable, and for opposing what is unjust and destructive. Therefore as you are to forbear till you see the supream Authority distinctly and rationally stated; so also you are not to engage till the Cause be expresly declared, lest after your next engagement you are as far to seek of a just cause as now you are; and after you have prevailed, in stead of finding your selves and your associates freemen, you find your selves more enslaved then you were formerly. For by experience you now find you may be made slaves as effectually by a Parliament, as by any other kind of Government; why then persist you to divide and fall into Factions? to kill and slay men for you know not what, to advance the honor and interest of you know not whom; the King, Parliament, great men in the City and Army can do nothing without you, to disturb the Peace of the Nation; upon you therefore both Soldiers and People, who fight, pay and disburse your estates, is to be charged all the evil that hath been done; if you on all hands had not been and were not so hasty to engage for the advancement of Interests to the prejudice of the Nation, it is very likely we had not only escaped those late bloody turmoils that have happened among us, but also might prevent greater threatned dangers, which like an inundation begin to break in upon us: And if you now stop not, your

Consciences will be loaded with all that is to come, which threatneth far worse then what is past; Therefore, if ye are either men or Christians, hold your hands till you know what you fight for, and be sure that you have the truth of Freedom in it, or never medle, but desist, and let who will both fight and pay.

Certainly there is none so vile, considering what hath been said, that will again incur the guilt of murtherers, and fight before the Cause be plainly stated and published, and if that were done as it ought to be, possibly it may be attained without fighting, and might have been all this while, the difference not being so great as was imagined; Besides, where is the man that would fight against the supream Authority, and a just Cause? and certainly there is none of you (whether Royalists, Presbyterians or Independents) so wicked as to desire to kill men without exceeding just grounds and upon the greatest necessity, it being the saddest work in the world.

For the preventing whereof, let us, I beseech you, examine what good things there are wanting, that are essential to the Peace, Freedom, and happiness of the Nation, that may not be obtained without fighting.

Is there wanting the certain knowledg where the supream Authority is, and of right ought to be; It is confest no one thing is more wanting, nor can the Nation ever be quiet, or happy without it.

But can it be any where justly and safely but in the House of Commons, who are chosen and trusted by the People? Certainly did men consider that in opposing thereof, they renounce and destroy their own freedoms, they would not do it for any thing in the world.

If the consideration of the manifold evils brought upon us by this House of Commons, deter them, the next thing that is wanting is, That a set time be appointed for the ending of this Parliament, and a certainty for future Parliaments, both for their due elections, meeting, and dissolving: And who will be so unreasonable as to oppose any of these? certainly the number cannot be considerable.

Is it also necessary That Parliaments be abridged the power of impressing men, to serve as bruit beasts in the Wars, who will be against their being bounded therein? a good Cause never wanted men, nor an authority that had money to pay them.

Hath it proved destructive in Parliaments to meddle in Religion, and to compel and restrain in matters of Gods worship? Are they evidently such things as cannot be submitted to Judgment? Doth every man find it so that hath a living Conscience? Who then will be against their binding herein, though they be entrusted to establish an uncompulsive publike way of worship for the Nation?

Is it unreasonable that any person should be exempt from those proceedings of Law, unto which the generality of the People are to be subject? Who is there then that will not willingly have all from the highest to the lowest bound alike?

That Parliaments should have no power to punish any person for doing that which is not against a known declared Law, or to take away general property, or to force men to answer to questions against themselves, or to order tryals, or proceed by any other ways then by twelve sworn men, who would not rejoyce to have such boundaries?

Then, that the proceedings in Law might be rectified, and all Laws and the duty of Magistrates written and published in English: That the Excise[a] might have a speedy end, and no Taxes but by way of subsidies: That Trade might be free, and a less burthensom way for the maintenance of Ministers be established, then that of Tythes; and that work and necessaries be provided for all kind of poor people. Certainly for the obtaining of these things a man may justly adventure his life; all these being for a common good, and tend not to the setting up of any one party or faction of men.

These then are the Causes to be insisted on, or nothing: And if the supream Authority adhere to this Cause, they need neither fear Scotch, French, nor English Enemies; but if they decline this Cause, they are to be declined; the just freedom and happiness of a Nation, being above all Constitutions, whether of Kings, Parliaments, or any other.

For shame therefore (Royalists, Presbyterians, Independents,) before you murther another man hold forth your Cause plainly and expresly; and if any Adversaries appear either within or without the Land, reason it out with them if it be possible, deal as becometh Christians, argue, perswade, and use all possible means to prevent another War, and greater blood-shed; your great ones, whether the King, Lords, Parliament men, rich Citizens, &c. feel not the miserable effects thereof, and so cannot be sensible; but you and your poor friends that depend on Farmes, Trades, and small pay, have many an aking heart when these live in all pleasure and deliciousness: The accursed thing is accepted by them, wealth and honor, and both comes by the bleeding miserable distractions of the Common-wealth, and they fear an end of trouble would put an end to their glory and greatness.

[a] Tax imposed under an Ordinance of 1643 on various foreign products, in addition to customs duty. It was highly unpopular.

Oh therefore all you Soldiers and People, that have your Consciences alive about you, put to your strength of Judgement, and all the might you have to prevent a further effusion of blood; let not the covetous, the proud, the blood-thirsty man bear sway amongst you; fear not their high looks, give no ear to their charms, their promises or tears; they have no strength without you, forsake them and ye will be strong for good, adhere to them, and they will be strong to evil; for which you must answer, and give an account at the last day.

The King, Parliament, great men in the City and Army, have made you but the stairs by which they have mounted to Honor, Wealth and Power. The only Quarrel that hath been, and at present is but this, namely, whose slaves the people shall be: All the power that any hath, was but a trust conveyed from you to them, to be employed by them for your good; they have mis-imployed their power, and instead of preserving you, have destroyed you: all Power and Authority is perverted from the King to the Constable, and it is no other but the policy of Statesmen to keep you divided by creating jealousies and fears among you, to the end that their Tyranny and Injustice may pass undiscovered and unpunished; but the peoples safety is the supream Law; and if a people must not be left without a means to preserve it self against the King, by the same rule they may preserve themselves against the Parliament and Army too; if they pervert the end for which they received their power, to wit the Nations safety; therefore speedily unite your selves together, and as one man stand up for the defence of your Freedom, and for the establishment of such equal rules of Government for the future, as shall lay a firm foundation of peace and happiness to all the people without partiallity: Let Justice be your breastplate, and you shall need to fear no enemies, for you shall strike a terrour to your now insulting oppressors, and force all the Nations Peace to fly before you. Prosecute[a] and prosper.
Vale.

Postscript

Can there be a more bloody Project then to engage men to kill one another, and yet no just cause declared? Therefore I advise all men that would be esteemed Religious or Rational, really to consider what may be done for the future that is conducible to the Peace of

[a] Persevere.

the Nation; If the Peace of the Nation cannot be secured without the Restauration of the King, let it be done speedily and honorably, and provide against his mis-government for the future; let his power be declared and limited by Law.

If the Peace of the Nation cannot be secured by the continuance of this Parliament, let a Period be set for the dissolution thereof, but first make certain provision for the successive calling, electing and sitting of Parliaments for the future; let their Priviledges be declared and power limitted, as to what they are empowred and what not; for doubtless in Parliaments rightly constituted consists the Freedom of a Nation: And in all things do as you would be done unto, seek peace with all men.

But above all things, abandon your former actings for a King against a Parliament, or an Army against both; for the Presbyterians against the Independents, &c. for in so doing you do but put a Sword into your enemies hands to destroy you, for hitherto, which of them soever were in power, they plaid the Tyrants and oppressed, and so it will ever be, when Parties are supported: Therefore if you engage at all, do it by Lawfull Authority, let your Cause be declared, and just also, and let it be for the good of the whole Nation, without which you will not only hazard being Slaves, but also contract upon your selves, and Posterities the guilt of Murtherers. *vale.*

FINIS

4. John Lilburne, 'Englands New Chains Discovered', February 1649

This pamphlet was presented on 26 February 1649 by Lilburne himself, 'with divers others', as an address to the House of Commons, and published immediately afterwards. There is a copy in the Thomason Collection, British Museum.

In *Legal Fundamental Liberties* (June 1649), Lilburne stated that on hearing of the Army Council's design to proceed against him and other Levellers, his 'spirit was all on fire'; it was this which 'justly and throughly ingaged me in the chief mannaging of the first and second part of *Englands new Chains discovered*'.

The pamphlet repeats the Levellers' demands and grievances set out in numerous petitions and manifestoes since the *Agreement of the People*, submitted to the Army Council in October 1647. But it adds treachery and tyranny to its charges against the leaders of the Long Parliament; demands specifically the dissolution of the Council of State and the ending of the revived political censorship; and warns ominously 'how dangerous it is for one and the same persons to be continued long in the highest commands of a Military power … the original of most Regalities and Tyrannies in the world'. Parliament took no action against the pamphlet; but, on the publication the following month of the much more vehement *Second Part*, the House voted that its authors were guilty of High Treason; and on 28 March Lilburne, Walwyn (who had taken no part in the pamphlet), Overton and Thomas Prince were committed to the Tower. Milton was directed by the Council of State 'to make some observations' on the pamphlet; but there is no evidence that he did so.

Our text is taken from W. Haller and G. Davies, eds., *The Leveller Tracts 1647–1653*.

Since you have done the Nation so much right, and your selves so much honour as to declare that the People (under God) are the original of all just Powers; and given us thereby fair grounds to hope, that you really intend their Freedom and Prosperity; yet the way thereunto being frequently mistaken, and through hast or error of judgment, those who mean the best, are many times mis-led so far to the prejudice of those that trust them, as to leave them in a condition neerest to bondage, when they have thought they had brought them into a way of Freedom. And since woful experience hath manifested this to be a Truth, there seemeth no small reason that you should seriously lay to heart what at present we have to offer, for discovery and prevention of so great a danger.

And because we have bin the first movers in and concerning an Agreement of the People, as the most proper and just means for the setling the long and tedious distractions of this Nation, occasioned by nothing more, than the uncertainty of our government; and

ENGLANDS
NEW CHAINS
DISCOVERED;

Or

The serious apprehensions of a part of the People, in behalf of the Commonwealth; (being Presenters, Promoters, and Approvers of the Large Petition of September 11. 1648.)

Presented to the Supreme Authority of England, the Representers of the people in Parliament assembled.

By Lieut. Col. John Lilburn, *and divers other Citizens of London, and Borough of Southwark; February 26. 1648. whereunto his speech delivered at the Bar is annexed.*

Since you have done the Nation so much right, and your selves so much honour as to declare that the People (under God) are the original of all just Powers; and given us thereby fair grounds to hope, that you really intend their Freedom and Prosp ity; yet the way thereunto being frequently mistaken, and through hast or error of judgement, those who mean the best, are many times mis-led so far to the prejudice of those that trust them, as to leave them in a condition neerest to bondage, when they have thought they had brought them into a way of Freedom. And since woful experience hath manifested this to be a Truth, there seemeth no small reason that you should seriously lay to heart what at present we have to offer, for discovery and prevention of so great a danger.

And because we have bin the first movers in and concerning an *Agreement of the People,* as the most proper and just means for the setling the long and tedious distractions of this Nation, occasioned by nothing more, than the uncertainty of our government; and since there hath bin an Agreement prepared and presented by some Officers of the Army to this honourable House, as what they thought requisite to be agreed unto by the People (you approving thereof) we shall in the first place deliver our apprehensions thereupon.

That an Agreement between those that trust, and those who are trusted, hath appeared a thing acceptable to this honorable House,

A   his

since there hath bin an Agreement prepared and presented by some Officers of the Army to this honourable House, as what they thought requisite to be agreed unto by the People (you approving thereof) we shall in the first place deliver our apprehensions thereupon.

That an Agreement between those that trust, and those who are trusted, hath appeared a thing acceptable to this honorable House, his Excellency, and the Officers of the Army, is as much to our rejoycing, as we conceive it just in it self, and profitable for the Common-wealth, and cannot doubt but that you will protect those of the people, who have no waies forfeited their Birth-right, in their proper liberty of taking this, or any other, as God and their own Considerations shall direct them.

Which we the rather mention, for that many particulars in the Agreement before you, are upon serious examination thereof, dis-satisfactory to most of those who are very earnestly desirous of an Agreement, and many very material things seem to be wanting therein, which may be supplyed in another: As

1. They are now much troubled there should be any Intervalls between the ending of this Representative, and the begining of the next as being desirous that this present Parliament that hath lately done so great things in so short a time, tending to their Liberties, should sit; until with certainty and safety they can see them delivered into the hands of another Representative, rather than to leave them (though never so small a time) under the dominion of a Councel of State; a Constitution of a new and unexperienced Nature, and which they fear, as the case now stands, may design to perpetuate their power, and to keep off Parliaments for ever.

2. They now conceive no less danger, in that it is provided that Parliaments for the future are to continue but 6. moneths, and a Councel of State 18. In which time, if they should prove corrupt, having command of all Forces by Sea and Land, they will have great opportunities to make themselves absolute and unaccountable: And because this is a danger, than which there cannot well be a greater; they generally incline to Annual Parliaments, bounded and limited as reason shall devise, not dissolvable, but to be continued or adjourned as shall seem good in their discretion, during that yeer, but no longer; and then to dissolve of course, and give way to those who shall be chosen immediatly to succeed them, and in the Intervals of their adjournments, to entrust an ordinary Committee of their own members, as in other cases limited and bounded with express instructions, and accountable to the next Session, which

will avoid all those dangers feared from a Councel of State, as at present this is constituted.

3. They are not satisfied with the clause, wherein it is said, that the power of the Representatives shall extend to the erecting and abolishing of Courts of Justice; since the alteration of the usual way of Tryals by twelve sworn men of the Neighborhood, may be included therein: a constitution so equal and just in it self, as that they conceive it ought to remain unalterable. Neither is it cleer what is meant by these words, (viz.) That the Representatives have the highest final judgment. They conceiving that their Authority in these cases, is onely to make Laws, Rules, and Directions for other Courts and Persons assigned by Law for the execution thereof; unto which every member of the Commonwealth, as well those of the Representative, as others, should be alike subject; it being likewise unreasonable in it self, and an occasion of much partiality, injustice, and vexation to the people, that the Law-makers, should be Law-executors.

4. Although it doth provide that in the Laws hereafter to be made, no person by vertue of any Tenure, Grant, Charter, Patent, Degree, or Birth, shall be priviledged from subjection thereunto, or from being bound thereby, as well as others; Yet doth it not null and make void those present Protections by Law, or otherwise; nor leave all persons, as well Lords as others, alike liable in person and estate, as in reason and conscience they ought to be.

5. They are very much unsatisfied with what is exprest as a reserve from the Representative, in matters of Religion, as being very obscure, and full of perplexity, that ought to be most plain and clear; there having occurred no greater trouble to the Nation about any thing than by the intermedling of Parliaments in matters of Religion.

6. They seem to conceive it absolutely necessary, that there be in their Agreement, a reserve from ever having any Kingly Government, and a bar against restoring the House of Lords, both which are wanting in the Agreement which is before you.

7. They seem to be resolved to take away all known and burdensome grievances, as Tythes, that great oppression of the Countries industry and hindrance of Tillage:[a] Excise, and Customs, Those secret thieves, and Robbers, Drainers of the poor and middle sort of People, and the greatest Obstructers of Trade, surmounting all the prejudices of Ship-mony, Pattents, and Projects, before this

---

[a] Cultivation of the land.

Parliament: also to take away all Monopolizing Companies of Marchants, the hinderers and decayers of Clothing and Cloth-working, Dying, and the like useful professions; by which thousands of poor people might be set at work, that are now ready to starve, were Marchandizing restored to its due and proper freedom: they conceive likewise that the three grievances before mentioned, (viz.) Monopolizing Companies, Excise, and Customes, do exceedingly prejudice Shiping, and Navigation, and Consequently discourage Sea-men, and Marriners, and which have had no smal influence upon the late unhappy revolts which have so much endangered the Nation, and so much advantaged your enemies. They also incline to direct a more equal and lesse burdensome way for levying monies for the future, those other fore-mentioned being so chargable in the receipt, as that the very stipends and allowance to the Officers attending there-upon would defray a very great part of the charge of the Army; whereas now they engender and support a corrupt interest. They also have in mind to take away all imprisonment of disabled men, for debt; and to provide some effectual course to enforce all that are able to a speedy payment, and not suffer them to be sheltered in Prisons, where they live in plenty, whilst their Creditors are undone. They have also in mind to provide work, and comfortable maintainance for all sorts of poor, aged, and impotent pepole, and to establish some more speedy, lesse troublesome and chargeable way for deciding of Controversies in Law, whole families having been ruined by seeking right in the wayes yet in being: All which, though of greatest and most immediate concernment to the People, are yet omitted in their Agreement before you.

These and the like are their intentions in what they purpose for an Agreement of the People, as being resolved (so far as they are able) to lay an impossibility upon all whom they shall hereafter trust, of ever wronging the Common wealth in any considerable measure, without certainty of ruining themselves, and as conceiving it to be an improper tedious, and unprofitable thing for the People, to be ever runing after their Representatives with Petitions for redresse of such Grievances as may at once be removed by themselves, or to depend for these things so essential to their happinesse and freedom, upon the uncertain judgements of several Representatives, the one being apt to renew what the other hath taken away.

And as to the use of their Rights and Liberties herein as becometh, and is due to the people, from whom all just powers are derived; they hoped for and expect what protection is in you and the Army to afford: and we likwise in their and our own behalfs do earnestly desire, that you will publikely declare your resolution to protect those who have not forfeited their liberties in the use thereof, lest they should conceive that the Agreement before you being published abroad, and the Commissioners therein nominated being at work in persuance thereof, is intended to be imposed upon them, which as it is absolutely contrary to the nature of a free Agreement, so we are perswaded it cannot enter into your thoughts to use any impulsion therein.

But although we have presented our apprehensions and desires concerning this great work of an Agreement, and are apt to perswade our selves that nothing shall be able to frustrate our hopes which we have built thereupon; yet have we seen and heard many things of late, which occasions not only apprehensions of other matters intended to be brought upon us of danger to such an Agreement, but of bondage and ruine to all such as shall pursue it.

Insomuch that we are even agast and astonished to see that notwithstanding the productions of the highest notions of freedom that ever this Nation, or any people in the world, have brought to light, notwithstanding the vast expence of blood and treasure that hath been made to purchase those freedoms, notwithstanding the many eminent and even miraculous Victories God hath been pleased to honour our just Cause withall, notwithstanding the extraordinary gripes and pangs, this House hath suffered more than once at the hands of your own servants, and that at least seemingly for the obtaining these our Native Liberties.

When we consider what rackings and tortures the People in general have suffered through decay of Trade, and deernesse of food, and very many families in particular, through Free-quarter,[a] Violence, and other miseries, incident to warre, having nothing to support them therein, but hopes of Freedom, and a well-setled Common-wealth in the end.

That yet after all these things have bin done and suffered, and whilst the way of an Agreement of the People is owned, and approved, even by your selves, and that all men are in expectation of being put into possession of so deer a purchase; Behold! in the close of all, we hear and see what gives us fresh and pregnant cause to believe that the contrary is really intended, and that all those specious pretenses, and high Notions of Liberty, with those extra-ordinary courses that have of late bin taken (as if of necessity for

---

[a] The enforced obligation on civilian families to quarter soldiers free.

liberty, and which indeed can never be justified, but deserve the greatest punishments, unless they end in just liberty, and an equal Government) appear to us to have bin done and directed by some secret powerful influences, the more securely and unsuspectedly to attain to an absolute domination over the Common-wealth: It being impossible for them, but by assuming our generally approved Principles, and hiding under the fair shew thereof their other designs, to have drawn in so many good and godly men (really aiming at what the other had but in shew and pretense) and making them unwittingly instrumental to their own and their Countries Bondage.

For where is that good, or where is that liberty so much pretended, so deerly purchased? If we look upon what this House hath done since it hath voted it self the Supreme Authority, and disburthened themselves of the power of the Lords. First, we find a high Court of Justice erected, for Tryal of Criminal causes; whereby that great and strong hold of our preservation, the way of tryal by 12. sworn men of the Neighborhood is infringed, all liberty of exception against the tryers, is over-ruled by a Court consisting of persons pickt and chosen in an un-usual way; the practise whereof we cannot allow of, though against open and notorious enemies; as well because we know it to be an usual policy to introduce by such means all usurpations, first against Adversaries, in hope of easier admission; as also, for that the same being so admited, may at pleasure be exercised against any person or persons whatsoever. This is the first part of our new liberty. The next is the censuring of a Member of this House, for declaring his judgment in a point of Religion, which is directly opposite to the Reserve in the Agreement concerning Religion. Besides the Act for pressing of Sea-men, directly contrary to the Agreement of the Officers. Then the stoping of our mouths from Printing, is carefully provided for, and the most severe and unreasonable Ordinances of Parliament that were made in the time of Hollis and Stapletons reign,[a] to gag us from speaking truth, and discovering the tyrannies of bad men, are refered to the care of the General, and by him to his Marshal, to be put in execution; in searching, fining, imprisoning, and other waies corporally punishing all that any waies be guilty of unlicensed Printing; They dealing with us as the Bishops of old did with the honest Puritan, who were exact in geting Laws made against the

---

[a] Denzil Holles (1599–1680) and Sir Philip Stapleton (1603–47), the leaders of the Presbyterians, impeached by the Army, with nine others, on 16 June 1647, accused of overthrowing the liberties of the subject.

Papist, but really intended them against the Puritan, and made them feel the smart of them: Which also hath bin, and is dayly exercised most violently, whereby our Liberties have bin more deeply wounded, than since the begining of this Parliament; and that to the dislike of the Souldiery, as by their late Petition in that behalf plainly appeareth. Then whereas it was expected that the Chancery, and Courts of Justice in Westminster, and the Judges and Officers thereof should have bin surveyed, and for the present regulated, till a better and more equal way of deciding controversies could have bin constituted, that the trouble and charge of the people in their suits should have bin abated: Insteed hereof, the old and advanced fees are continued, and new thousand pounds Annual stipends alotted; when in the corruptest times the ordinary fees were thought a great and a sore burden; in the mean time, and in lieu thereof, there is not one perplexity or absurdity in proceedings taken away. Those Petitioners that have moved in behalf of the people, how have they bin entertained? Sometimes with the complement of empty thanks, their desires in the mean time not at all considered; at other times meeting with Reproches and Threats for their constancy and publike affections, and with violent motions, that their Petitions be burnt by the common Hangman, whilst others are not taken in at all; to so small an account are the people brought, even while they are flattered with notions of being the Original of all just power. And lastly, for compleating this new kind of liberty, a Councel of State is hastily erected for Guardians thereof, who to that end are possessed with power to order and dispose all the forces appertaining to England by Sea or Land, to dispose of the publike Treasure, to command any person whatsoever before them, to give oath for the discovering of Truth, to imprison any that shall dis-obey their commands, and such as they shall judge contumatious. What now is become of that liberty that no mans person shall be attached or imprisoned, or otherwise dis-eased of his Free-hold, or free Customs, but by lawful judgement of his equals? We entreat you give us leave to lay these things open to your view, and judge impartially of our present condition, and of your own also, that by strong and powerfull influences of some persons, are put upon these and the like proceedings, which both you and we ere long (if we look not to it) shall be inforced to subject our selves unto; then we have further cause to complain, when we consider the persons: as first, the chief of the Army directly contrary to what themselves thought meet in their Agreement for the People. 2. Judges of the Law. and Treasurers for monies. Then 5. that were Members of the Lords House, and most of them such as have refused to approve of your Votes and proceedings, concerning the King and Lords. 2. of them Judges in the Star-chamber, and approvers of the bloudy and tyrannical sentences issuing from thence.

Some of your own House, forward men in the Treaty, and decliners of your last proceedings; all which do cleerly manifest to our understandings that the secret contrivers of those things doe think themselves now so surely guarded by the strength of an Army, by their dayly Acts and Stratagems, to their ends inclined, and the captivation of his House, that they may now take off the Vail and Cloak of their designes as dreadlesse of what ever can be done against them. By this Councel of State, all power is got into their own hands, a project which hath been long and industriously laboured for; and which being once firmly and to their liking established their next motions may be upon pretense of ease to the People, for the dissolution of this Parliament, half of whose time is already swallowed up by the said Councel now, because no obstacle lies in their way, to the full establishment of these their ends, but the uncorrupted part of the Souldiery, that have their eyes fixed upon their ingagements and promises of good to the People, and resolve by no threats or allurements to decline the same; together with that part of the people in Citie and Countries, that remain constant in their motions for Common good, and still persist to run their utmost hazards for procurement of the same, by whom all evil mens designes both have, and are still likely to find a check and discovery. Hereupon the grand contrivers fore-mentioned, whom we can particular by name, do begin to raise their spleen, and manifest a more violent enmitie against Souldiers and People, disposed as afore-said, than ever theretofore, as appeareth by what lately past, at a meeting of Officers, on Feb. 22. last, at White-Hall, where after expressions of much bitternesse against the most Conscientious part of the Souldiery, and others, it was insisted upon, (as we are from very credible hands certainly informed) that a motion should be made to this House for the procurement of a Law enabling them to put to death all such as they should judge by Petitions or otherwise to disturbe the present proceedings; and upon urging that the Civil Magistrate should do it, It was answered, that they could hang twenty ere the Magistrate one. It was likewise urged that Orders might be given to seize upon the Petitioners, Souldiers, or others, at their meetings, with much exclamation against some of greatest integritie to your just Authority, whereof they have given continual and undenyable assurances. A Proclamation was likewise appointed, forbidding the Souldiers to Petition you, or any but their Officers, prohibiting their correspondencies: And private Orders to be given out for seizing upon Citizens and Souldiers at their meetings. And thus after these fair blossoms of hopefull liberty, breaks forth this bitter fruit, of the vilest and basest bondage that ever English men groan'd under: whereby this notwithstanding is gained (viz.) an evident and (we hope) a timely discovery of the instruments, from whence all the evils, contrivances, and designes (which for above these eighteen moneths have been strongly suspected) took their rise and original, even ever since the first breach of their Promises and engagements made at New Market, Triploe Heath, with the Agitators and People.[a] It being for these ends that they have so violently opposed all such as manifested any zeal for Common Right, or any regard to the Faith of the Army, sentencing some to death, others to reproachful punishments, placing and dis-placing Officers according as they shewed themselves serviceable or opposite to their designes, listing as many as they thought good, even of such as have served in Arms against you: And then again upon pretence of easing the charge of the People, disbanding Supernumeraries,[b] by advantage thereof picking out, such as were most cordial and active for Common good; thereby moulding the Army (as far as they could) to their own bent and ends premised; exercising Martial Law with much cruelty, thereby to debase their spirits, and make them subservient to their wils and pleasures; extending likewise their power (in many cases) over persons not Members of the Army.

And when in case of opposition and difficult services, they have by their creatures desired a Reconciliation with such as at other times they reproached, vilified, and otherwise abased; and through fair promises of good, and dissembled repentance gained their association and assistance, to the great advantage of their proceedings: yet their necessities being over, and the Common enemy subdued, they have sleighted their former promises, and renewed their hate and bitternesse against such their assistances, reproaching them with such appellations as they knew did most distaste the People, such as Levellers, Jesuites, Anarchists, Royalists,

---

[a] The *Solemn Engagement* of 5 June 1647 between the Army and Parliament, which first refers to Agitators; and the *Declaration, or, Representation* 'Concerning the just and Fundamental Rights and Liberties of themselves and the Kingdom'. Both were entered into at Newmarket Heath, the Army rendezvous.

[b] Officers not formally belonging to the Army, summoned in an emergency.

names both contradictory in themselves, and altogether groundlesse in relation to the men so reputed; meerly relying for releese thereof upon the easinesse and credulity of the People.

And though the better to insinuate themselves, and get repute with the People, as also to conquer their necessities, they have bin fane to make use of those very principles and productions, the men they have so much traduced, have brought to light: yet the producers themselves they have and doe still more eagerly maligne than ever, as such whom they know to bee acquainted to their deceipts, and deviations and best able to discover the same.

So that now at length, guessing all to be sure, and their own (the King being removed, the House of Lords nulled, their long plotted Councel of State erected, and this House awed to their ends,) the edge of their mallice is turning against such as have yet so much courage left them as to appear for the well establishment of Englands Liberties: and because God hath preserved a great part of the Army untainted with the guilt of the designes afore-mentioned, who cannot without much danger to the designers themselves be suppressed, they have resolved to put this House upon raising more new forces, (notwithstanding the present necessities of the People, in maintaining those that are already) in doing whereof, though the pretence be danger, and opposition, yet the concealed end is like to be the over-ballancing those in the Army, who are resolved to stand for true Freedome, as the end of all their labours, the which (if they should be permitted to do) they would not then doubt of making themselves absolute seizures, Lords and Masters, both of Parliament and People; which when they have done we expect the utmost of misery, nor shall it grieve us to expire with the liberties of our native Country: for what good man can with any comfort to himself survive then? But God hath hitherto preserved us, and the Justice of our desires, as integrity of our intentions are dayly more and more manifest to the impartial and unprejudiced part of men; insomuch that it is no smal comfort to us, that notwithstanding we are upon all these disadvantages that may be, having neither power nor preheminence, the Common Idols of the world; our Cause and principles, do through their own natural truth and lustre get ground in mens understandings, so that where there was one, twelve moneths since, that owned our principles, we beleeve there are now hundreds, so that though we fail, our Truths prosper.

And posterity we doubt not shall reap the benefit of our endeavours, what ever shall become of us. However though we have neither strength nor safety before us, we have discharged our

Consciences, and emptied our breasts unto you, knowing well that if you will make use of your power, and take unto you that courage which becomes men of your Trust and condition, you may yet through the goodnesse of God prevent the danger and mischief intended, and be instrumental in restoring this long enthralled and betrayed Nation into a good and happy condition.

For which end we most earnestly desire and propose, as the main prop and support of the work, [1] that you will not dissolve this House, nor suffer your selves to be dissolved, until as aforesaid, you see a new Representative the next day ready to take your room; which you may confidently and safely insist upon, there being no considerable number in the Army or else-where, that will be so unworthy as to dare to disturb you therein.

2. That you will put in practise the self-denying Ordinance,[a] the most just and useful that ever was made, and continually cryed out for by the people; whereby a great infamy that lies upon your cause will be removed, and men of powerful influences, and dangerous designes, deprived of those means and opportunities which now they have, to prejudice the publike.

3. That you will consider how dangerous it is for one and the same persons to be continued long in the highest commands of a Military power, especially acting so long distinct, and of themselves, as those now in being have done, and in such extraordinary waies whereunto they have accustomed themselves, which was the original of most Regalities and Tyrannies in the world.

4. That you appoint a Committee of such of your own members, as have bin longest establisht upon those rules of Freedom upon which you now proceed; to hear, examine, and conclude all controversies between Officers and Officers, and between Officers and Souldiers; to consider and mitigate the Law-Martial; and to provide that it be not exercised at all upon persons not of the Army: Also to release and repair such as have thereby unduly suffered, as they shall see cause: To consider the condition of the private Souldiers, both Horse and Foot in these deer times, and to allow them such increase of pay, as wherewithal they may live comfortably, and honestly discharge their Quarters: That all disbanding be referred to the said Committee, and that such of the Army as have served the King, may be first disbanded.

5. That you will open the Press, whereby all trecherous and tyranical designes may be the easier discovered, and so prevented, which is a liberty of greatest concernment to the Commonwealth, and

[a] Under which no member of either Lords or Commons could hold office in the Army; finally passed by the Lords on 3 April 1645.

which such only as intend a tyrannie are engaged to prohibit: The mouths of Adversaries being best stopped, by the sensible good which the people receive from the actions of such as are in Authority.

6. That you wil (whilst you have opportunity) abate the charge of the Law, and reduce the stipends of Judges, and all other Magistrates and Officers in the Common-wealth, to a less, but competent allowance, converting the over-plus to the publike Treasury, whereby the taxes of the people may be much eased.

7. But above all, that you will dissolve this present Councel of State, which upon the grounds fore-mentioned so much threatneth Tyrannie; and mannage your affairs by Committees of short continuance, and such as may be frequently and exactly accountable for the discharge of their Trusts.

8. That you will publish a strict prohibition, and severe penalty against all such, whether Committees, Magistrates, or Officers of what kind so-ever, as shall exceed the limits of their Commission, Rules, or Directions, and incourage all men in their informations and complaints against them.

9. That you will speedily satisfie the expectations of the Souldiers in point of Arrears, and of the people in point of Accounts, in such a manner, as that it may not as formerly, prove a snare to such as have bin most faithful, and a protection to the most corrupt, in the discharge of their trust and duties.

10. That the so many times complained of Ordinance for Tyths upon treble damages,[a] may be forthwith taken away; all which, together with due regard shewed to Petitioners, without respect to their number and strength, would so fasten you in the affections of the people, and of the honest Officers and Souldiers, as that you should not need to fear any opposite power whatsoever: and for the time to come, of your selves enjoy the exercise of your Supreme Authority, whereof you have yet but the name onely; and be inabled to vindicate your just undertakings; wherein we should not onely rejoyce to have occasion to manifest how ready we should be to hazard our lives in your behalf, but should also bend all our studies and endeavours to render you Honorable to all future generations.

Febr. 26. 1648. Being ushered in by the Sergeant at Arms, and called to the Bar, with all due respects given unto the House, Lieutenant Colonel John Lilburn, with divers others, coming to

---

[a] The penal proceedings for recovery of unpaid tithes in the ecclesiastical courts.

the Bar next the Mace, with the Address in his hand, spake these words, or to this effect, as followeth.

M. Speaker,

I am very glad that without any inconvenience unto my self, and those that are with me, I may freely and cheerfully address my self to this honorable House, as the Supreme Authority of England (time was when I could not) and it much refresheth my spirit, to live to see this day, that you have made such a step to the Peoples Liberties, as to own and declare your selves to be (as indeed you are) the Supreme Authority of this Nation.

M. Speaker, I am desired by a company of honest men, living in and about London, who in truth do rightly appropriate to themselves, the title of the Contrivers, Promoters, Presenters, and Approvers of the late Large London Petition of the 11. of Sept. last,[a] (which was the first Petition I know of in England, that was presented to this honorable House against the late destructive Personal Treaty with the late King) to present you with their serious apprehensions; And give me leave (I beseech you) for my self and them, to say thus much; That for the most part of us, we are those that in the worst of times durst own our Liberties and Freedoms, in the face of the greatest of our adversaries; and from the begining of these Wars, never shrunk from the owning of our Freedoms, in the most tempestuous times, nor changed our Principles: Nay Sir, let me with truth tell you, that to the most of us, our Wives, our Children, our Estates, our Relations, nay our Lives, and all that upon earth we can call Ours, have not bin so highly valued by us, as our Liberties and Freedoms; which our constant Actions (to the apparent hazard of our Bloud and Lives) have bin a cleer and full demonstration of, for these many yeers together.

And M. Speaker, give me leave to tell you, that I am confident our Liberties and Freedoms (the true and just end of all the late Wars) are so deer and precious to us, that we had rather our Lives should breath out with them, than to live one moment after the expiration of them.

M. Speaker, I must confess I am to present you with a paper, something of a new kind, for we have had no longer time to consider of it, than from Thursday last, and Warrants (as we are informed) issuing out against us to take us, from those that have no power over us; we durst not well go our ordinary way to work, to

---

[a] The Levellers' *Humble Petition* of 11 Sept. 1648.

get Subscriptions to it, lest we should be surprised before we could present it to this honorable House, and so be frustrated in that benefit or relief that we justly expect from you; and to present it with a few hands, we judged inconsiderable in your estimation, and therefore chuse in the third place (being in so much hast as we were to prevent our eminent and too apparent ruine) in person to bring it to your Bar, and avowedly to present it here: And therefore without any further question, give me leave to tell you, I own it, and I know so doth all the rest of my Friends present; and if any hazard should ensue thereby, Give me leave resolvedly to tell you, I am sorry I have but one life to lose, in maintaining the Truth, Justice, and Righteousness, of so gallant a piece.

M. Speaker, We own this honorable House (as of right) the true Guardian of our Liberties and Freedoms; and we wish and most heartily desire, you would rouse up your spirits (like men of gallantry) and now at last take unto your selves a magnanimous resolution, to acquit your selves (without fear or dread) like the chosen and betrusted Trustees of the People, from whom (as your selves acknowledge and declare) all just power is derived, to free us from all bondage and slavery, and really and truly invest us into the price of all our bloud, hazards, and toyls; Our Liberties and Freedoms, the true difference and distinction of men from beasts.

M. Speaker, Though my spirit is full in the sad apprehension of the dying condition of our Liberties and Freedoms: Yet at present I shall say no more, but in the behalf of my self and my friends, I shall earnestly entreat you to read these our serious Apprehensions seriously, and debate them deliberatley.

Friends,

This we have adventured to publish for the timely information and benefit of all that adhere unto the common interest of the people, hoping that with such, upon due consideration, it will find as large an acceptance, as our late Petition of Sept. 11. 1648. And we thought good (in regard we were not called in to receive an answer to the same) to acquaint you, that we intend to second it with a Petition sufficiently subscribed, we doubt not with many thousands, earnestly to solicite for an effectual Answer.

FINIS

5. John Milton, 'The Tenure of Kings and Magistrates', February 1649

The text is that of the first edition. In the second edition, February 1650, Milton added a list of Protestant apologists for tyrannicide, led by Luther and Calvin. Thomason dated his copy of the first edition 13 February 1649. It was almost certainly conceived and mainly written during Charles's trial, and completed after his execution on 30 January. It is both a passionately argued and biblically and historically supported defence of tyrannicide: of the people's right to depose and punish unjust kings; and a polemic against the Presbyterians, who were now arguing against Charles's deposition and execution. Its central argument against tyranny goes back to Aristotle in the *Nicomachean Ethics* (VIII, x); but its justification of government as made necessary by the Fall shows the link between Milton's political thought and that of the opening tract in this collection, Parker's *Observations Upon Some of His Majesties Late Answers and Expresses*. Our text is taken from John T. Shawcross, ed., *The Tenure of Kings and Magistrates* in *The Prose of John Milton*, ed. J. Max Patrick (New York, 1967).

THE TENURE OF KINGS AND MAGISTRATES:

PROVING, THAT IT IS LAWFULL, AND HATH BEEN HELD SO THROUGH ALL AGES, FOR ANY, WHO HAVE THE POWER, TO CALL TO ACCOUNT A TYRANT, OR WICKED KING, AND AFTER DUE CONVICTION, TO DEPOSE, AND PUT HIM TO DEATH; IF THE ORDINARY MAGISTRATE HAVE NEGLECTED, OR DENY'D TO DOE IT. AND THAT THEY, WHO OF LATE, SO MUCH BLAME DEPOSING, ARE THE MEN THAT DID IT THEMSELVES.

THE AUTHOR, J. M.

LONDON, Printed by Matthew Simmons, at the Gilded Lyon in Aldersgate Street, 1649.

If Men within themselves would be govern'd by reason, and not generally give up their understanding to a double tyrannie, of custome from without, and blind affections within, they would discerne better what it is to favour and uphold the Tyrant of a Nation. But being slaves within doores, no wonder that they strive so much to have the public State conformably govern'd to the inward vitious rule, by which they govern themselves. For indeed none can love freedom heartilie, but good men; the rest love not freedom, but licence; which never hath more scope or more indulgence than under Tyrants. Hence is it that Tyrants are not oft offended, nor stand much in doubt of bad men, as being all naturally servile,[1] but in whom vertue and true worth most is eminent, them they feare in earnest, as by right their Masters, against them lies all their hatred and suspicion. Consequentlie neither doe bad men hate Tirants, but have been alwaies readiest with the falsifi'd names of *Loyalty* and *Obedience*, to colour over their base compliances. And although sometimes for shame, and when it comes to their owne grievances, of purse especially, they would seeme good Patriots, and side with the better cause, yet when others for the deliverance of their Countrie, endu'd with fortitude and Heroick vertue, to feare nothing but the curse written against those *That doe the worke of the Lord negligently*,[2] would goe on to remove, not onely the calamities and thraldomes of a people, but the roots and causes whence they spring, streight these men,[a] and sure helpers at need, as if they hated onely the miseries but not the mischiefes, after they have juggl'd and palter'd with the World, bandied and borne armes against their King, devested him, disanointed him, nay curs'd him all over in thir Pulpits, and their Pamphlets, to the ingaging of sincere and reall men, beyond what is possible or honest to retreat from, not onely turne revolters from those principles, which onely could at first move them, but lay the staine of disloyaltie, and worse, on those proceedings, which are the necessarie consequences of their owne former actions; nor dislik'd by themselves, were they manag'd to the intire advantages of their owne Faction; not considering the while that he toward whom they boasted their new fidelitie, counted them accessory, and by those Statutes and Laws which they so impotently brandish against others, would have doom'd them to a traytors death for what they have done alreadie. Tis true, that most men are apt anough to civill Wars and commotions as a noveltie, and for a flash, hot and active;

[a] The Presbyterians.

but through sloth or inconstancie, and weakness of spirit either fainting, ere their owne pretences, though never so just, be halfe attain'd, or through an inbred falshood and wickednesse, betray oft times to destruction with themselves, men of noblest temper join'd with them for causes which they in their rash undertakings were not capable of. If God and a good cause give them Victory, the prosecution whereof for the most part, inevitably drawes after it the alteration of Lawes, change of Government, downfall of Princes with their Families; then comes the task to those Worthies which are the soule of that Enterprize, to bee swett[a] and labour'd out amidst the throng and noises of vulgar and irrationall men. Some contesting for Privileges, customes, formes, and that old intanglement of iniquitie, their gibrish Lawes,[b] though the badge of their ancient slavery. Others who have been fiercest against their Prince, under the notion of a Tyrant, and no meane incendiaries of the Warre against him, when God out of his providence and high disposall hath deliver'd him into the hand of their brethren, on a suddaine and in a new garbe of Allegiance, which their doings have long since cancell'd; they plead for him, pity him, extoll him, protest against those that talke of bringing him to the tryall of Justice, which is the Sword of God, superiour to all mortall things, in whose hand soever by apparent signes his testified wil is to put it. But certainely, if we consider who and what they are, on a suddaine growne so pitifull, wee may conclude, their pity can be no true and Christian commiseration, but either levitie and shallownesse of minde, or else a carnall admiring of that worldly pompe and greatness, from whence they see him fall'n; or rather lastly a dissembl'd and seditious pity, fain'd of industry to beget new commotions. As for mercy, if it bee to a Tyrant, under which name they themselves have cited him so oft in the hearing of God, of Angels, and the holy Church assembl'd, and there charg'd him with the spilling of more innocent blood by farre, than ever *Nero* did, undoubtedly the mercy which they pretend, is the mercy of wicked men; and their mercies, wee read, are cruelties;[3] hazarding the welfare of a whole Nation, to have sav'd one, whom so oft they have tearm'd *Agag*,[c] and villifying the blood of many *Jonathans* that have sav'd *Israel*;[d] insisting with much nicenesse on the unnecessariest clause[e] of their Covnant; wherein the feare of change, and the absurd contradiction of a flattering hostilitie had hamperd them,

---

[a] Sweated.   [b] The Anglo-Norman laws of the Conquest.
[c] King of the Amalekites, spared by Saul against God's will (1 Sam. xv, 9–11).
[d] As his father Saul had planned to do.   [e] To preserve the King's person and authority.

but not scrupling to give away for complements, to an implacable revenge, the heads of many thousand Christians more.

Another sort there is, who comming in the course of these affaires, to have thir share in great actions above the forme of Law or Custome, at least to give thir voice and approbation, begin to swerve and almost shiver at the majesty and grandeur of som noble deed, as if they were newly enter'd into a great sin; disputing presidents,[a] formes, and circumstances, when the Common wealth nigh perishes for want of deeds in substance, don with just and faithfull expedition. To these I wish better instruction, and vertue equall to their calling; the former of which, that is to say Instruction, I shall indeavour, as my dutie is, to bestow on them; and exhort them not to startle[b] from the just and pious resolution of adhering with all their assistance to the present Parlament and Army, in the glorious way wherein Justice and Victorie hath set them; the onely warrants through all ages, next under immediate Revelation, to exercise supreme power; in those proceedings which hitherto appeare equali to what hath been don in any age or Nation hertofore, justly or magnanimouslie. Nor let them be discourag'd or deterr'd by any new Apostate Scarcrowes,[c] who under show of giving counsell, send out their barking monitories and *mimento's*,[d] emptie of ought else but the spleene of a frustrated Faction. For how can that pretended counsell, bee either sound or faithfull, when they that give it, see not for madnesse and vexation of their ends lost, that those Statutes and Scriptures which both falsly and scandalously, they wrest against their Friends and Associates, would by sentence of the common adversarie, fall first and heaviest upon their owne heads. Neither let milde and tender dispositions be foolishly softn'd from their dutie and perseverance with the unmasculine Rhetorick of any puling Priest or Chaplain, sent as a friendly Letter of advice, for fashion-sake in private, and forthwith publish't by the Sender himselfe, that wee may know how much of friend there was in it, to cast an odious envie upon them, to whom it was pretended to be sent in charitie. Nor let any man bee deluded by either the ignorance or the notorious hypocrisie and selfe-repugnance of our dancing Divines,[e] who have the conscience and the boldnesse, to come with Scripture in their mouthes, gloss'd and fitted for thir turnes with a double contradictory sense, transforming the sacred veritie of God, to an Idol with two faces,

---

[a] Precedents.　[b] Swerve.　[c] William Prynne, in particular.
[d] Prynne's *A Briefe Memento*, 4 Jan. 1649, attacking the leaders of the Rump Parliament.
[e] Such as Charles's chaplain, Henry Hammond, who had appealed to Fairfax to save him.

looking at once two several ways; and with the same quotations to charge others, which in the same case they made serve to justifie themselves. For while the hope to bee made Classic and Provinciall Lords[a] led them on, while pluralities[b] greas'd them thick and deepe, to the shame and scandall of Religion, more than all the Sects and Heresies they exclaime against, then to fight against the Kings person, and no lesse a party of his Lords and Commons, or to put force upon both the Houses was good, was lawfull, was no resisting of Superiour powers; they onely were powers not to be resisted, who countenanc'd the good and punish't the evill. But now that thir censorious domineering is not suffer'd to be universall, truth and conscience to be freed, Tithes and Pluralities to be no more, though competent allowance provided, and the warme experience of large gifts, and they so good at taking them; yet now to exclude and sieze on impeach't Members,[c] to bring Delinquents without exemption to a faire Tribunall by the common Nationall Law against murder, is now to be no lesse than *Corah, Dathan*, and *Abiram*.[d] He who but erewhile in the Pulpits was a cursed Tyrant, an enemie to God and Saints, laden with all the innocent blood spilt in three Kingdomes, and so to bee fought against, is now though nothing penitent or alter'd from his first principles, a lawfull Magistrate, a Sovrane Lord, the Lords Annointed, not to bee touch'd, though by themselves imprison'd. As if this onely were obedience, to preserve the meere uselesse bulke of his person, and that onely in prison, not in the field, and to disobey his commands, denie him his dignitie and office, every where to resist his power but where they thinke it onely surviving in thir owne faction.

But who in particular is a Tyrant cannot be determined in a generall discourse, otherwise than by supposition; his particular charge, and the sufficient proofe of it must determine that: which I leave to Magistrates, at least to the uprighter sort of them, and of the people, though in number lesse by many, in whom faction least hath prevaild above the Law of nature and right reason, to judge as they finde cause. But this I dare owne as part of my faith, that if such a one there be by whose Commission, whole massacres have been committed on his faithfull Subjects,[e] his Provinces offerd to pawne or elienation,[f] as the hire of those whom he had sollicited to

---

[a] Presbyterian administrators who worked through the synod (*classic*) and the provinces.
[b] The holding of several livings together.
[c] Eleven members of Parliament charged in July 1647 with corresponding with the Queen.
[d] Rebels against Moses and Aaron – cited against Parliament's leaders by the Presbyterians.
[e] Charles was held responsible by Parliament for the massacre of English Protestants in Ulster in 1641.
[f] To win Irish Catholic support, Charles had given up his rights to five Irish counties.

come in and destroy whole Cities and Countries; be hee King, or Tyrant, or Emperour, the Sword of Justice is above him; in whose hand soever is found sufficient power to avenge the effusion, and so great a deluge of innocent blood. For if all humane power to execute, not accidentally but intendedly, the wrath of God upon evill doers without exception, be of God; then that power, whether ordinary, or if that faile, extraordinary so executing that intent of God, is lawfull, and not to be resisted. But to unfold more at large this whole Question, though with all expedient brevity, I shall here set downe, from first beginning, the originall of Kings; how and wherefore exalted to that dignitie above their Brethren; and from thence shall prove, that turning to tyranny they may bee as lawfully deposd and punishd, as they were at first elected: This I shall doe by autorities and reasons, not learnt in corners among Schismes and Herisies, as our doubling Divines are ready to calumniate, but fetch't out of the midst of choicest and most authentic learning, and no prohibited Authors, nor many Heathen, but Mosaical, Christian, Orthodoxal, and which must needs be more convincing to our Adversaries, Presbyterial.

No man who knows ought, can be so stupid to deny that all men naturally were borne free, being the image and resemblance of God himselfe, and were by privilege above all the creatures, borne to command and not to obey: and that they livd so, till from the root of *Adams* transgression, falling among themselves to doe wrong and violence, and foreseeing that such courses must needs tend to the destruction of them all, they agreed by common league to bind each other from mutual injury, and joyntly to defend themselves against any that gave disturbance or opposition to such agreement. Hence came Cities, Townes and Common-wealths. And because no faith in all was found sufficiently binding, they saw it needfull to ordaine some authoritie, that might restraine by force and punishment what was violated against peace and common right: This autoritie and power of self-defence and preservation being originally and naturally in every one of them, and unitedly in them all, for ease, for order, and least each man should be his owne partial judge, they communicated and deriv'd either to one, whom for the eminence of his wisdom and integritie they chose above the rest, or to more than one whom they thought of equal deserving: the first was calld a King; the other Magistrates. Not to be thir Lords and Maisters (though afterward those names in som places were giv'n voluntarily to such as had bin authors of inestimable good to the people) but, to be thir Deputies and Commissioners, to execute, by vertue of thir intrusted power, that justice which else every man by the bond of nature and of Cov'nant must have executed for himselfe, and for one another. And to him that shall consider well why among free persons, one man by civill right should beare autority and jurisdiction over another, no other end or reason can be imaginable. These for a while governd well, and with much equitie decided all things at thir owne arbitrement: till the temptation of such a power left absolute in thir hands, perverted them at length to injustice and partialitie. Then did they who now by tryall had found the danger and inconveniences of committing arbitrary power to any, invent Lawes either fram'd or consented to by all, that should confine and limit the autority of whom they chose to govern them: that no man of whose failing they had proof, might no more rule over them, but law and reason abstracted as much as might be from personal errors and frailties. When this would not serve, but that the Law was either not executed, or misapply'd, they were constraind from that time, the onely remedy left them, to put conditions and take Oaths from all Kings and Magistrates at their first instalment to doe impartial justice by Law: who upon those termes and no other, receav'd Allegeance from the people, that is to say, bond or Covnant to obey them in execution of those Lawes which they the people had themselves made or assented to. And this oft times with express warning, that if the King or Magistrate prov'd unfaithfull to his trust, the people would be disingag'd. They added also Counselors and Parlaments, not to be onely at his beck, but with him or without him, at set times, or at all times, when any danger threatn'd, to have care of the public safety. Therefore saith *Claudius Sesell*[4] a French Statesman, *The Parlament was set as a bridle to the King*; which I instance rather, because that Monarchy is granted by all to be a farre more absolute than ours. That this and the rest of what hath hitherto been spok'n is most true, might be copiously made appeare throughout all Stories Heathen and Christian; eev'n of those Nations where Kings and Emperours have sought meanes to abolish all ancient memory of the peoples right by their encroachments and usurpations. But I spare long insertions, appealing to the German, French, Italian,[5] Arragonian, English, and not least the Scottish Histories. Not forgetting this onely by the way, that *William* the Norman though a Conqueror, and not unsworne at his Coronation, was compelld a second time to take oath at S. *Albanes*, ere the people would be brought to yeild obedience.

It being thus manifest that the power of Kings and Magistrates is nothing else, but what is onely derivative, transferrd and committed to them in trust from the people to the Common good of them all, in whom the power yet remaines fundamentally, and cannot be tak'n from them, without a violation of thir natural birthright, and seeing that from hence *Aristotle*[6] and the best of Political writers have defin'd a King, him who governs to the good and profit of his people, and not for his owne ends, it follows from necessary causes that the titles of Sovran Lord, naturall Lord, and the like, are either arrogancies, or flatteries, not admitted by Emperors and Kings of best note, and dislikt by the Church both of Jews, *Isai*. 26.13. and ancient Christians as appears by *Tertullian*[7] and others, Although generally the people of Asia and with them the Jews also, especially since the time they chose a King,[a] against the advice and counsel of God, are noted by wise authors much inclinable to slavery.[b]

Secondly, that to say, as is usual, the King hath as good right to his crown and dignitie, as any man to his inheritance, is to make the subject no better than the Kings slave, his chattell, or his possession that may be bought and sould. And doubtless if hereditary title were sufficiently inquir'd, the best foundation of it would be found but either in courtesie or convenience. But suppose it to be of right hereditarie, what can be more just and legal, if a subject for certaine crimes be to forfet by Law from himselfe and posterity, all his inheritance to the King, than that a King for crimes proportionall, should forfet all his title and inheritance to the people: unless the people must be thought created all for him, he not for them, and they all in one body inferior to him single, which were a kinde of treason against the dignity of mankind to affirm.

Thirdly it followes, that to say Kings are accountable to none but God, is the overturning of all Law and government. For if they may refuse to give account, then all covnants made with them at Coronation; all Oathes are in vaine, and meer mockeries, all Lawes which they sweare to keep, made to no purpose; for if the King feare not God, as how many of them doe not? we hold then our lives and estates, by the tenure of his meer grace and mercy, as from a God, not a mortall Magistrate, a position that none but Court parasites or men besotted would maintain. And no Christian Prince not drunk with high mind, and prouder than those Pagan *Caesars*, that deifi'd themselves, would arrogate so unreasonably above human condition, or derogate so basely from a whole Nation of men his brethren, as if for him onely subsisting, and to serve his glory, valuing them in comparison of his owne brute will and pleasure no more than so many beasts, or vermine under his feet,

---

[a] Saul, against Samuel's warning (1 Sam. VIII, 4–5).   [b] By Aristotle, e.g., in *Politics*, VII, 7.

not to be reasond with, but to be injurd; among whom there might
be found so many thousand men for wisdome, vertue, nobleness of
mind and all other respects, but the fortune of his dignity, farr
above him. Yet some would perswade us that this absurd opinion
was King *Davids*; because in the 51 *Psalm* he cries out to God,
Against thee onely have I sinn'd; as if *David* had imagind that to
murder *Uriah* and adulterate his wife, had bin no sinne against his
neighbor,[8] when as the law of *Moses* was to the King expresly, *Deut.*
17. not to think so highly of himself above his Brethren. *David*
therefore by those words could mean no other, than either that the
depth of his guiltness was known to God onely, or to so few as had
not the will or power to question him, or that the sin against God
was greater beyond compare than against *Uriah*. Whatever his
meanings were, any wise man will see that the patheticall words of a
Psalme can be no certaine decision to a point that hath abundantly
more certaine rules to goe by. How much more rationally spake the
Heathen King *Demophoon* in a Tragedy of *Euripides*[9] than these
interpreters would put upon King *David, I rule not my people by
tyranny, as if they were Barbarians, but am my self liable, if I doe
unjustly to suffer justly*. Not unlike was the speech of *Trajan* the
worthy Emperor, to one whom he made General of his Praetorian
Forces. Take this drawne sword, saith he, to use for me, if I reigne
well, if not, to use against me. Thus *Dion* relates.[10] And not *Trajan*
onely, but *Theodosius* the younger, a Christian Emperor and one of
the best, causd it to be enacted as a rule undeniable and fit to be
acknowledgd by all Kings and Emperors, that a Prince is bound to
the Laws; that on the autority of Law the autority of a Prince
depends, and to the Laws ought submit. Which Edict of his
remaines yet unrepeald in the *Code* of *Justinian*. 1.1. *tit.* 24, as a
sacred constitution to all the succeeding Emperors. How then can
any King in Europe maintaine and write himselfe accountable to
none but God, when Emperors in thir owne imperiall Statutes have
writt'n and decreed themselves accountable to Law. And indeed
where such account is not fear'd, he that bids a man reigne over him
above Law, may bid as well a savage beast.

It follows lastly, that since the King or Magistrate holds his
autoritie of the people, both originally and naturally for their good
in the first place, and not his owne, then may the people as oft as
they shall judge it for the best, either choose him or reject him,
retaine him or depose him though no Tyrant, merely by the libertie
and right of free born men to be govern'd as seems to them best.
This, though it cannot but stand with plaine reason, shall be made

good also by Scripture, *Deut*. 17.14. *When thou art come into the Land which the Lord thy God giveth thee, and shalt say I will set a King over mee, like as all the Nations about mee.* These words confirme us that the right of choosing, yea of changing thir owne goverment is by the grant of God himself in the people. And therefore when they desir'd a King, though then under another forme of goverment, and though thir changing displeasd him, yet he that was himself thir King,[a] and rejected by them, would not be a hindrance to what they intended, furder than by perswasion, but that they might doe therin as they saw good, 1 *Sam*. 8, onely he reserv'd to himself the nomination of who should reigne over them. Neither did that exempt the King as if hee were to God onely accountable, though by his especiall command anointed. Therefore *David first made a Covnant with the Elders of Israel, and so was by them anointed King, Chron*. 11. And *Jehoiada* the Priest making *Jehoash* King, made a Cov'nant between him and the people, 2 *Kings* 11.17. Therefore when *Roboam*[b] at his comming to the Crowne, rejected those conditions which the Israelites brought him, heare what they answer him, *what portion have we in David, or inheritance in the son of Jesse. See to thine own house David.* And for the like conditions not perform'd, all Israel before that time deposd *Samuell*; not for his own default, but for the misgoverment of his Sons. But som will say to both these examples, it was evilly don. I answer, that not the latter, because it was expressely allow'd them in the Law to set up a King if they pleas'd; and God himself joynd with them in the work; though in some sort it was at that time displeasing to him, in respect of old *Samuell* who had governd them uprightly. As *Livy* praises the Romans who took occasion from *Tarquinius* a wicked Prince to gaine their libertie,[11] which to have extorted, saith hee, from *Numa* or any of the good Kings before, had not bin seasonable. Nor was it in the former example don unlawfully; for when *Roboam* had prepar'd a huge Army to reduce the Israelites, he was forbidd'n by the Profet, 1 *Kings* 12.24. *Thus saith the Lord yee shall not goe up, nor fight against your brethren, for this thing is from me.* He calls them thir brethren, not Rebels, and forbidds to be proceeded against them, owning the thing himselfe, not by single providence, but by approbation, and that not onely of the act, as in the former example, but of the fitt season also; he had not otherwise forbidd to molest them. And those grave and wise Counsellors whom *Rehoboam* first advis'd with, spake no such thing, as our old gray headed Flatterers

[a] God Himself. [b] The tyrant Rehoboam, rejected by the Israelites (1 Kings XII, 16).

now are wont, stand upon your birth-right, scorne to capitulate, you hold of God, and not of them; for they knew no such matter, unless conditionally, but gave him politic counsel, as in a civil transaction. Therefore Kingdom and Magistracy, whether supreme or subordinat is calld *a human ordinance*, 1 *Pet.* 2.13, etc. which we are there taught is the will of God wee should submitt to, so farr as for the punishment of evill doers, and the encouragement of them that doe well. *Submitt* saith he, *as free men.* And *there is no power but of God*, said *Paul, Rom.* 13, as much as to say, God put it into mans heart to find out that way at first for common peace and preservation, approving the exercise therof; els it contradicts *Peter* who calls the same autority an Ordinance of man. It must be also understood of lawfull and just power, els we read of great power in the affaires and Kingdomes of the World permitted to the Devill: for saith he to Christ, *Luke* 4.6, *all this power will I give thee and the glory of them for it is delivered to me, and to whomsoever I will, I give it:* neither did hee ly, or Christ gainsay what hee affirm'd: for in the thirteenth of the *Revelation* wee read how the Dragon gave to the beast *his power, his seat, and great autority:* which beast so autoriz'd most expound to be the tyrannical powers and Kingdomes of the earth.[a] Therfore Saint *Paul* in the forecited Chapter tells us that such Magistrates hee meanes, as are, not a terror to the good but to the evill, such as beare not the sword in vaine, but to punish offenders, and to encourage the good. If such onely be mentioned here as powers to be obeyd, and our submission to them onely required, then doubtless those powers that doe the contrary, are no powers ordaind of God, and by consequence no obligation laid upon us to obey or not to resist them. And it may be well observd that both these Apostles, whenever they give this precept, express it in termes not *concret* but *abstract*, as Logicians are wont to speake, that is, they mention the ordinance, the power, the autoritie before the person that execute it, and what that power is, lest we should be deceavd, they describe exactly. So that if the power be not such, or the person execute not such power, neither the one nor the other is of God, but of the Devill, and by consequence to bee resisted. From this exposition *Chrysostome*[12] also on the same place dissents not; explaining that these words were not writt'n in behalf of a tyrant. And this is verify'd by *David*, himself a King, and likeliest to bee Author of the *Psalm* 94.20. which saith, *Shall the throne of iniquity have fellowship with thee.* And it were worth the knowing, since Kings, and that by

---

[a] The Beast was traditionally identified by Protestants with the Papacy.

Scripture boast the justness of thir title, by holding it immediately of God, yet cannot show the time when God ever set on the throne them or thir forefathers, but onely when the people chose them; why by the same reason, since God ascribes as oft to himself the casting down of Princes from the throne, it should not be thought as lawful, and as much from God when none are seen to do it but the people, and that for just causes. For if it needs must be a sin in them to depose, it may as likely be a sin to have elected. And contrary if the peoples act in election be pleaded by a King, as the act of God, and the most just title to enthrone him, why may not the peoples act of rejection, be as well pleaded by the people as the act of God, and the most just reason to depose him? So that we see the title and just right of reigning or deposing in reference to God, is found in Scripture to be all one; visible onely in the people, and depending meerly upon justice and demerit.[a] Thus farr hath bin considerd briefly the power of Kings and Magistrates; how it was, and is originally the peoples, and by them conferrd in trust onely to bee imployd to the common peace and benefit; with libertie therfore and right remaining in them to reassume it to themselves, if by Kings or Magistrates it be abus'd; or to dispose of it by any alteration, as they shall judge most conducing to the public good.

Wee may from hence with more ease, and force of argument determin what a Tyrant is, and what the people may doe against him. A Tyrant whether by wrong or by right comming to the Crowne, is he who regarding neither Law nor the common good, reigns onely for himself and his faction: Thus St *Basil*[13] among others defines him. And because his power is great, his will boundless and exorbitant, the fulfilling whereof is for the most part accompanied with innumerable wrongs and oppressions of the people, murders, massacres, rapes, adulteries, desolation, and subversion of Citties and whole provinces; look how great a good and happiness a just King is, so great a mischeife is a Tyrant; as hee the public Father of his Countrie, so this the common enemie. Against whom what the people lawfully may doe, as against a common pest, and destroyer of mankinde, I suppose no man of cleare judgment need goe furder to be guided than by the very principles of nature in him. But because it is the vulgar folly of men to desert thir owne reason, and shutting thir eyes to think they see best with other mens, I shall shew by such examples as ought to have most waight with us, what hath bin don in this case heretofore. The *Greeks* and

[a] Ill desert.

Romans as thir prime Authors witness held it not onely lawfull, but a glorious and Heroic deed, rewarded publicly with Statues and Garlands, to kill an infamous Tyrant at any time without tryal; and but reason, that he who trod down all Law, should not bee voutsaf'd the benefit of Law. Insomuch that *Seneca* the Tragedian brings in *Hercules* the grand suppressor of Tyrants, thus speaking,

> *. . . Victima haud ulla amplior*
> *Potest, magisque opima mactari Jovi*
> *Quam Rex iniquus . . .*[14]

> *. . . There can be slaine*
> *No sacrifice to God more acceptable*
> *Than an unjust and wicked King . . .*

But of these I name no more, lest it bee objected they were Heathen; and come to produce another sort of men that had the knowledge of true Religion. Among the Jews this custome of tyrant-killing was not unusual. First *Ehud*, a man whom God had raysd to deliver Israel from *Eglon* King of *Moab*, who had conquerd and rul'd over them eighteene yeares, being sent to him as an Ambassador with a present slew him in his owne house[15] But hee was a forren Prince, an enemie, and *Ehud* besides had special warrant from God. To the first I answer, it imports not whether forren or native: For no Prince so native but professes to hold by Law; which when he himselfe overturnes, breaking all the Covnants and Oaths that gave him title to his dignity, and were the bond and alliance between him and his people, what differs he from an outlandish[a] King or from an enemie? For looke how much right the King of *Spaine* hath to govern us at all, so much right hath the King of *England* to govern us tyrannically. If he, though not bound to us by any league, comming from *Spaine* in person to subdue us or to destroy us, might lawfully by the people of *England* either bee slaine in fight, or put to death in captivity, what hath a native King to plead, bound by so many Covnants, benefits and honours to the welfare of his people, why he through the contempt of all Laws and Parlaments, the onely tie of our obedience to him, for his owne wills sake, and a boasted praerogative unaccountable,[b] after sev'n years warring and destroying of his best subjects, overcom, and yeilded prisoner, should think to scape unquestionable, as a thing divine, in respect of whom so many thousand Christians destroy'd should lye unaccounted for, polluting with thir slaughterd carcasses all the Land over, and crying for vengeance against the living that should

[a] Foreign.   [b] Not responsible to Parliament.

have righted them. Who knows not that there is a mutual bond of amity and brotherhood between man and man over all the World, neither is it the English Sea that can sever us from that duty and relation: a straiter bond yet there is between fellow-subjects, neighbours, and friends; But when any of these doe one to another so as hostility could doe no worse, what doth the Law decree less against them, than open enemies and invaders? or if the Law be not present, or too weake, what doth it warrant us to less than single defence or civil warre? and from that time forward the Law of civill defensive Warr differs nothing from the Law of forren hostility. Nor is it distance of place that makes enmitie, but enmity that makes distance. He therefore that keeps peace with me neer or remote of whatsoever Nation, is to mee as farr as all civil and human offices an Englishman and a nighbour: but if an Englishman forgetting all Laws, human, civil and religious offend against life and libertie, to him offended and to the Law in his behalf, though born in the same womb, he is no better than a Turk, a Sarasin, a Heathen. This is Gospel, and this was ever Law among equals; how much rather than in force against any King whatsoever, who in respect of the people is confessd inferior and not equal: to distinguish therfore of a Tyrant by outlandish, or domestic is a weak evasion. To the second that he was an enemie, I answer, what Tyrant is not? yet *Eglon* by the Jewes had bin acknowledgd as thir Sovran, they had servd him eighteen yeares, as long almost as wee our *William* the Conqueror, in all which time he could not be so unwise a Statesman but to have tak'n of them Oaths of Fealty and Allegeance by which they made themselves his proper subjects, as thir homage and present sent by *Ehud* testifyd. To the third, that he had special warrant to kill *Eglon* in that manner, it cannot bee granted, because not expressd; tis plain that he was raysd by God to be a Deliverer, and went on just principles, such as were then and ever held allowable, to deale so by a Tyrant that could not otherwise be dealt with. Neither did *Samuell* though a Profet, with his owne hand abstain from *Agag*; a forren enemie no doubt; but mark the reason, *As thy Sword hath made women childless*;[16] a cause that by the sentence of Law it selfe nullifies all relations. And as the Law is between Brother and Brother, Father and Son, Maister and Servant, wherfore not between King or rather Tyrant and People? And whereas *Jehu* had special command to slay *Jehoram*[a] a successive and hereditarie Tyrant, it seemes not the less imitable for that; for where

---

[a] The son of Ahab.

a thing grounded so much on naturall reason hath the addition of a command from God, what does it but establish the lawfulness of such an act. Nor is it likely that God who had so many wayes of punishing the house of *Ahab* would have sent a subject against his Prince, if the fact in it selfe as don to a Tyrant had bin of bad example. And if *David* refus'd to lift his hand against the Lords anointed,[17] the matter between them was not tyranny, but private enmity, and *David* as a private person had bin his own revenger, not so much the peoples; but when any tyrant at this day can shew to be the Lords anointed, the onely mention'd reason why *David* withheld his hand, he may then but not till then presume on the same privilege.[a]

We may pass therfore hence to Christian times. And first our Saviour himself, how much he favourd tyrants and how much intended they should be found or honourd among Christians, declares his minde not obscurely; accounting thir absolute autoritie no better than Gentilisme, yea though they flourishd it over with the splendid name of Benefactors;[18] charging those that would be his Disciples to usurp no such dominion; But that they who were to bee of most autoritie among them, should esteem themselves Ministers and Servants to the public. *Matt.* 20.25. *The Princes of the Gentiles exercise Lordship over them*, and *Mark* 10.42. *They that seem to rule*, saith he, either slighting or accounting them no lawful rulers, *but yee shall not be so, but the greatest among you shall be your servant.* And although hee himself were the meekest, and came on earth to be so, yet to a tyrant we hear him not voutsafe an humble word: but *Tell that Fox, Luc.* 13.[b] And wherfore did his mother the Virgin *Mary* give such praise to God in her profetic song,[c] that he had now by the comming of Christ *Cutt down Dynasta's or proud Monarchs from the throne*,[d] if the Church, when God manifests his power in them to doe so, should rather choose all miserie and vassalage to serve them, and let them still sit on thir potent seats to bee ador'd for doing mischiefe. Surely it is not for nothing that tyrants by a kind of natural instinct both hate and feare none more than the true Church and Saints of God, as the most dangerous enemies and subverters of Monarchy, though indeed of tyranny; hath not this bin the perpetual cry of Courtiers, and Court Prelates? whereof no likelier cause can be alleg'd, but that they well discern'd the mind and principles

---

[a] The status the Royalists claimed for Charles.

[b] Christ's answer to the Pharisees when they told him of Herod's threat to kill him (Luke XIII, 31–2).

[c] The Magnificat.   [d] 'He hath put down the mighty from their seats.'

of most devout and zealous men, and indeed the very discipline of Church, tending to the dissolution of all tyranny. No marvel then if since the faith of Christ receav'd, in purer or impurer times, to depose a King and put him to death for tyranny hath bin accounted so just and requisit, that neighbour Kings have both upheld and tak'n part with subjects in the action. And *Ludovicus Pius*,[a] himself an Emperor, and sonne of *Charles* the great, being made Judge, *Du Haillan*[b] is my author, between *Milegast* King of the *Vultzes* and his subjects who had depos'd him, gave his verdit for the subjects, and for him whom they had chos'n in his room. Note here that the right of electing whom they please is by the impartial testimony of an Emperor in the people. For, said he, *A just Prince ought to be prefer'd before an unjust, and the end of goverment before the prerogative.* And *Constantinus Leo*,[c] another Emperor in the *Byzantine* Laws saith, *that the end of a King is for the general good, which he not performing is but the counterfet of a King.* And to prove that some of our owne Monarchs have acknowledg'd that thir high office exempted them not from punishment, they had the Sword of St *Edward*[d] born before them by an Officer who was calld Earle of the palace eev'n at the times of thir highest pomp and solemnitie, to mind them, said *Mathew Paris*,[e] the best of our Historians, that if they errd, the Sword had power to restraine them. And what restraint the Sword comes to at length, having both edge and point, if any *Sceptic* will needs doubt, let him feel. It is also affirm'd from diligent search made in our ancient books of Law, that the Peers and Barons of England had a legall right to judge the King: which was the cause most likely, for it could be no slight cause, that they were call'd his Peers, or equals. This however may stand immovable, so long as man hath to deale with no better than man; that if our Law judge all men to the lowest by thir Peers, it should in all equity ascend also, and judge the highest. And so much I find both in our own and forren Storie, that Dukes, Earles, and Marqueses were at first not hereditary, not empty and vain titles, but names of trust and office, and with the office ceasing, as induces me to be of opinion, that every worthy man in Parlament, for the word Baron[f] imports no more, might for the public good be thought a fit Peet and judge of the King; without regard had to petty caveats,[g] and circumstances, the chief impediment in high affaires, and ever stood upon most by

---

[a] Louis the Pious, Holy Roman Emperor (AD 818–40).
[b] Girard du Haillan (c. 1535–1610), in *Histoire de France*, IV, p. 248.   [c] Leo III.
[d] King Edward the Confessor (1042–66).   [e] Matthew the Monk (d. 1259).
[f] Originally, a vassal of the King or other feudal lord.
[g] Process to suspend legal proceedings.

circumstantial men. Whence doubtless our Ancestors who were not ignorant with what rights either Nature or ancient Constitution had endowd them, when Oaths both at Coronation, and renewd in Parlament would not serve, thought it no way illegal to depose and put to death thir tyrannous Kings. Insomuch that the Parlament drew up a charge against *Richard the second*, and the Commons requested to have judgment decree'd against him, that the realme might not bee endangerd. And *Peter Marty* a Divine of formost rank, on the third of *Judges* approves thir doings.[19] Sir *Thomas Smith* also a Protestant and a Statesman in his Commonwealth of *England* putting the question whether it be lawful to rise against a Tyrant, answers that the vulgar judge of it according to the event, and the learned according to the purpose of them that do it.[20] But far before those days *Gildas*[a] the most ancient of all our Historians, speaking of those times wherein the Roman Empire decaying quitted and relinquishd what right they had by Conquest to this Iland, and resign'd it al into the peoples hands, testifies that the people thus re-invested with thir own original right, about the year 446, both elected them Kings, whom they thought best (the first Christian Brittish Kings that ever raign'd heer since the Romans) and by the same right, when they apprehended cause, usually depos'd and put them to death.[21] This is the most fundamental and ancient tenure that any King of *England* can produce or pretend to; in comparison of which, all other titles and pleas are but of yesterday. If any object that *Gildas* condemns the Britanes for so doing, the answer is as ready; that he condemns them no more for so doing, then hee did before for choosing such, for saith he, *They anointed them, Kings, not of God, but such as were more bloody than the rest.* Next hee condemns them not at all for deposing or putting them to death, but for doing it over hastily, without tryal or well examining the cause, and for electing others worse in thir room. Thus we have here both Domestic and most ancient examples that the people of Britain have deposd and put to death thir Kings in those primitive Christian times. And to couple reason with example, if the Church in all ages, Primitive, Romish, or Protestant held it ever no less thir duty than the power of thir Keyes,[b] though without express warrant of Scripture, to bring indifferently both King and Peasant under the utmost rigor of thir Canons and Censures Ecclesiastical, eev'n to the smiting him with a final excommunion,[c] if he persist impenitent,

---

[a] AD 516–70.
[b] The Keys of the Kingdom of Heaven given by Christ to Peter (Matt. xvi, 19).
[c] Excommunication.

what hinders but that the temporal Law both may and ought, though without a special Text, or president, extend with like indifference the civil Sword, to the cutting off without exemption him that capitally offends. Seeing that justice and Religion are from the same God, and works of justice ofttimes more acceptable. Yet because that some[a] lately with the tongues and arguments of Malignant backsliders have writt'n that the proceedings now in Parlament against the King, are without president from any Protestant State or Kingdom, the examples which follow shall be all Protestant and chiefly Presbyterian.

In the yeare 1546. The *Duke of Saxonie, Lantgrave of Hessen,* and the whole Protestant league raysd open Warr against *Charles the fifth* thir Emperor, sent him a defiance, renounc'd all faith and allegeance toward him, and debated long in Counsell whether they should give him so much as the title of *Caesar. Sleidan. l.* 17.[b] Let all men judge what this wanted of deposing or of killing, but the power to doe it.

In the yeare 1559. the Scotch Protestants claiming promise of thir Queen Regent[c] for libertie of conscience, she answering that promises were not to be claim'd of Princes beyond what was commodious for them to grant, told her to her face in the Parlament then at *Sterling,* that if it were so, they renokunc'd thir obedience; and soone after betooke them to Armes. *Buchanan Histl. l.* 16[d] certainely when allegeance is renounc'd, that very hour the King or Queen is in effect depos'd.

In the yeare 1564. *John Knox* a most famous Divine and the reformer of *Scotland* to the Presbyterian discipline, at a generall Assembly maintaind op'nly in a dispute against *Lethington*[e] the Secretary of State, that Subjects might and ought execute Gods judgments upon thir King; that the fact of *Jehu* and others against thir King having the ground of Gods ordinary command to put such and such offenders to death was not extraordinary, but to bee imitated of all that prefer'd the honour of God to the affection of flesh and wicked Princes, that Kings, if they offend, have no privilege to be exempted from the punishments of Law more than any other subject; so that if the King be a Murderer, Adulterer, or Idolater, he should suffer not as a King, but as an offender; and this position hee repeates againe and againe before them.[22] Answerable was the opinion of *John Craig*[f] another learned Divine, and that Lawes made by the tyranny of Princes, or the

---

[a] Presbyterian pamphleteers.
[b] I.e. Johann Philippson (1506–56), in his *General History of the Reformation of the Church,* XVII (English trans. 1556).
[c] Mary of Lorraine, widow of James V and mother of Mary, Queen of Scots.
[d] George Buchanan, *Rerum Scoticarum Historia* (1582), bk. XVI.
[e] William Maitland of Lethington (1528–73) who, although a Protestant, remained loyal to Mary.
[f] 1512–1600; Knox's strongest supporter.

negligence of people, thir posterity might abrogate, and reform all things according to the original institution of Common-welths. And *Knox* being commanded by the Nobilitie to write to *Calvin* and other learned men for thir judgments in that question refus'd; alleging that both himselfe was fully resolv'd in conscience, and had heard thir judgments, and had the same opinion under hand-writing of many the most godly and most learned that he knew in Europe; that if he should move the question to them againe, what should he doe but shew his owne forgetfulness or inconstancy. All this is farr more largely in the Ecclesiastic History of *Scotland l.* 4.[23] with many other passages to this effect all the book over; set out with diligence by Scotchmen of best repute among them at the beginning of these troubles, as if they labourd to inform us what wee were to doe and what they intended upon the like occasion.

And to let the world know that the whole Church and Protestant State of *Scotland* in those purest times of reformation were of the same beleif, three years after, they met in the feild *Mary* thir lawful and hereditary Queen, took her prisoner yeilding before fight, kept her in prison and the same yeare deposed her.[a] *Buchan. Hist. l.* 18.

And four years after that, the Scots in justification of thir deposing Queen *Mary*, sent Embassadors to Queen *Elizabeth*, and in a writt'n Declaration alleag'd that they had us'd towards her more lenity than shee deservd; that thir Ancestors had heretofore punishd thir Kings by death or banishment; that the Scots were a free Nation, made King whom they freely chose, and with the same freedome un-Kingd him if they saw cause, by right of ancient laws and Ceremonies yet remaining, and old customes yet among the High-landers in choosing the head of thir Clanns, or Families; all which with many other arguments bore witness that regal power was nothing else but a mutuall Covnant or stipulation between King and people. *Buch. Hist. l.* 20. These were Scotchmen and Presbyterians; but what measure then have they lately offerd, to think such liberty less beseeming us than themselves, presuming to put him upon us for a Maister whom thir Law scarce allows to be thir own equall?[b] If now then we heare them in another straine than heretofore in the purest times of thir Church, we may be confident it is the voice of Faction speaking in them, not of truth and Reformation.

In the yeare 1581, the States of *Holland* in a general Assembly at the *Hague*, abjur'd all obedience and subjection to *Philip* King of *Spaine*; and in a Declaration justifie thir so doing; for that by this tyrannous

[a] In 1567. [b] I.e. Charles I, still accepted by the Scottish Presbyterians as legitimate King.

goverment against faith so oft'n giv'n and brok'n he had lost his right to all the Belgic Provinces;[a] that therfore they deposd him and declar'd it lawful to choose another in his stead. *Thuan. l.* 74.[b] From that time, to this no State or Kingdom in the World hath equally prosperd: But let them remember not to look with an evil and prejudicial eye upon thir neighbours walking by the same rule.[c]

But what need these examples to Presbyterians, I meane to those who now of late would seem so much to abhorr deposing, whenas they to all Christendom have giv'n the latest and the liveliest example of doing it themselves. I question not the lawfulness of raising Warr against a Tyrant in defence of Religion, or civil libertie; for no Protestant Church from the first *Waldenses*[d] of *Lyons*, and *Languedoc* to this day but have don it round, and maintaind it lawfull. But this I doubt not to affirme, that the Presbyterians, who now so much condemn deposing, were the men themselves that deposd the King, and cannot with all thir shifting and relapsing, wash off the guiltiness from thir owne hands. For they themselves, by these thir late doings have made it guiltiness, and turnd thir owne warrantable actions into Rebellion.

There is nothing that so actually makes a King of *England*, as rightful possession and Supremacy *in all causes both civil and Ecclesiastical*: and nothing that so actually makes a Subject of *England*, as those two Oaths of Allegeance and Supremacy observd *without equivocating, or any mental reservation*. Out of doubt then when the King shall command things already constituted in Church, or State, obedience is the true essence of a subject, either to doe, if it be lawful, or if he hold the thing unlawful, to submit to that penaltie which the Law imposes, so long as he intends to remaine a subject. Therefore when the people or any part of them shall rise against the King and his autority executing the Law in any thing establishd civil or Ecclesiastical, I doe not say it is rebellion, if the thing commanded though establishd be unlawfull, and that they sought first all due means of redress (and no man is furder bound to Law) but I say it is an absolute renouncing both of Supremacy and Allegeance, which in one word is an actual and total deposing of the King, and the setting up of another supreme autority over them. And whether the Presbyterians have not don all this and much

---

[a] Holland and the Spanish Netherlands.
[b] Jacques-Auguste de Thon (1553–1617), in his *History of his Own Times* (1604).
[c] The Dutch States General had sent ambassadors to protest against Charles's trial.
[d] Followers of Peter Waldo of Lyons, who had broken away from the Papacy after the Lateran Council of 1179.

more, they will not put mee, I suppose, to reck'n up a seven yeares story fresh in the memory of all men. Have they not utterly broke the Oath of Allegeance, rejecting the Kings command and autority sent them from any part of the Kingdom whether in things lawful or unlawful? Have they not abjur'd the Oath of Supremacy by setting up the Parlament without the King, supreme to all thir obedience, and though thir Vow and Covnant bound them in general to the Parlament, yet sometimes adhering to the lesser part of Lords and Commons that remain faithful as they terme it, and eev'n of them, one while to the Commons without the Lords, another while to the Lords without the Commons.[a] Have they not still declar'd thir meaning, whatever their Oath were, to hold them onely for supreme whom they found at any time most yeilding to what they petitiond? Both these Oaths which were the straitest bond of an English subject in reference to the King, being thus broke and made voide, it follows undeniably that the King from that time was by them in fact absolutely deposd, and they no longer in reality to be thought his subjects, notwithstanding thir fine clause in the Covnant to preserve his person, Crown, and dignitie, set there by som dodging Casuist with more craft than sinceritie to mitigate the matter in case of ill success, and not tak'n I suppose by any honest man, but as a condition subordinate to every the least particle that might more concern Religion, liberty, or the public peace. To prove it yet more plainly that they are the men who have deposd the King, I thus argue. We know that King and Subject are relatives, and relatives have no longer being than in the relation; the relation between King and Subject can be no other than regal autority and subjection. Hence I inferr past their defending, that if the Subject who is one relative, takes away the relation, of force he takes away also the other relative; but the Presbyterians who were one relative, that is to say Subjects, have for this sev'n years tak'n away the relation, that is to say the Kings autoritie, and thir subjection to it, therefore the Presbyterians for these sev'n yeares have removd and extinguishd the other relative, that is to say the King, or to speake more in brief have depos'd him; not onely by depriving him the execution of his autoritie, but by conferring it upon others. If then thir Oathes of subjection brok'n, new Supremacy obey'd, new Oaths and Covnants tak'n, notwithstanding frivolous evasions, have in plaine tearmes unking'd the King, much more than hath thir sev'n yeares Warr, not depos'd him onely, but

[a] Most Presbyterians voted with the Independent minority throughout 1648.

outlawd him, and defi'd him as an alien, a rebell to Law, and enemie
to the State, it must needs be cleare to any man not averse from
reason, that hostilitie and subjection are two direct and positive
contraries; and can no more in one subject stand together in respect
of the same King, than one person at the same time can be in two
remote places. Against whom therfore the Subject is in act of
hostility we may be confident that to him he is in no subjection: and
in whom hostility takes place of subjection, for they can by no
meanes consist together, to him the King can bee not onely no
King, but an enemie. So that from hence wee shall not need dispute
whether they have depos'd him, or what they have defaulted
towards him as no King, but shew manifestly how much they have
don toward the killing him. Have they not levied all these Warrs
against him whether offensive or defensive (for defence in Warr
equally offends, and most prudently before hand) and giv'n Commission to slay where they knew his person could not bee exempt
from danger? And if chance or flight had not sav'd him, how oft'n
had they killd him, directing thir Artillery without blame or
prohibition to the very place where they saw him stand? Have they
not converted his revenue to other uses, and detain'd from him all
meanes of livelyhood, so that for them long since he might have
perisht, or have starv'd? Have they not hunted and pursu'd him
round about the Kingdom with sword and fire? Have they not
formerly deny'd to Treat with him,[a] and thir now recanting
Ministers preach'd against him, as a reprobate incurable, an enemy
to God and his Church markt for destruction, and therfore not to
bee treated with? Have they not beseig'd him and to thir power
forbid him Water and Fire, save what they shot against him to the
hazard of his life? Yet while they thus assaulted and endangerd it
with hostile deeds, they swore in words to defend it with his Crown
and dignity; not in order, as it seems now, to a firm and lasting
peace, or to his repentance after all this blood; but simply, without
regard, without remorse or any comparable value of all the miseries
and calamities sufferd by the poore people, or to suffer hereafter
through his obstinacy or impenitence. No understanding man can
bee ignorant that Covnants are ever made according to the present
state of person and of things; and have ever the more general laws
of nature and of reason included in them, though not express'd. If I
make a voluntary Covnant as with a man to doe him good, and hee
prove afterward a monster to me, I should conceave a diso-

---

[a] In the bill of 'No More Addresses', 3 Jan., 1648, Parliament had resolved to allow no further
negotiations with Charles.

bligement.[a] If I Covnant, not to hurt an enemie, in favour of him and
forbearance, and hope of his amendment, and he, after that, shall doe
me tenfould injury and mischief to what hee had don when I so
Covnanted, and stil be plotting what may tend to my destruction, I
question not but that his after actions release me; nor know I Covnant
so sacred that withholds mee from demanding Justice on him.
Howbeit, had not thir distrust in a good cause, and the fast and loos of
our prevaricating Divines oversway'd, it had bin doubtless better, not
to have inserted in a Covnant unnecessary obligations, and words not
works of a supererogating[b] Allegeance to thir enemy; no way
advantageous to themselves, had the King prevail'd, as to thir cost
many would have felt; but full of snare and distraction to our friends,
usefull onely, as we now find, to our adversaries, who under such a
latitude and shelter of ambiguous interpretation have even since been
plotting and contriving new opportunities to trouble all againe. How
much better had it bin, and more becomming an undaunted vertue to
have declard op'nly and boldly whom and what power the people were
to hold Supreme, as on the like occasion Protestants[c] have don before,
and many conscientious men now in these times have more than once
besought the Parlament to doe, that they might go on upon a sure
foundation, and not with a ridling Covnant in thir mouthes, seeming
to sweare counter almost in the same breath Allegeance and no
Allegeance; which doubtless had drawn off all the minds of sincere
men from siding with them, had they not discern'd thir actions farr
more deposing him than thir words upholding him; which words
made now the subject of cavillous[d] interpretations, stood ever in the
Covnant by judgment of the more discerning sort an evidence of thir
feare not of thir fidelity. What should I return to speak on, of those
attempts for which the King himself hath oft'n charg'd the Presbyterians of seeking his life, whenas in the due estimation of things they
might without a fallacy be sayd to have don the deed outright. Who
knows not that the King is a name of dignity and office, not of person:
Who therfore kils a King, a must kill him while he is a King. Then they
certainly who by deposing him have long since tak'n from him the life
of a King, his office and his dignity, they in the truest sence may bee
said to have killd the King: nor onely by thir deposing and waging
Warr against him, which besides the danger to his personal life, set him
in the fardest opposite point from any vital function of a King, but by
thir holding him in prison vanquishd and yeilded into thir absolute and
despotic power, which brought him to the lowest degradement and

[a] Release from obligation. [b] Beyond what is necessary for salvation. [c] The Dutch.
[d] Carping.

incapacity of the regal name. I say not by whose matchless valour[a] next under God, lest the story of thir ingratitude thereupon carry me from the purpose in hand, which is to convince them that they, which I repeat againe, were the men who in the truest sense killd the King, not onely as is provd before, but by depressing him thir King farr below the rank of a subject to the condition of a Captive, without intention to restore him, as the Chancellour of *Scotland*[b] in a speech told him plainly at *Newcastle*,[c] unless hee granted fully all thir demands, which they knew he never meant. Nor did they Treat or think of Treating with him, till thir hatred to the Army that deliverd them, not thir love or duty to the King, joyn'd them secretly with men sentencd so oft for Reprobates in thir owne mouthes, by whose suttle inspiring they grew madd upon a most tardy and improper Treaty.[d] Whereas if the whole bent of thir actions had not bin against the King himselfe, but against his evill Councel, as they faind, and publishd, wherefore did they not restore him all that while to the true life of a King, his Office, Crown, and Dignity, when he was in thir power, and they themselves his neerest Counselers. The truth therefore is, both that they would not, and that indeed they could not without thir own certaine destruction, having reduc'd him to such a final pass, as was the very death and burial of all in him that was regal, and from whence never King of *England* yet revivd, but by the new re-inforcement of his own party, which was a kind of resurrection to him. Thus having quite extinguisht all that could be in him of a King, and from a total privation clad him over like another specifical[e] thing with formes and habitudes destructive to the former, they left in his person dead as to Law and all the civil right either of King or Subject the life onely of a Prisner, a Captive and a Malefactor. Whom the equal and impartial hand of justice finding, was no more to spare than another ordnary man; not onely made obnoxious to the doome[f] of Law by a charge more than once drawn up against him, and his owne confession to the first Article at *Newport*,[g] but summond and arraignd in the sight of God and his people, curst and devoted to perdition worse than any *Ahab*, or *Antiochus*,[h] with exhortation to

---

[a] Cromwell's. [b] John Campbell, 1st Earl of Loudoun (1598–1663).
[c] Where Charles was taken prisoner in May 1646.
[d] The Treaty of Newport, negotiated with Charles in the Isle of Wight, Sept.–Nov. 1648.
[e] Species of. [f] Decree.
[g] The preamble stated that Parliament had been forced to 'undertake a war in their just and lawful defence'.
[h] Antiochus IV (175–164 BC), persecutor of the Jews; overthrown by Judas Maccabeus.

curse all those in the name of God that made not Warr against him, as bitterly as *Meroz* was to be curs'd,[a] that went not out against a Canaanitish King, almost in all the Sermons, Prayers, and Fulminations that have bin utterd this sev'n yeares by those clov'n tongues of falshood and dissention, who now, to the stirring up of new discord, acquitt him; and against thir owne discipline, which they boast to be the throne and scepter of Christ, absolve him, unconfound him, though unconverted, unrepentant, unsensible of all thir pretious Saints and Martyrs whose blood they have so oft layd upon his head: and now againe with a new sovran anointment can wash it all off, as if it were as vile, and no more to be reckn'd for than the blood of so many Dogs in a time of Pestilence: giving the most opprobrious lye to all the acted zeale that for these many yeares hath filld thir bellies, and fed them fatt upon the foolish people. Ministers of sedition, not of the Gospell, who while they saw it manifestly tend to civil Warr and bloodshed, never ceasd exasperating[b] the people against him; and now that they see it likely to breed new commotion, cease not to incite others against the people that have savd them from him, as if sedition were thir onely aime whether against him or for him. But God as we have cause to trust, wil put other thoughts into the people, and turn them from looking after these firebrands, of whose fury, and fals prophecies we have anough experience; and from the murmurs of new discord will incline them to heark'n rather with erected minds to the voice of our supreme Magistracy, calling us to liberty and the flourishing deeds of a reformed Common-wealth;[c] with this hope that as God was heretofore angry with the Jews who rejected him and his forme of Goverment to choose a King, so that he will bless us, and be propitious to us who reject a King to make him onely our leader, and supreme governour in the conformity as neer as may be of his own ancient goverment; if we have at least but so much worth in us to entertaine the sense of our future happiness, and the courage to receave what God voutsafes us: wherin we have the honour to precede other Nations who are now labouring to be our followers. For as to this question in hand what the people by thir just right may doe in change of goverment, or of governour, we see it cleerd sufficiently; besides other ample autority eev'n from the mouths of

[a] The inhabitants of Meroz were cursed because 'they came not to the help of the Lord . . . against the mighty' (Judges v, 23).
[b] Incensing.
[c] *The Joynt Resolution and Declaration of the Parliament and Counsell of the Army*, 11 Jan, 1649, declared that 'the Commons of England, in parliament assembled, have the supreme power in this nation'.

Princes themselves. And surely they that shall boast, as we doe, to be a free Nation, and not have in themselves the power to remove, or to abolish any governour supreme, or subordinate with the goverment it self upon urgent causes, may please thir fancy with a ridiculus and painted freedom, fit to coz'n babies; but are indeed under tyranny and servitude; as wanting that power, which is the root and sourse of all liberty, to dispose and *oeconomize*ᵃ in the Land which God hath giv'n them, as Maisters of Family in thir own house and free inheritance. Without which natural and essential power of a free Nation, though bearing high thir heads, they can in due esteem be thought no better than slaves and vassals born, in the tenure and occupation of another inheriting Lord. Whose goverment, though not illegal, or intolerable, hangs over them as a Lordly scourge, not as a free goverment; and therfore to be abrogated. How much more justly then may they fling off tyranny, or tyrants? who being once depos'd can be no more than privat men, as subject to the reach of Justice and arraignment as any other trangressors. And certainly if men, not to speak of Heathen, both wise and Religious have don justice upon Tyrants what way they could soonest, how much more mild and human then is it to give them fair and op'n tryall? To teach lawless Kings and all that so much adore them, that not mortal man, or his imperious will, but Justice is the onely true sovran and supreme Majesty upon earth. Let men cease therfore out of faction and hypocrisie to make outcrys and horrid things of things so just and honorable. And if the Parlament and Military Councel do what they doe without president,ᵇ if it appeare thir duty, it argues the more wisdom, vertue, and magnanimity, that they know themselves able to be a president to others. Who perhaps in future ages, if they prove not too degenerat, will look up with honour and aspire toward these exemplary, and matchless deeds of thir Ancestors, as to the highest top of thir civil glory and emulation. Which heretofore in the persuance of fame and forren dominion spent it self vain-gloriously abroad; but henceforth may learn a better fortitude to dare execute highest Justice on them that shall by force of Armes endeavour the oppressing and bereaving of Religion and thir liberty at home: that no unbridl'd Potentate or Tyrant, but to his sorrow for the future, may presume such high and irresponsible licence over mankind to havockᶜ and turn upside-down whole Kingdoms of men as though they were no more in respect of his perverse will than a Nation of

---

ᵃ Administer itself.   ᵇ Precedent.   ᶜ Cause havoc to.

Pismires.ᵃ As for the party calld Presbyterian, of whom I beleive
very many to be good and faithful Christians, though misled by som
of turbulent spirit, I wish them earnestly and calmly not to fall off
from thir first principles; nor to affect rigor and superiority over
men not under them; not to compell unforcible things in Religion
especially, which if not voluntary, becomes a sin; nor to assist the
clamor and malicious drifts of men whom they themselves have
judg'd to be the worst of men, the obdurat enemies of God and his
Church: not to dart against the actions of thir brethren, for want of
other argument those wrested Lawes and Scriptures thrown by
Prelats and Malignants against thir own sides, which though they
hurt not otherwise, yet tak'n up by them to the condemnation of
thir owne doings give scandal to all men and discoverᵇ in themselves either extreame passion or apostacy. Let them not oppose thir
best friends and associats who molest them not at all, infringe not
the least of thir liberties; unless they call it thir liberty to bind other
mens consciences, but are still seeking to live at peace with them and
brotherly accord. Let them beware an old and perfet enemy,ᶜ who
though he hope by sowing discord to make them his instruments,
yet cannot forbeare a minute the op'n threatning of his destind
revenge upon them when they have servd his purposes. Let them
feare therefore, if they bee wise, rather what they have don already,
than what remaines to doe, and be warn'd in time they put no
confidence in Princes whom they have provokd, lest they be added
to the examples of those that miserably have tasted the event.
Storiesᵈ can inform them how *Christiern* the second, King of
Denmark not much above a hundred yeares past, driv'n out by his
Subjects, and receavd againe upon new Oaths and conditions, broke
through them all to his most bloody revenge; slaying his cheif
opposers when he saw his time, both them and thir children invited
to a feast for that purpose.²⁴ How *Maximilian*ᵉ dealt with those of
Bruges, though by mediation of the *German* Princes reconcil'd to
them by solem and public writings drawn and seald. How the
massacre at *Paris*ᶠ was the effect of that credulous peace which the
French Protestants made with *Charles* the ninth thir King: and that
the main visible cause which to this day hath sav'd the *Netherlands*
from utter ruine, was thir finall not beleiving the perfidious cruelty
which as a constant maxim of State hath bin us'd by the Spanish
Kings on thir Subjects that have tak'n armes and after trusted them;

ᵃ Ants. ᵇ Expose. ᶜ Charles. ᵈ Histories.
ᵉ Holy Roman Emperor (he revenged himself on Bruges in 1490).
ᶠ On St Bartholomew's Eve, 24 Aug, 1572.

as no later age but can testifie, heretofore in *Belgia* it self, and this very yeare[a] in *Naples*. and to conclude with one past exception, though farr more ancient, *David* after once hee had tak'n armes, never after that trusted *Saul*, though with tears and much relenting he twise promis'd not to hurt him.[25] These instances, few of many, might admonish them both English and Scotch not to let thir owne ends, and the driving on of a faction betray them blindly into the snare of those enemies whose revenge looks on them as the men who first begun, fomented and carri'd on beyond the cure of any sound or safe accommodations[b] all the evil which hath since unavoidably befall'n them and thir King.

I have something also to the Divines, though brief to what were needfull; not to be disturbers of the civil affairs, being in hands better able and more belonging to manage them; but to study harder and to attend the office of good Pastors, knowing that he whose flock is least among them hath a dreadfull charge, not performd by mounting twise into the chair[c] with a formal preachment huddl'd up at the od hours of a whole lazy week, but by incessant pains and watching *in season and out of season, from house to house* over the soules of whom they have to feed. Which if they ever well considerd, how little leasure would they find to be the most pragmatical Sidesmen[d] of every popular tumult and Sedition? And all this while are to learne what the true end and reason is of the Gospel which they teach; and what a world it differs from the censorious and supercilious lording over conscience. It would be good also they liv'd so as might perswade the people they hated covetousness, which worse than heresie, is idolatry; hated pluralities and all kind of Simony; left rambling from Benefice to Benefice, like ravnous Wolves seeking where they may devour the biggest. Of which if som, well and warmely seated from the beginning, be not guilty, twere good they held not conversation with such as are: let them be sorry that being call'd to assemble about reforming the Church, they fell to progging[e] and sollicting the Parlament, though they had renouncd the name of Priests, for a new setling of thir Tithes and Oblations; and double lin'd themselves with spiritual places of commoditie beyond the possible discharge of thir duty. Let them assemble in Consistory[f] with thir Elders and Deacons, according to ancient Ecclesiastical rule, to the preserving of Church discipline, each in his several charge, and not a pack of Clergie men by themselves to belly cheare[g] in thir presumptuous Sion,[h] or to

[a] 1648. [b] Settlement. [c] Pulpit. [d] Officious intruders. [e] Importuning.
[f] Diocesan disciplinary court. [g] Guzzle.
[h] Sion College, seat of the Presbyterian London assembly, 1647–59.

promote designes, abuse and gull the simple Laity, and stirr up tumult, as the Prelats did, for the maintenance of thir pride and avarice. These things if they observe and waite with patience, no doubt but all things will goe well without their importunities or exclamations: and the Printed letters which they send subscrib'd with the ostentation of great Characters[a] and little moment, would be more considerable than now they are. But if they be the Ministers of Mammon instead of Christ, and scandalise his Church with the filthy love of gaine, aspiring also to sit the closest and the heaviest of all Tyrants, upon the conscience, and fall notoriously into the same sins, whereof so lately and so loud they accus'd the Prelates, as God rooted out those immediately before, so will he root out them thir imitators: and to vindicate his own glory and Religion, will uncover thir hypocrisie to the open world; and visit upon thir own heads that *curse ye Meroz*,[26] the very *Motto* of thir Pulpits, wherwith so frequently, not as *Meroz*, but more like Atheists they have mock'd the vengeance of God, and the zeale of his people.

[a] The title-pages of Presbyterian published letters and tracts were notorious for their large capitals.

6. *Richard Overton,*
'The Baiting of the Great Bull of Bashan',[a]
July 1649

There is a copy in the Thomason Collection, British Museum, dated by Thomason 16 July 1649. It was Overton's last pamphlet, written as a prisoner in the Tower, a final attempt to rally the Levellers. Cromwell's suppression of the Army mutiny at Burford on 15 May had in fact made their defeat – with that of the Agitators – certain. It fully confirms Overton's reputation as the wittiest and most scathing of the Leveller pamphleteers.

Our text is taken from A. L. Morton, ed., *Freedom in Arms: A Selection of Leveller Writings* (London, 1975).

Gentlemen,

Being necessitated (by some over-sudden misdeemings from amongst you) some few dayes since to assert and avow the continuance of my integrity to those sure foundations of Peace and Freedom, offered to the people of this Nation under the forme or draught of an Agreement of the People, May 1. 1649.[b]

It hath happened with me, as with other adventurers into the publick: All pallates are not pleased with that Sheet intituled *Overtons Defiance &c.*[c] yet falleth it out no other wise then I expected; it seems many are weak and as many are offended, and chiefly with that figurative passage of the Bull;[1] especially at the word Pox; but they need not much, did they but also take into their thoughts, the adulterous and wicked generation, on whom that Metaphor is made good, a people whose heart is waxed grosse, and their ears dull of hearing, having closed their eyes, least at any time they should see, hear, understand and be converted.

To such a people Christ spake not but in Parables: why then to such might not I use the Figure of the Bull of Bason, or rather of the Bull-baiting, with all the circumstances *Emphasis Gratia* thereunto appertaining? But ther's uncivill language, such as becommeth not

---

[a] I.e. Cromwell. The Bull of Bashan was the Old Testament type of the oppressor: see Amos IV, I and Psalm XXII, 12.
[b] *An Agreement of the Free People of England*, issued from the Tower by Lilburne, Walwyn, Prince and Overton.
[c] *Overton's Defyance of the Act of Pardon*, 4 July 1649.

THE BAITING OF THE GREAT

BULL *of* BASHAN

Unfolded and
Presented to the Affecters and approvers
of the PETITION of the
11 *Sept.* 1648.

Especially, to the *Citizens* of London usually
meeting at the *Whale-bone* in LOTHBURY
behind the Royal Exchange, Commonly
(though unjustly) styled

LEVELLERS.

By *Richard Overton* Close-prisoner in the
Tower of LONDON.

Psal. 22. 12. 13. Psal. 68. 28. 30.

*Many Bulls have compassed me: strong Buls of Bashan
have beset me round.*
*They opened their mouths against me, as a ravening and a
roaring Lion.*
Strengthen O God that which thou hast wrought for us.
*Rebuke the Company of Spearmen, the multitude of the
Bulls, with the Calves of the people, til every one
submit. Scatter thou the people that delight in war.*

Imprinted at *London*, 1649.

the Gospell of Christ. I answer (my Brethren) he or she (how pure or nice soever to the eye) that is not guilty of reall grosse incivilities both in word and deed, let him or her throw the first stone at that seeming incivillity, for at most you can make it but so in appearance, and no like is the same. The figure is but the shell; will you not crack the shell to take out the kernell? passe through the Parable to the Morall thereof? I, but it jears and thats not the language of Canaan, and be it so: Is it not recorded that Eliah[a] mocked the Priests of Baal, and said, Cry aloud for he is god, either he is talking or he is pursuing his Enemy, or he is in a journey, or peradventure he sleepeth, and must be waked.[2]

Sure this was a jear to some purpose: here Eliah bid them cry aloud &c. and 'tis justified; then why now may I not cry ha-looe-ha-looe-&c. and not be condemned? What if I had turn'd Fidler in that Paper, Christ himselfe useth the simile of a Piper, saying, we have Piped unto you and ye have not danced (*Mat.* ii. 17.) And truly I think we (the four poor Sea-green[b] Fidlers in the Tower) may take up the same saying, We have Piped unto you ever since the first of May, the most pleasant tune of the AGREEMENT of the PEOPLE, but yee have not danced up so roundly as so sprightly a tune deserves. But you will say (it may be) I am still in the language of Ashdod[c] (as perchance you may take it) or that this Dialect is of Consanguinity with the other: Tis true; things (however in themselves) are to others as they are taken. He that should take the Parable of Dives and Lazarus[d] in the bare letter (how known Cannonical soever in its own genuine sence) he must explode[e] it the Scriptures and at best give it but a place in the Apocrypha, for the Letter or character thereof (if that must be the sense) is contradictory to the body of divinity, except you wil say, to beleeve that the rich Glutton and the Begger let not their eyes, tongues, fingers, &c. in the grave is Orthodox.[f] And so of my Metaphor of the Bull, the use of the word Genitals, Pox, &c. you may say is uncivill in the Letter, but how uncivill I pray in the Morall? Know yee not that whosoever shall but fasten on the Genitors or Parents of the peoples ruine, so, as to pinch the grand Imposters and deluders of the times, he burns his Fingers, is smit with the *Morbus Gallicus* of the enslaving Sword; For, what's he, that is precisely honest to the Common-wealth, that

---

[a] Elijah.   [b] The colour adopted by the Levellers.[3]
[c] The chief city of the Philistines.   [d] The rich man and the beggar (Luke xvi).
[e] Expel it from.
[f] In the parable, Lazarus is in 'Abraham's bosom' and the rich man suffering bodily torments in hell.

can scape persecution? As it hath been of old and is still in things spirituall, He that will live godly in Christ Jesus shall suffer persecution; so he now, that will but faithfully discharge his duty to the publick, shall be sure to be cast upon the Fiery Tryall, that Dogs mouth (as after the Metaphor) shall be sure to be burnt,[a] and tis well he scapes hanging as the time goes.

Now I pray, to how much incivility doth this amount? Is it so worthy your second condemnings as it may not be indulg'd with a favourable eye? Love envyeth not, it judgeth the best; I had thought with two or three merry Jiggs to attempt an uproar in all the laughers in England, but I see you are a company of dull souls, mirth with you is like a Shoulder of Mutton to a sick Horse, or worse, you strait convert into malancholy, trample it under your feet, turne againe, and are (some of you) ready to rent me; He that had cast Pearls before Swine could have expected no lesse.

Indeed, you looked (many of you) upon me as in a Sownd[b] at my close Imprisonment; but truly, when I came abroad with that ignorant Sheet, it found you in a dead sleep, as men in a Trans, portending, as if the Champions of the Eleventh of September[c] had been Sparrow-blasted with the businesse of Burford:[d] and I essayed, to put you out of your dumps, and mind you of the *Agreement of the People* as the center, or *ne plus ultra* of all our Engagements; but it seems it proved but as musick to the house of Mourning: yet however, it hath so far gained its end; if by it you wil not be provoked to your duties equally with us, it hath awaked you into a little discourse *pro & con*, though it be but to point at my weaker parts, and that's better then nothing, if rightly applyed, for *ex nihilo nil fit*:[e] by this you may take notice of your own infirmities in so wire-drawing[f] of mine: Certainly, it may provoke you to consider of what spirits you are, not unlike such as strain at a Gnat & swallow a Camel, that usually in any discourse passe over what concerneth themselves, though of never so serious and weighty consideration in point of their duties, and betake themselves wholly to spye out the spots and infirmities thereof, and of the Author, and fall foul thereupon, and so sleight their duties, stifle and smother the thing that is good: And now (my tender friends) I pray tell me what Spirit is this? 'tis a foul spirit, away with't for shame; go purge, goe purge;

[a] The allusion is to bull-baiting: see passage quoted from *Overton's Defyance* above.
[b] Swoon.
[c] *The Humble Petition* of 11 Sept. 1648, probably drafted by Lilburne, with the other Leveller leaders, and regarded as a key statement of Leveller principles.
[d] Cromwell's suppression of the Army mutiny on 15 May.
[e] 'Nothing comes from nothing'.   [f] Spinning out.

one penniworth of the *Agreement of the people*, with a little good
resolution taken morning and evening, will work out this corruption, cleanse and purifie the bloud, and put a period to this
distinction of parties, allay the feude and division of the people, and
state us in firme Freedom, Safety and Peace; and then there will be
none of this catching and carping, this lying in wait to snap at
infirmities; and till the Agreement be setled, this is not to be
expected.

I have known, when things as unserious as my last sheet, drest
out in the youthfull attire of mirth, hath found a very large
acceptance not only with you, but even with this generation of men,
that are now the Enemies of the People; and I think if I have not
forgot the *Arraignment of Persecution*,[a] and some other things of that
nature, that I myself have been one of those who have had the
honour of such acceptances: But *O tempora! O Mores!*[b] how few are
the same yesterday and to day? successe changeth mens minds as the
wind doth the weathercock.

But (my friends) your gravity (which I am affraid hath too much
of Melancholy in it) cannot more move me to a more serious
Dialect, then my own affections incline me, I prize both in their
places; as I affect the one, I respect the other: for sure, modest mirth
tempered with due gravity makes the best composition, most
naturall and harmonious: God in the temper of our natures as he
hath made us Earth, so hath he enlivened that dull lump with the
Element of Fire, which is the *forma formans*, the giver and preserver
of being and motion, and the Original of that habit of laughter:
Therefore Mirth sure is of Divine instinct, and I think I may boldly
say, more naturall then Melancholy, and lesse savours of the Curse.
Nature in its Creation was pure and good, void of corruption, or
any thing obnoxious or destructive: all misery and mischiefe came
in with the fall, as a Curse upon the Creature, as Death, sorrow,
tears, pains, &c, in which number you may reckon Melancholy, for
'tis both unnaturall and destructive to nature, and so fitly reputed a
branch of the Curse, and 'tis the root of the root of all wickednesse,
Coveteousnesse; for where have you seen a Melancholy man that's
not covetous? and a covetous man seldom proves a good
Common-wealths man: yet this ill Weed is gotten into so religious
an esteem that all our Religion is turn'd into Melancholy; that, he
that cannot whine, pipe, weep and hang down his head like a
Bulrush and seem sad unto men, is prophane, light, hath not any

---

[a] Overton's *Araignement of Mr. Persecution*, 1645, a scathing attack on the Presbyterians.
[b] 'What times! what manners!' (Terence, *Adelphoe*, 1, 758).

thing of God in him, is a Reprobate, is condemned and censured of all, as neither fit for Church nor Common-wealth; And thus comes it to passe; my mirth is heightened to such a transgression, even to cast me under the present *Anathama* of the now godly party.[4]

But my Brethren of the Sea green Order, take a little wine with your water, and Ile take a little water with my wine, and it will temper us to the best constitution. I wonder what meaneth your late dulnesse of motion, appearing as men in a dream, or as if you were another sort of people then the Authors, promoters, approvers and presenters of the Petition of the II of Sept. that people use to be the most active and vigorous People in England for publick Freedom and safety, they use to fear no colours, the more they were prest down the more they prest forward, and the more they encreased: few months have passed that they have not in point of Common-Right produced some eminent peece: but your heads have drooped of late, nothing hath appeared, not one punctilio in supportation and promotion of the *Agreement*; deep silence hath covered you; fie, fie; be not cow'd out of your abilities and principles by the present rage of the wicked: compare but the strength of your principles and the strength of an Army, and tell me which is stronger: How many persecuting powers have fallen before your principles as Dagon before the Ark?[5] and who hath been able to stand before them, even from Episcopacy to this whited and Jesabel like painted Independency? Think you, that this unparallell'd tyranny, under this new name, more fierce and cruel then his fellows, trampling the residue under its feet, that it shall scape the vengeance of Gods wrath more than its Predecessors? no, no; Gods Motto is *Semper Idem*.[a] Be not therefore dismayed or daunted at the height and magnificence of this insolent faction, the new sons of Perdition, that are set up to deceive if it were possible the very Elect.

It is your own evill and weaknesse, and of those that are Professors and pretenders to the same principles with you, that our Cause is thus under a Cloud: would you all act together, all suffer together, all be as one; and not thus (as some amongst you Commonally use) hang back in the adversity, and be seen in the Van of Prosperity (not daring when the storme rageth, to peep into the tempest for fear of being blowne away) we should not be at this passe with our Cause.

Where there is any thing of venture or hazard, while 'tis in the *Embrio*, who's not then busie and forward? but when 'tis put upon the personall test for execution, O then one hath bought a piece of ground, and must be excused; another a yoke of Oxen, and he must

[a] 'Always the same'.

goe see them; and a third hath marryed a wife and therefore must please her.

Friends, be not offended, this is a crime deserves your repentance; I condemn you not all, it is but some few; A little Leaven you know leaveneth the whole Lump; therefore do ye beware of the Leaven of the pharisees; it much retardeth your motions and blasteth their fruits; the publick is a loser thereby, and your Cause receiveth dammage: let those whome this pincheth, be thereby provoked to amendment, it is worthy their care: For know you not, that it is many hands make light work? If the stresse or weight of the work be laid upon one, or some 3 or 4, it must needs goe on slowly: Why, is not he that's most backward as forward as the best? it is his Cause as much as it is any mans, and thereto in duty as much obliged as any. We are no more concerned than your selves, 'tis but upon the point of common duty (which binds all) to our Country, that we suffer, and we count it our Joy, for that we know we suffer for well-doing, and though we perish in the Work, our Reward is our stay. Therefore why stand you still, and are not provoked to this good Emulation; be as active and vigilant, and you shall share in the rejoycing, and 'tis such (I must tell you my Friends) is worth your having; *Dulce est pro patria pati.*[a]

Fear not those Hils and Mountains that are in your way; it is but your want of faith that they are not removed, and cast into the bottome of the sea: While you lift up your heads, are vigorous and active, your principles present you as Steeples above the rest of the people; every man is a strong Barricado in the way of the Enemy, and your principles flourish and get ground, but when you are fearfull, are flat or remisse, then they retire and fade; for they are said to increase or diminish, as they get or lose ground in the understanding or acceptance of others: And this ever take as a sure Rule, That the most vertuous and saving principles in a person most undaunted and faithfull, the more they are supprest, and the more he is persecuted, the more they prosper and spread; of so mighty an efficacy are his sufferings and testimony; as, in the case of Paul is witnessed, Now I would (saith he) ye should understand, Brethren, that the things that hapned unto me, have faln out rather to the furtherance of the Gospel; so that my bonds in Christ are manifest in all the Pallace, and in all other places, and many of the Brethren in the Lord waxed confident by my Bonds, are much-more bold to speak the Word without fear: And this is all the persecutor gaineth

---

[a] 'It is sweet to suffer for one's country.' (Cf. 'It is sweet and glorious to die for one's country', Horace, *Odes*, III, 2.)

upon the undaunted Asserters of righteousness; his own sword is turned into his own bowels: persecution, as the Viper, devoureth its own parent. Then faint ye not (my friends) rouse up your heads and be valiant; lift up your *Agreement of the people* again, and put it upon the publick stage for promotion and subscription, and doubt not: What man that there is amongst you, that is fearfull and faint-hearted, let him depart your Meetings, and return to his house: the more the Enemy stormeth, the more resolute and vigorous be ye; give them enough of persecution; the more they persecute, the more doe ye appear, that your Bands may be famous; for with fetters, Irons, and prison-walls you may shake them to pieces; 'tis their tyrannies, cruelties and oppressions must be their Fall, through which you must eat your way for the *Agreement*.

I highly honor the fidelity and valor of Mr. Chrestopher Chisman[a] who notwithstanding his Imprisonment, his abuses and sufferings, hath not wrapt up his talent in a napkin, but like a good and faithful servant hath improv'd his imprisonment to the publick advantage; see his Book, entituled, *The Lamb contending with the Lion*[b] 'tis worthy your imitation. Let your light (as his) so shine before men, that they may see your good Works,[6] and glorifie your Cause; fear no dangers; the high and mighty Cedars[c] are never able to overtop your principles; what though Ambition hath mounted to the title of Lord Govenour[d] (forsooth) hath not your vigorous principles slain both the Lyon and the Bear, and shall not this uncircumcised Philistine be as one of them?

But (my friends) I am informed those painted Sepulchers of Independency desire your complyance and treaty with them:[e] But touch pitch, and you shall be defiled, have nothing to do with them; touch not, tast not, handle not, which all are to perish with the using; Remember the fidelity of Uriah to David:[f] The Ark, and Israel, and Judah abide in Tents, and my Lord Joab, and the servants of my Lord are encamped in the open fields, shall I then go into my house, to eat and to drink, and to lye with my wife? As thou livest and as thy soul liveth, I wil not do this thing.[g] Your *Agreement* lyeth

---

[a] Cornet Christopher Cheeseman, arrested by Cromwell for delivering a petition from the imprisoned Army Agitator, Captain Bray, to the Speaker of the House of Commons.

[b] Published in 1649. It describes his arrest, court-martial and imprisonment for eighteen days, and adds a defiant letter to Cromwell.

[c] The Army 'Grandees'.   [d] I.e. Cromwell.

[e] The leading Independent ministers had recently attempted to persuade Lilburne and his three associates in the Tower to submit to Cromwell's régime.

[f] David had committed adultery with Uriah's wife and afterwards had him put in the forefront of the battle, where he was killed (2 Sam. XI, 17).

[g] Uriah's answer to David: 2 Sam. XI, II.

half dead in the streets, your friends and its assertors are in prison, with sentinels at their doors, denied the access and visitation of friends, have the catch-poles of the Counsel of State enter their chambers when they are in bed, with Musketteers at their heels, search, rifle, catch and take away any thing that any way they may wrest unto their bloody ends against them, as formerly, and now, the other day (July 4.) they have done, and all the land mourneth and groaneth at the calamity and miseries upon it for want of the settlement of a just constitution of Government; and shall you go unto them (those pests and vipers of the Nation) to treat or comply? As you live and as your soul liveth you must not do this thing:

While your agreement is trod under their feet, your freinds under their cruel captivity, &c. let him that treateth with them amongst you, or with any of their creatures, or keepeth any correspondency with them, be to you as a Reprobate, let the Marke of Cain be set upon him, that every finger may point at him for a Traytor, and a Judas to the people that meeteth him.

If a wife or child be like to be destroyed by fire, water, or thieves, he accounts himself base that dare not venture his own life to save theirs: our cause is of a more transcendent value, and we suffer for it; and can you see it destroyed in us, and we for it, and not be as naturall as in a private relation? the lives, liberties, and freedomes of all is contained in it? If your neighbours Oxe or his Asse were in a ditch, it is a shame to passe by and not to help; and behold, here's all in the ditch, then, why venture you not your time, your labours, your monies, &c. to redeeme out all, our Cause, the nation, and us in it, and with it.

I confesse no people in England have been more vigorous, more active and diligent, and more adventurous for the Cause of the Nation, and for our Liberties than most of you: we have been as precious to you as the apple of your eye; you have spared no hazard, no toyle or time to get us at freedome, and I hope we shall never be so ungratefull as not thankfully to remember that service of Love: To you we are obliged in the deepest obligations of any others in England.

But now considering the extream necessity of your still constant unwearied prosecution, I have emboldened my self to presse you forward to the good work of the people, that at this time you may be as vigilant and industrious as at any other, that publick life and spirit may still be preserved and encreased in our cause, even in the worst of times.

And if I have been a little too sharp in my advice, and admonishment, impute it I pray you to the heat of my zeal and ardent

affections to the promotion of that Cause; for truly to me it is as the
life of my life; without it I'm nothing, with it I live, and therein am
Yours and every mans as my own
RICHARD OVERTON

From my close imprisonment
in the tower of London
July the ninth, 1649

FINIS

7. Gerrard Winstanley, 'A New-Yeers Gift Sent to the Parliament and Armie', December 1649 (first part)

There is a copy in the Thomason Collection, British Museum. The first twenty-four pages of the manifesto are given, as virtually a complete argument in itself; the second section (pp. 25–43), separately headed 'The Curse and Blessing that is in Mankind', repeats many of Winstanley's mythological interpretations of the Bible given in support of his Communism both here and in his earlier pamphlets, *The New Law of Righteousness* and *The True Levellers Standard Advanced*.

The title-page is dated 1650; Thomason dated his copy 1 January, almost a year after the execution of Charles I and nine months after Winstanley had set up his Digger colony on St George's Hill, Cobham. The pamphlet is probably the most effective of Winstanley's many pleas for realising the Diggers' radical belief, revealed to him, he claimed, in a vision: that the poor should have the right to cultivate the common or waste land customarily claimed by the Lords of Manors. By persecuting the Diggers, the landowners were perpetuating the kingly power in the new Commonwealth; breaking their covenant with the common people and soldiers, who had won Parliament the victory; and continuing the Norman yoke, the people's dispossession of the land by William the Conqueror and his barons, supported by lawyers and priests. This was the rule of covetousness, the Devil. Against it, Winstanley proclaims the 'new Righteousness', realised in the Diggers' colony, held together by love and co-operation, with no private property, no money and no buying and selling: the first Communist utopia.

Our text is taken from G. H. Sabine, ed. *The Works of Gerrard Winstanley*.

Gentlemen of the Parliament and Armie; you and the Common people have assisted each other, to cast out the Head of oppression which was Kingly power, seated in one mans hand, and that work is now done, and till that work was done you called upon the people to assist you to deliver this distressed bleeding dying nation out of bondage. And the people came and failed you not, counting neither purse not blood too dear to part with to effect this work.

The Parliament after this have made an Act to cast out Kingly power, and to make *England* a free Common-wealth.[a] These Acts the People are much rejoyced with, as being words forerunning their freedome,

---

[a] An Act abolishing 'the office' of King was passed on 19 March 1649 and proclaimed on 30 May. An Act declaring England to be a free commonwealth was passed on 19 May.

and they wait for their accomplishment that their joy may be full; for as words without action are a cheat, and kills the comfort of a righteous spirit, so words performed in action does comfort and nourish the life thereof.

Now Sirs, wheresoever we spie out Kingly power, no man I hope shall be troubled to declare it, nor afraid to cast it out, having both Act of Parliament, the Souldiers Oath, and the common peoples consent on his side, for Kingly power is like a great spread tree, if you lop the head or top-bow, and let the other Branches and root stand, it will grow again and recover fresher strength.

If any ask me, What Kingly power is? I Answer there is a twofold Kingly power. The one is, The Kingly power of right-eousnesse, and this is the power of Almightie God, ruling the whole creation in peace, and keeping it together. And this is the power of universall love, leading people into all truth, teaching every one to doe as he would be done unto, now once more striving with fresh and blood, shaking down every thing that cannot stand, and bringing every one into the Unitie of himself, the one Spirit of love and righteousnesse, and so will work a thorough restauration. But this Kingly power is above all, and will tread all covetousness, pride, envy, and self-love, and all other enemies whatsoever, under his feet, and take the kingdom and government of the Creation out of the hand of self-seeking and self-honouring Flesh, and rule the alone King of Righteousness in the earth; and this indeed is Christ himself, who will cast out the curse; But this is not that Kingly power intended by that Act of Parliament to be cast out, but pretended to be set up, though this Kingly power be much fought against both by Parliament, Armie, Clergie, and people; but when they are made to see him, then they shall mourn, because they have persecuted him.

But the other Kingly power, is the power of unrighteousness, which indeed is the Devil; And O that there were such a heart in Parliament and Army, as to perform your own Act; then People would never complain of you for breach of Covenant, for your Covetousness, Pride, and too much Self-seeking that is in you. And you on the other side would never have cause to complain of the Peoples murmurings against you. Truly this jarring that is between you and the People is The Kingly Power; yea that very Kingly power which you have made an Act to cast out; therefore see it be fulfilled on your part; for the Kingly power of Righteous-ness expects it, or else he will cast you out for Hypocrites and unsavory Salt; for he looks upon all your Actions, and truly there is abundance of Rust about your Actings, which makes them that they do not shine bright.

This Kingly power is covetousness in his branches, or the power of self-love, ruling in one or in many men over others, and enslaving those who in the Creation are their equals; nay, who are in the strictness of equity rather their Masters: And this Kingly power is usually set in the Chair of Government, under the name of Prerogative, when he rules in one over other: And under the name of State Priviledge of Parliament, when he rules in many over others: and this Kingly power, is alwayes raised up, and established by the Sword, and therefore he is called the Murderer, or the great red Dragon, which fights against *Michael*,[a] for he enslaves the weakness of the People under him, denying an equal freedom in the Earth to every one, which the Law of Righteousness gave every man in his creation. This I say is Kingly power under darkness, and as he rules in men, so he makes men jar one against another, and is the cause of all Wars and Complainings; he is known by his outward actions, and his action at this very day fills all places; for this power of darkness rules, and would rule, and is that only Enemy that fights against Creation and National Freedom: And this Kingly power is he, which you have made an Act of Parliament to cast out. And now your Rulers of *England*, play the men, and be valiant for the Truth, which is Christ: for assure your selves God will not be mocked, nor the Devil will not be mocked; for First you say and profess you own the Scriptures of Prophets and Apostles, and God looks that you should perform that Word in action: Secondly you have Declared against the Devil, and if you do not now go through with your work, but slack your hand by hypocritical self-love, and so suffer this dark Kingly power to rise higher and Rule, you shall find he will maule both you and yours to purpose.

The life of this dark Kingly power, which you have made an Act of Parliament and Oath to cast out, if you search it to the bottom, you shall see it lies within the iron chest of cursed Covetousness, who gives the Earth to some part of mankind, and denies it to another part of mankind: and that part that hath the Earth, hath no right from the Law of creation to take it to himself, and shut out others; but he took it away violently by Theft and Murder in Conquest: As when our Norman *William* came into *England* and conquered, he turned the English out, and gave the Land unto his

---

[a] Revelation, XII, 7: the war in Heaven, in which Michael and his angels overcame the Dragon, or Satan, and sent him to Hell.

Norman Souldiers every man his parcel to inclose, and hence rose up Propriety;[a] for this is the fruit of War from the beginning, for it removes Propriety out of a weaker into a stronger hand, but still upholds the curse of Bondage; and hereby the Kingly power which you have made an Act, and Sworn to cast out, does remove himself from one chair to another; and so long as the Sword rules over brethren, (mind what I say) so long the Kingly power of darkness Rules, and so large as yet is his Kingdom; which spreds from Sea to Sea, and fills the Earth; but Christ is rising who will take the Dominion and Kingdom out of his hand, and his power of Righteousness shall rise and spred from East to West, from North to South, and fill the Earth with himself, and cast the other cursed power out; when Covetousness sheaths his Sword, and ceases to rage in the field, he first makes sharp Laws of Bondage, That those that are conquered, and that by him are appointed not to enjoy the Earth, but are turned out, shall be Servants, Slaves, and Vassals to the Conquerers party: so those Laws that upholds Whips, Prisons, Gallows is but the same power of the Sword that raged, and that was drunk with Blood in the field.

King *Charles*, it is true, was the Head of this Kingly power in *England*, and he Reigned as he was a Successor of the last Norman Conquerer: and whosoever you be, that hath Propriety of Land, hath your Titles and Evidences made to you in his or his Ancestors Name, and from his and their Will and Kingly power; I am sure, he was not our Creator, and therefore parcelled out the Earth to some, and denied it to others, therefore he must needs stand as a Conquerer, and was the Head of this Kingly power, that burdens and oppresses the People, and that is the cause of all our Wars and Divisions; for if this Kingly power of Covetousness, which is the unrighteous Divider, did not yet Rule: both Parliament, Army, and rich People, would cheerfully give consent that those we call Poor should Dig and freely Plant the Waste and Common Land for a livelihood, seeing there is Land enough, and more by half then is made use of, and not be suffered to perish for want. And yet O ye Rulers of *England*, you make a blazing profession, That you know, and that you own God, Christ, and the Scriptures: but did Christ ever declare such hardness of heart? did not he bid the rich man go and sell all that he hath and give to the Poor? and does not the Scripture say, If thou makest a Covenant, keep it, though it be to thy loss: But truly it will not be to your loss, to let your fellow

---

[a] The myth that private ownership of land had begun with the Conquest had already been used by the Levellers.

Creatures, your equals in the Creation, nay those that have been
faithful in your Cause, and so your Friends; I say it will not be to
your loss to let them quietly improve the Waste and Common Land,
that they may live in peace, freed from the heavie burdens of
Poverty; for hereby our own Land will be increased with all sorts of
Commodities, and the People will be knit together in love, to keep
out a forreign Enemy that endeavours, and that will endeavour as
yet, to come like an Army of cursed Batts and Mice to destroy our
inheritance; so that if this Freedom be quietly granted to us, you
grant it but to your selves, to English-men, to your own flesh and
blood: and you do but give us our own neither, which Covetousness, in the Kingly power hath, and yet does hold from us; for the
Earth in the first Creation of it, was freely given to whole mankind,
without respect of Persons; therefore you Lords of Mannors, and
you Rulers of *England*, if you own God, Christ and Scripture, now
make Restitution, and deliver us quiet possession of our Land,
which the Kingly power as yet holds from us.

While this Kingly power raigned in one man called *Charls*, all
sorts of people complained of oppression, both Gentrie and Common people, because their lands, Inclosures,[a] and Copieholds were
intangled, and because their Trades were destroyed by Monopolis-
ing Patentees[b] and your troubles were that you could not live free
from oppression in the earth: Thereupon you that were the Gentrie,
when you were assembled in Parliament, you called upon the poor
Common-People to come and help you, and cast out oppression;
and you that complained are helped and freed, and that top-bow is
lopped off the tree of Tyrannie, and Kingly power in that one
particular is cast out; but alas oppression is a great tree still, and
keeps off the sun of freedome from the poor Commons still, he hath
many branches and great roots which must be grub'd up, before
every one can sing Sions[c] songs in peace.

As we spie out Kinglie power we must declare it, and cast it out,
or else we shall deny the Parliament of *England* and their Acts, and
so prove Traitors to the Land, by denying obedience thereunto.
Now there are Three Branches more of Kinglie power greater then
the former that oppresses this Land wonderfully; and these are the
power of the Tithing Priests over the Tenths of our labours; and the
power of Lords of Mannors, holding the free use of the Commons,

---

[a] Common land enclosed by lords of manors and farmers for grazing by sheep or cattle.[1]
[b] Those holding sole and exclusive privileges of buying and selling in a given market by the Crown.[2]
[c] I.e. Zion, one of the hills of Jerusalem: here an emblem of the Christian Church.

and wast Land from the poor, and the intolerable oppression either of bad Laws, or of bad Judges corrupting good Laws; these are branches of the Norman conquest and Kingly power still, and wants a Reformation.

For as for the first, *William* the Conqueror promised, That if the Clergie would preach him up, so that the people might be be-witched, so as to receive him to be Gods Anointed over them, he would give them the Tenths of the Lands increase yeerly; and they did it, and he made good his Promise; and do we not yet see, That if the Clergie can get Tithes or Money, they will turn as the Ruling power turns, any way; to Popery, to Protestanisme; for a King, against a King, for Monarchy, for State-Government; they cry who bids most wages, they will be on the strongest side, for an Earthly maintenance; yea, and when they are lifted up, they would Rule too, because they are called Spiritual men: It is true indeed, they are spiritual; but it is of the spiritual power of Covetousness and Pride; for the spiritual power of Love and Righteousness they know not; for if they knew it, they would not persecute and raile against him as they do.

The Clergie will serve on any side, like our ancient Laws, that will serve any Master: They will serve the Papists, they will serve the Protestants, they will serve the King, they will serve the States; they are one and the same Tools for Lawyers to work with under any Government. O you Parliament-men of *England*, cast those whorish Laws out of doors, that are so Common, that pretend love to every one, and is faithful to none; for truly, he that goes to Law, as the Proverb is, shall die a Beggar: so that old Whores, and old Laws, picks men pockets, and undoes them: If the fault lie in the Laws, and much does, burn all your old Law-Books in *Cheapside*, & set up a Government upon your own Foundation: do not put new Wine into old Bottles; but as your Government must be new, so let the Laws be new, or else you will run farther into the Mud, where you stick already, as though you were fast in an *Irish* Bogge; for you are so far sunke, that he must have good eyes that can see where you are: but yet all are not blind, there are eyes that sees you: but if the fault lies in the Judges of the Law, surely such men deserve no power in a Reforming Common-wealth, that burdens all sorts of People.

And truly Ile tell you plain, your Two Acts of Parliament are excellent and Righteous: The One to cast out Kingly power; The Other to make *England* a Free Common-wealth: build upon these Two, it is a firm Foundation, and your House will be the glory of the World; and I am confident, the righteous Spirit will love you: do not stick in the Bogge of covetousness; Let not self-love so be-muddy your brain, that you should lose your selves in the thicket of bramblebush-words, and set never a strong Oak of some stable Action for the Freedome of the poor Oppressed that helped you when you complained of Oppression. Let not Pride blind your eyes, that you should forget you are the Nations Servants, and so prove *Solomons* words good in your selves. That Servants ride on Horse-back and Coaches, when as Princes, such as Chose you, and set you there, go on foot: and many of them, through their love to the Nation, have so wasted themselves, that now they can hardly get Bread, but with great difficulty. I tell you this is a sore Evil, and this is truth; therefore think upon it, it is a poor mans Advice, and you shall finde weight in it, if you Do as well as Say.

Then Secondly for Lords of Mannors, They were *William* the Conquerors Colonels and Favourites, and he gave a large circuit of Land to every one, called A Lord-ship, that they might have a watchful eye, that if any of the conquered English should begin to Plant themselves upon any Common or waste Land, to live out of sight or out of slavery, that then some Lord of Mannor or other might see and know of it, and drive them off, as these Lords of Mannors now a dayes, endeavours to drive off the Diggers from Digging upon the Commons; but we expect the Rulers of the Land will grant unto us their Friends, the benefit of their own Acts against Kingly power, and not suffer that Norman power to crush the poor Oppressed, who helped them in their straits, nor suffer that Norman power to bud fresher out, & so in time may come to over-top our deer bought Freedom more then ever.

Search all your Laws, and Ile adventure my life, for I have little else to lose, That all Lords of Mannors hold Title to the Commons by no stronger hold then the Kings Will,[3] whose Head is cut off; and the King held Title as he was a Conqueror; now if you cast off the King who was the Head of that power, surely the power of Lords of Mannors is the same; therefore performe your own Act of Parliament, and cast out that part of the Kinglie power likewise, that the People may see you understand what you Say and Do, and that you are faithful.

For truly the Kinglie power reigns strongly in the Lords of Mannors over the Poor; for my own particular, I have in other Writings as well as in this, Declared my Reasons, That the common Land is the poor Peoples Proprietie; and I have Digged upon the Commons, and I hope in time to obtain the Freedom, to get Food and Raiment therefrom by righteous labour, which is all I desire; and for so doing, the supposed Lord of that Mannor hath Arrested me twice,[4] First, in an Action of 20.l. Trespass for Plowing upon the Commons, which I never did; and because they would not suffer me to Plead my own Cause, they made shift to pass a Sentence of Execution against some Cows I kept, supposing they had been mine, and took them away; but the right Owner reprieved them & fetched the Cowes back; so greedy are these Theeves and Murderers after my life for speaking the truth, and for maintaining the Life and Marrow of the Parliaments Cause in my Actions.

And now they have Arrested me again in an Action of £4 trespas for digging upon the Comons, which I did, & own the work to be righteous, & no trespas to any: This was the Attorney of *Kingstone's* Advice, either to get Money on both sides, for they love Mony as deerly as a poor mans dog do his breakfast in a cold morning (but regard not justice) or else, That I should not remove it to a higher Court, but that the cause might be tryed there, and then they know how to please the Lords of Mannors, that have resolved to spend hundreds of pounds but they will hinder the poor from enjoying the Commons; for they will not suffer me to plead my own Cause, but I must Fee an enemie, or else be condemned and executed without mercy or Justice as I was before, and so to put me in Prison till I pay their unrighteous Sentence; for truly Attourneys are such neat workmen, that they can turn a Cause which way those that have the biggest purse will have them: and the Countrie knows very well, That *Kingstone* court is so full of the Kinglie power; that some will rather lose their Rights, then have their causes tryed there: one of the Officers of that court, told a friend of mine, That if the Diggers cause was good, he would pick out such a Jurie as should overthrow him: And upon my former Arrest, they picked out such a Jurie as Sentenced me to pay 10.l. damages for plowing upon the commons, which I did not do, neither did any witness prove it before them: So that from *Kingstone* Juries, Lords of Mannors, and Kinglie power, *Good Lord deliver us*.

Do these men obey the Parliaments Acts, to throw down Kinglie power? O no: The same unrighteous doing that was complained of in King *Charles* dayes, the same doings is among them still: Monies will buy and sell Justice still: and is our 8 yeers Wars come round about to lay us down again in the kennel of injustice as much or more then before? are we no farther learned yet? O ye Rulers of *England*, when must we turn over a new leaf? will you alwayes hold us in one Lesson? surely you will make Dunces of us; then all the

Boyes in other Lands will laugh at us: come, I pray let us take forth, and go forward in our learning.

You blame us who are the Common people as though we would have no government; truly Gentlemen, We desire a righteous government with all our hearts, but the government we have gives freedom and livelihood to the Gentrie, to have abundance, and to lock up Treasures of the Earth from the poor, so that rich men may have chests full of Gold and Silver, and houses full of Corn and Goods to look upon; and the poor that works to get it, can hardly live, and if they cannot work like Slaves, then they must starve. And thus the Law gives all the Land to some part of mankind whose Predecessors got it by conquest, and denies it to others, who by the righteous Law of Creation may claim an equall portion; and yet you say this is a righteous government, but surely it is no other but selfishnes, which is the great Red Dragon, the Murtherer.

England is a Prison; the variety of subtilties in the Laws preserved by the Sword, are bolts, bars, and doors of the prison; the Lawyers are the Jaylors, and poor men are the prisoners; for let a man fall into the hand of any from the Bailiffe to the Judge, and he is either undone, or wearie of his life.

Surely this power [of] the Laws, which is the great Idoll that people dote upon, is the burden of the Creation, a Nurserie of Idleness, luxurie, and cheating, the only enemie of Christ the King of righteousness; for though it pretend Justice, yet the Judges and Law-Officers, buy and sell Justice for money, and wipes their mouths like *Solomons* whore, and says it is my calling, and never are troubled at it.

Two things must cast out this Idoll: First, Let not people send their children to those Nurseries of Covetousness, *The Innes of Court*. Secondly, let not people live in contention, but fulfill Christs last commandment, *Love*; and endeavour to practice that full point for the Law and the Prophets. *Doe as you would be done by*, and so cast out envie and discontent. Woe to you Lawyers, for your trade is the bane and miserie of the world; your power is the only power that hinders Christ from rising; the destruction of your power will be the life of the World; it is full of confusion, it is Babylon, and surely its fall is neer, in regard the light of truth is rising, who will consume your power, but save your persons by the words of his mouth, and brightnesse of his coming.

The Lawyers trade is one of the false Prophets, that says, Lo here is Christ, Ile save you in this Court, and lo there is Christ, Ile save you in that Court: but when we have tried all, we are lost, and not saved, for we are either utterly made Beggars by this Saviour, the Law, or else we are nursed up in hardnesse of heart and cruelty against our fellow creature whom we ought to love and preserve, and not destroy: This Saviour jeeres righteousness, and bids every man save himself, and never regard what becomes of another, and so is a plain destroyer of the Creation; Surely that Wo pronounced against Lawyers by the Man Christ must be fulfilled, delay is no payment: Therefore you Parliament and Army that have power in your hands, reform the Law; and suffer none to be called to practice Law but reformed ones; may suffer every man to plead his own cause, and choose his own Lawyer, where he finds the most ingenuous man: Wel, every mans burthen in this Age fills their mouths with words of Lamentation against Law and Lawyers sufficiently; therefore you that have an opportunitie to ease the cry of the oppressed, shut not your eies and eares, but cast out this covetous corruption whereby corrupt Lawyers doe oppress the People; it is another Branch of the Kingly power.

You Gentlemen of *Surrey*, and Lords of Mannors and you Mr. Parson *Platt*[a] especially that lay almost a fortnight waiting and tempting the Lord *Fairfax*[b] to send Souldiers to drive off the Diggers; when he granted your Desire, it was but to secure[c] the Sheriff, for he did not give them commission to beat us, which we thank him for; and we thank the Souldiers for their moderation, that they would not strike poor wormes, *Englands* and the creations faithful friends, though you would have moved them thereunto. My Advice to you Gentlemen is this, Hereafter to lie still and cherish the Diggers, for they love you, and would not have your finger ake if they could help it; and why should you be so bitter against them? O let them live by you; some of them have been Souldiers, and some countrie-men that were alwayes friends to the Parliaments cause, by whose hardship and meanes you enjoy the creatures about you in peace, and will you now destroy part of them that have preserved your lives? O do not do so; be not so besotted with the Kinglie power; hereafter let not the Attourneyes or Lawyers neatly councel your Money out of your purses, and stir you up to beat and abuse the Diggers, to make all rational men laugh at your folly, and condemn you for your bitterness: If you have yet so much Money, give it not away to destroy men, but give it to some poor or other to be a Stock, and bid them go and Plant the common; this will be

---

a Presbyterian rector of West Horsley and lord of the manor of Cobham by marriage; he led the opposition to the Digger colony.
b Commander-in-Chief of the Army.   c I.e. support.

your honour, and your comfort; assure your selves you never must have true comfort tell you be friends with the poor; therefore come, come, love the Diggers, and make restitution of their Land you hold from them; for what would you do if you had not such labouring men to work for you?

And you great Officers of the Army and Parliament, love your common Souldiers, (I plead for Equity and Reason) and do not force them by long delay of Payment to sell you their deer bought Debenters[a] for a thing of naught, and then to go and buy our common Land, and crown Land, and other Land that is the spoil one of another, therewith: Remember you are Servants to the commons of *England*, and you were Volunteers in the Wars, and the common people have paid you for your pains so largely, that some of us have not left our selves hardly bread to eate; and therefore if there be a spoil to be gathered of crown Lands, Deans, Bishops, Forrests Lands and commons, that is to come to the poor commons freely; and you ought to be content with your wages, unless you will denie Christ and the Scriptures; and you ought not to go and buy one of another that which is common to all the Nation; for you ought neither to buy nor sell other mens Proprietie by the Law of creation; for Christ gives you no such Warrant. As soon as you have freed the Earth from one intanglement of Kinglie power, will you intangle it more, and worse by another degree of Kinglie power? I pray consider what you do, and do righteously: We that are the poor commons, that paid our Money, and gave you free Quarter, have as much Right in those crown Lands and Lands of the spoil as you; therefore we give no consent That you should buy and sell our crown Lands and waste Lands, for it is our purchased inheritance from under Oppression, it is our own, even the poor common peoples of *England*: It was taken from us, and hath been held from us by former conquests, whereof the Norman conquest was the last, which is cast out by yours and our joynt Assistance, therefore you cannot in Equity take it from us, nor we cannot in Equity take it from you, for it is our joynt purchased inheritance; we paid you your wages to help us to recover it, but not to take it to your selves, and turn us out, and buy and sell it among your selves, for this is a cheat of the Kinglie swordlie power which you hold up; and we profess to all the world, in so doing you denie God, Christ, and the Scriptures whom ye professed you own: for God, Christ, and Scriptures owne no such practice: Likewise we

---

[a] I.e. debentures: claims to land issued to the soldiers in lieu of wages, which they had to sell at a discount to obtain cash.

profess to all the Creation, That in so doing, you rob us of our Rights; & you kill us, by denying to give us our livelihood in our own inheritance freely, which is the crown Land and Comon Land and waste Lands, Bishops & Deans, which some of you begin to say you are not satisfied in your conscience to let us have: I, well spoke, tender hearted Covetousness; if you do so, you will uphold the Kinglie power, and so disobey both Acts of Parliament, and break your Oath, and you will live in the breach of those Two Commandements, *Thou shalt not kill: Thou shalt not steal*; by denying us the Earth which is our Livelyhood, and thereby killing us by a lingring death.

Well, the end of all my Speech is to point out the Kingly power, where I spie it out, and you see it remains strongly in the hands of Lords of Mannors, who have dealt discourteously with some who are sincere in heart, though there have some come among the Diggers that have caused scandall, but we dis-own their wayes.[a]

The Lords of Mannors have sent to beat us, to pull down our houses, spoil our labours; yet we are patient, and never offered any violence to them again, this 40 weeks past, but wait upon God with love till their hearts thereby be softned; and all that we desire is, but to live quietly in the land of our nativity, by our righteous labour, upon the common Land which is our own, but as yet the Lords of the Mannor so formerly called, will not suffer us, but abuse us. Is not that part of the Kingly power? In that which follows I shall cleerly prove it is, for it appears so cleer that the understanding of a child does say, It is Tyranny, it is the Kingly power of darkness, therefore we expect that you will grant us the benefit of your Act of Parliament that we may say, Truly *England* is a Common-wealth, and a free people indeed.

Sir, Though your Tithing Priests and other tell you, That we Diggers do deny God, Christ, and the Scripture, to make us odious, and themselves better thought of; yet you will see in time when the King of Righteousness whom we serve does cleer our innocencie, That our actions and conversation is the very life of the Scripture, and holds forth the true power of God and Christ. For is not the end of all preaching, praying, and profession wrapped up in this action, namely, *Love your enemies, and doe to all men, as you would they should do to you, for this is the very Law and the Prophets*. This is the New Commandement that Christ left behind him. Now if any seem to say this, and does not do this, but acts

[a] A reference to the Ranters who, unlike the Diggers, admitted women to their colonies.[5]

contrary, for my part I owne not their wayes, they are members that uphold the curse.

Bare talking of righteousnesse, and not acting, hath ruled, and yet does rule king of darkness in the creation; and it is the cause of all this immoderate confusion and ignorance that is in men.

But the actings of righteousnesse from the inward power of love, shall rule King of righteousnesse in the creation now in these later dayes, and cast the other Serpent and fiery scorpion out; for this is Christ the restoring power: and as he rises up, so multitude of words without action (which is hypocrisie) is to die, his judgment hastens apace.

If any sort of people hold the earth to themselves by the dark Kingly power, and shut out others from that freedom, they deny God, Christ, and Scriptures, and they overthrow all their preaching, praying, and profession; for the Scriptures declare them to be Hypocrites, Scribes and Pharisees, *that say, and do not*; they have words, and no deeds: Like Parson *Platt* the Preacher at *Horsley* in *Surrey*, a Lord of Mannor (by marriage) of the place where we digg, who caused a poor old mans house that stood upon the Common, to be pulled down in the evening of a cold day, and turned the old man, and his wife, and daughter to lie in the open field, because he was a Digger: and he, and other Lords of Mannors, and Gentlemen sent their servants up and down the Town, to bid their Tenants and neighbours, neither to give the Diggers lodging nor victuals, on pain of their displeasure. Though this Parson *Platt* preach the Scriptures, yet I'll affirm, he denyes God, Christ, and Scriptures, and knowes nothing of them, for covetousness, pride, and envie hath blinded his eyes. A man knowes no more of righteousness than he hath power to act; and surely, this cruelty of preaching *Platt* is an unrighteous act.

If the Diggers were enemies, (oh you Lords of Mannors) as they are not, you ought to love them: I am sure, they love you, and if you doubt it, put them to the tryall; you shall find them more faithfull than many of those pick-thank slaves, and belly-god servants to whom your ears are open, when they bring tales full of envie to you against us.

We are told likewise, That to make us who are called Diggers, odious, and to incense you against us, there came to the Generall and Councell of State, divers Justices, and others, and told you, that we Diggers were Cavaliers, and that we waited an opportunity, and gathered together to stand up for the Prince.

But all that know us can prove that to be a false report, to the dishonour of those Justices; for we have been friends to the Parliaments cause, and so do continue, and will continue; for this work of digging, to make *England* a free Common-wealth, is the life and marrow of the Parliaments cause. And the two Acts of Parliament, the One, to cast out Kingly power, the Other, to make *England* a free Common-wealth, declares it: and we do obey those Acts, and will obey them, for they hold forth righteousnesse.

But for our rising in arms for the Prince, or any other, let any come and see our strength and work, and they will say, It is a meer envious slander cast upon us, to incense you against us.

Besides, You shall see by and by, That our principles are wholly against Kingly power in every one, as well as in one. Likewise we hear, that they told you, that the Diggers do steal and rob from others. This likewise is a slander: we have things stolen from us; but if any can prove that any of us do steal any mans proper goods, as Sheep, Geese, Pigs, as they say, let such be made a spectacle to all the world: For my part, I own no such doing, neither do I know any such thing by any of the Diggers. Likewise they report, that we Diggers hold women to be common, and live in that bestialnesse: For my part, I declare against it; I own this to be a truth, That the earth ought to be a common Treasury to all; but as for women, *Let every man have his own wife, and every woman her own husband*; and I know none of the Diggers that act in such an unrationall excesse of female communitie: If any should, I professe to have nothing to do with such people, but leave them to their own Master, who will pay them with torment of minde, and diseases in their bodies.

These and such-like tales, we hear, are brought to you, to incense you against us: but we desire you to mark them that bring them, for we partly know who they be, and we can tell them to their faces, they were Cavaliers, and had hands in the Kentish Rising,[a] and in stirring up that offensive *Surrey* Petition,[b] which was the occasion of bloodshed in *Westminster*-yard, and they would rejoyce to see the Prince come with an Armie to over-top you: for we know, they love you not but from the teeth outwards, for their own ends: And these are the proud *Hamans*,[c] that would incense you against the *Mordecaies* of the Land, even your true-hearted friends, the Diggers. Well, in the midst of our slanders we rejoyce in the uprightness of our hearts, and we do *commit our cause to him that judgeth righteously*.

Upon these lying reports, and importunitie to the General, it

[a] In May 1648.

[b] Presented to Parliament on 16 May 1648, asking that the King be 'restored to his due honor and just right'. It led to a riot, in which ten were killed and a hundred injured.

[c] Haman was an inveterate enemy of the Jews and persecutor of the family of Mordecai, Esther's foster-father (Esther).

seems the General granted the Lords of Mannor to have some souldiers to go along with the Sheriff, to pull down the Diggers houses; and so the souldiers did come: but they were very moderate and rationall men, and as they were sent to secure the Sheriff, so they did: but there was no cause; for, though the Gentlemen possess'd the General, that they feared opposition from the Diggers, yet the souldiers saw they lifted not up a finger in discontent, but fought against those dragons, the Lords of Manors, with the spirit of love and patience: for when the two Lords of Manor sat among the souldiers on horseback and coach, and commanded their fearfull tenants to pull down one of the Diggers houses before their faces, and rejoyced with shouting at the fall; yet some of the Diggers stood by, and were very chearfull, and preached the Gospel to those Turkish *Bashaws*, which are words of life, and in time will prove words of terrour, to torment their awakened consciences.

And the poor tenants that pulled down the house, durst do no other, because their Landlords and Lords looked on, for fear they should be turned out of service, or their livings; as a poor honest man, because he looked with a cheerfull countenance upon the Diggers (though he was affraid to come neer, or affraid to speak openly, lest his Landlords setting-dogs should smell the sound of his words, and carry a pick-thank tale, which his Lords ears are much open to) a Baily was sent presently to him, to warn him out of his house.

Can the Turkish Bashaws hold their slaves in more bondage than these Gospel-professing Lords of Manors do their poor tenants? and is not this the Kingly power? O you Rulers of *England*, I pray see that your own acts be obeyed, and let the oppressed go free.

And when the poor enforced slaves had pulled down the house, then their Lords gave them ten shillings to drink, and there they smiled one upon another; being fearfull, like a dog that is kept in awe, when his Master gives him a bone, and stands over him with a whip; he will eat, and look up, and twinch his tail; for they durst not laugh out, lest their Lords should hear they jeer'd them openly; for in their hearts they are Diggers. Therefore, you Lords of Manors, if you have none to stand for you but whom you force by threatning, then leave off striving against the spirit, and say you are fallen, and come in and embrace righteousnesse, that you may finde mercy betimes.

The next day after this, there came two souldiers and three Country-men to another house which the Diggers had set up, (which the Sheriff the day before had let alone, for, as some say, he was grieved to see what was done,) one of these souldiers was very civill, and walked lovingly with the Diggers round their corn which they had planted, and commended the work, and would do no harm (as divers others were of the same minde) and when he went his way, gave the Diggers 12*d*. to drink: but the other souldier was so rude, that he forced those three Country-men to help him to pull down the house, and railed bitterly: the men were unwilling to pull it down; but for fear of their Landlords, and the threatening souldier, they did put their hands to pull it down.

And seeing Parson *Platt* (the Lord of that Manor) will not suffer the Diggers to have a house (wherein he forgets his Master Christ, that is persecuted in naked, hungry, and houselesse members) yet the Diggers were mighty cheerfull, and their spirits resolve to wait upon God, to see what he will do, and they have built them some few little hutches like calf-cribs, and there they lie anights, and follow their work adayes still with wonderfull joy of heart, taking the spoyling of their goods cheerfully, counting it a great happinesse to be persecuted for righteousnesse sake, by the Priests and Professors,[a] that are the successors of *Judas*, and the bitter-spirited Pharisees that put the man Christ *Jesus* to death. And they have planted divers Acres of Wheat and Rye, which is come up, and promises a very hopefull crop, committing their cause to God, and wait upon him, saying, O thou King of righteousnesse, do thine own work.

O that you would search and try our wayes narrowly, and see whether we deny God, Christ, Scriptures, as the Priests slander us we do; and you shall finde, that the Scriptures warrant our action, and God in Christ is the life of our souls, and the support of our spirits in the midst of this our sharp persecution from the hands of unreasonable men, who have not faith in Christ, but uphold the Kingly power, which you have Voted down.

Likewise, you shall see, that we live in the performance of that work which is the very life and marrow of the Parliaments Cause, whereby we honour the Parliament and their Cause: as you shall see by this following Declaration, unfolding the foundation whereupon *Englands* Laws are, or the Freedom of a Common-wealth ought to be built, which is Equity and Reason.

In the time of the Kings, who came in as Conquerors, and ruled by the power of the Sword, not only the Common land, but the Inclosures also were captivated under the will of those Kings, till

---

[a] I.e. those who only profess religion.

now of late that our later Kings granted more freedom to the
Gentry than they had presently after the Conquest; yet under
bondage still: for what are prisons, whips and gallows in the times
of peace, but the laws and power of the sword, forcing and
compelling obedience, and so enslaving, as if the sword raged in the
open field?

England was in such a slavery under the Kingly power, that both
Gentry and Commonaltie groaned under bondage; and to ease
themselves, the endeavoured to call a Parliament, that by their
counsels and decrees they might find some freedom.

But *Charles* the then King perceiving that the Freedom they
strove for, would derogate from his Prerogative tyranny, therupon
he goes into the North, to raise a War against the Parliament, and
took WILLIAM *the Conqueror's* Sword into his hand again, thereby
to keep under the former conquered English, and to uphold his
Kingly power of self-will and Prerogative, which was the power got
by former Conquests; that is, to rule over the lives and estates of all
men at his will, and so to make us pure slaves and vassals.

Well, This Parliament, that did consist of the chief Lords, Lords
of Manors, and Gentry, and they seeing that the King, by raising an
Army, did thereby declare his intent to enslave all sorts to him by
the sword; and being in distresse, and in a low ebb, they call upon
the common people to bring in their Plate, Moneys, Taxes,
Free-quarter, Excise, and to adventure their lives with them, and
they would endeavour to recover *England* from that *Norman* yoak,
and make us a free people: and the common people assent hereunto,
and call this the Parliaments Cause, and own it, and adventure
person and purse to preserve it; and by the joynt assistance of
Parliament and People, the King was beaten in the field, his head
taken off, and his Kingly power voted down; and the Norman
Conquest, we want nothing but possession of the spoyl, which is a
free use of the Land for our livelyhood.

And from hence we the common people, or younger brothers,
plead our propriety in the Common land, as truly our own by
vertue of this victory over the King; as our elder brothers can plead
proprietie in their Inclosures; and that for three reasons in *Englands*
law.

First, By a lawfull purchase or contract between the Parliament
and us; for they were our Landlords and Lords of Mannors that
held the freedom of the Commons from us, while the King was in
his power; for they held title thereunto from him, he being the
head, and they branches of the Kingly power, that enslaved the

people by that ancient Conquerors Sword, that was the ruling power. For they said, Come and help us against the King that enslaves us, that we may be delivered from his Tyranny, and we will make you a free People.

Now they cannot make us free, unlesse they deliver us from the bondage which they themselves held us under; and that is, they held the freedom of the Earth from us: for we in part with them have delivered our selves from the King: now we claim freedom from that bondage you have, and yet do hold us under, by the bargain and contract between Parliament and us, who (I say) did consist of Lords of Manors, and Landlords, whereof Mr. *Drake*, who hath arrested me for digging upon the Common was one at that time: Therefore by the law of Bargain and Sale, we claim of them our freedom, to live comfortably with them in this Land of our Nativity; and this we cannot do, so long as we lie under poverty, and must not be suffered to plant the commons and waste land for our livelihood: for, take away the land from any people, and those people are in a way of continuall death and misery; and better not to have had a body, than not to have food and rayment for it. But (I say) they have sold us our freedom in the common, and have been largely paid for it; for by means of our bloods and money, they sit in peace: for if the King had prevailed, they had lost all, and been in slavery to the meanest Cavalier, if the King would. Therefore we the Commons say, Give us our bargain: if you deny us our bargain, you deny God, Christ, and Scriptures; and all your profession then is and hath been hypocrisie.

Secondly, The Commons and Crown land is our propriety by equall conquest over the Kingly power: for the Parl. did never stir up the people by promises and covenant to assist them to cast out the King, and to establish them in the Kings place and prerogative power: No, but all their Declarations were for the safety and peace of the whole Nation.

Therefore the common-people being part of the Nation, and especially they that bore the greatest heat of the day in casting out the oppressor: and the Nation cannot be in peace, so long as the poor oppressed are in want, and the land is intangled and held from them by bondage.

But the Victory being obtained over the King, the spoyl which is properly the Land, ought in equity to be divided now between the two Parties, that is, Parliament and Common-people. The Parliament, consisting of Lords of Manors, and Gentry, ought to have their inclosure Lands free to them without molestation, as they are freed from the Court of Wards.[6]

And the Common-people, consisting of Souldiers, and such as paid Taxes and Free-quarter, ought to have the freedom of all waste and common land, and Crown-land equally among them; the Souldiery ought not in equity to have all, nor the other people that paid them to have all; but the spoyle ought to be divided between them that stay'd at home, and them that went to Warr; for the Victory is for the whole Nation.

And as the Parliament declared, they did all for the Nation, and not for themselves onely; so we plead with the Armie, they did not fight for themselves, but for the freedom of the Nation: and I say, we have bought our Freedom of them likewise by Taxes and Free-quarter: therefore we claim an equall Freedom with them in this Conquest over the King.

Thirdly, We claim an equall portion in the Victory over the King, by vertue of the two Acts of Parliament, the One to make *England* a Free Common-wealth; the Other to take away Kingly power. Now the Kingly power (you have heard) is a power that rules by the Sword in covetousnesse and self, giving the earth to some, and denying it to others: and this Kingly power was not in the hand of the King alone; but Lords, and Lords of Manors, and corrupt Judges, and Lawyers especially, held it up likewise; for he was the head, and they, with the Tything-priests[a] are the branches of that Tyrannical Kingly power; and all the several limbs and members must be cast out, before Kingly power can be pulled up root and branch. Mistake me not, I do not say, Cast out the persons of men.[b] No, I do not desire their fingers to ake: but I say, Cast out their power, whereby they hold the people in bondage, as the King held them in bondage. And I say, it is our own Freedom we claim, both by bargain, and by equality in the Conquest; as well as by the Law of righteous Creation, which gives the Earth to all equally.

And the power of Lords of Mannors lies in this: They deny the Common people the use and free benefit of the Earth, unless they give them leave, and pay them for it, either in Rent, in Fines, in Homages, or Heriots.[c] Surely the Earth was never made by God, that the Younger brother should not live in the Earth, unless he would work for, and pay his Elder brother Rent for the Earth: No; this Slavery came in by Conquest, and it is part of the Kingly power; and *England* cannot be a Free Common-wealth, till this Bondage be taken away. You have taken away the King; you have

a The clergy had the right to take a tithe (a tenth) of the labourers' produce for their support.
b Winstanley never advocated the ejection of lords of manors or landlords.
c Originally, restoration of weapons to the lord on the tenant's death.

taken away the House of Lords: Now step two steps further, and take away the power of Lords of Mannors, and of Tything Priests, and the intolerable oppressions of Judges, by whom Laws are corrupted; and your work will be honourable.

Fourthly, if this Freedom be denied the Common people, To enjoy the Common Land; then Parliament, Army and Judges will deny Equity and Reason, whereupon the Laws of a well-governed Common-wealth ought to be built: And if this Equity be denied, then there can be no Law, but Club-Law,[a] among the people: and if the Sword must raign, then every Party will be striving to bear the Sword; and then farewel Peace; nay, farewel Religion and Gospel, unless it be made use of to intrap one another, as we plainly see some Priests and others make it a Cloke for their Knavery. If I adventure my life, and fruit of my labour, equal with you, and obtain what we strive for; it is both Equity and Reason, that I should equally divide the Spoil with you, and not you to have all, and I none: And if you deny us this, you take away our Propriety from us, our Moneys and Blood, and give us nothing for it.

Therefore, I say, the Common Land is my own Land, equal with my fellow-Commoners; and our true Propriety, by the Law of Creation: it is every ones, but not one single ones: Yea, the Commons are as truly ours by the last excellent two Acts of Parliament, the Foundation of *Englands* new righteous Government aimed at, as the Elder brothers can say the Inclosures are theirs: for they adventured their Lives, and covenanted with us to help them to preserve their Freedom: And we adventured our lives, and they covenanted with us, to purchase and to give us our Freedom, that hath been hundreds of yeers kept from us.

Dæmona non Armis, sed Morte subegit Jesus.[b]

By patient Sufferings, not by Death[c]
Christ did the Devil kill;
And by the same, still to this day,
his Foes be conquers still.

True Religion, and undefiled, is this, To make restitution of the Earth, which hath been taken and held from the Common people, by the power of Conquests formerly, and so *set the oppressed free*. Do not All strive to enjoy the Land? The Gentry strive for Land, the

---

[a] The countrymen of the West and South who had taken up arms in 1645 against Royalists and Parliamentarians alike were known as Clubmen.
[b] 'Jesus vanquished the devils not by arms, but by His death': the quotation, not biblical, has not been traced.
[c] I.e. not by destroying the Devil.

Clergie strive for Land, the Common people strive for Land; and Buying and Selling is an Art, whereby people endeavour to cheat one another of the Land. Now if any can prove, from the Law of Righteousness, that the Land was made peculiar to him and his successively, shutting others out, he shall enjoy it freely, for my part: But I affirm, It was made for all; and true Religion is, To let every one enjoy it. Therefore, you Rulers of *England*, make restitution of the Lands which the Kingly power holds from us: *Set the oppressed free*; and come in, and honour Christ, who is the Restoring Power, and you shall finde rest.

8. James Harrington, 'Valerius and Publicola', 1659

Valerius and Publicola was published on 22 October 1659, ten days after Major General John Lambert had dissolved the recalled Rump Parliament and set up a Committee of Public Safety in its stead. This latest crisis between Army and Parliament causes Harrington's Valerius to say: 'I must confess that our army hath it now in their power to introduce a commonwealth.'

To this end Harrington uses the dialogue form to urge the possibility of establishing in England a balanced gentry republic which will guarantee religious and political liberty. He proposes a bicameral representative constitution, to consist of a popular assembly of a thousand and a senate of three hundred. The nation will be divided into fifty electoral districts and in each year a third of each chamber will be elected for three years, and a third retire for at least the same period. A property qualification governs eligibility to stand: for the assembly four candidates having less than £100 a year may stand for every six having that much or more; for the senate £100 a year at least is required. Harrington does not discuss the extent of the franchise. He does discuss the relation of the two chambers, seeking to reconcile the few and the many by having the upper house debate and propose, and the lower house never debate, but rather accept or reject by vote the proposals of the upper house.

This brief and simple scheme is closely related to the balanced republican constitution fully expounded in Harrington's major and most famous work, *Oceana* (1656). The Venetian constitution is Harrington's general model in each case. *Valerius and Publicola* is, however, consistent with *Oceana* rather than an exact brief version of its proposals. Of the two great principles of *Oceana*, the rotation of office, and the recurrent correction of imbalance in property, the former is seen here in the rules for elections, while the latter is not described but taken for granted: 'That which I have long since proved, and you granted: the balance, the distribution of property, and the power thence naturally deriving . . .'.

Publicola speaks particularly for Harrington in the dialogue, and it may be that petitions produced by Publicola are, or closely resemble, actual petitions submitted by Harrington and his Rota Club to the Rump during the last month of its 1659 session. At the same time the dialogue is used not merely to propose, but to arouse the awareness of political possibility: to stir fresh thought and urge wise innovation.

Harrington has been re-edited and fully discussed in J. G. A. Pocock, *The Political Works of James Harrington*. The present text is from that edition.

Valerius and Publicola

Or the true
FORM
OF
A POPULAR
COMMONWEALTH
Extracted
E puris naturalibus.[a]

Quos perdere vult Jupiter, hos dementat prius.[b]

LONDON:
Printed by J. C. for Henry Fletcher, at the Three
Gilt Cups in St Paul's Churchyard. 1659.

To the Reader

The way of dialogue, being not faithfully managed, is of all other the most fraudulent; but being faithfully managed, is the clearest and most effectual for the conveying a man's sense unto the understanding of his reader. There is nothing in this world, next the favour of God, I so much desire as to be familiarly understood; which that great men have thought below them, hath proved hitherto but the ruin of themselves and the detriment of the public; for which cause, having tried all other means, I now add this. My work, if I be not given over unto utter blindness, is the same with, or nearest, that of the nation; and the work of the nation, being not understood, is in horrid danger of utter ruin.

Valerius: Dearest Publicola, how have I longed to meet you, and in the favourable silence of this long walk!

Publicola: What has my noble friend Valerius to command his faithful servant?

Valerius: Why really, notwithstanding the tumult of these extravagant changes[1] your last discourse had so much of my attention then, and hath had such digestion with me since, that I feel it running in my veins.

Publicola: Find you in that any temptation to the buckling on of high shoon?[c]

---

[a] From simple and natural things.
[b] Those whom Jupiter wishes to destroy, he first makes mad.
[c] Adopting the cause of the people.

Valerius: My thoughts, Publicola, are quite of another strain; sometimes methinks I see England grasping at empire, like Rome itself.

Publicola: Why then, Valerius, my discourses are not such as they say; there runneth nothing of them in your veins that hath imbased your noble blood.

Valerius: The heraldry of them is of as high a pitch as the policy; but I would have them be somewhat lower in some things.

Publicola: What are those?

Valerius: The vulgar complain of you that you are too learned.

Publicola: I thought it was not you, Valerius.

Valerius: For all that, I could be contented to see you raise your structure by your own strength, and without the help of other authors.

Publicola: That I dare say you may, when you please.

Valerius: I must see it then, before I lose the covert of these reverend elms.

Publicola: You take care that the building should be well situated; and for the foundation, I may presume, by what hath already passed between you and me, that we are long since agreed.

Valerius: That the threefold balance or distribution of property is the cause of the triple way of government, I fully consent with you; as also that the balance now in England is in the people plainly, and exclusively both to a king and lords.

Publicola: You are not of them that grant this, and then ask which way a commonwealth should be introduced in England.

Valerius: Why truly, yes; seeing not only the people are so wholly unacquainted with the means, but their leaders so adverse to it.

Publicola: Think you that a plant grows the worse for not understanding the means?

Valerius: A plant is not a free agent; but among men, who are free agents, the introduction of government seemeth to be arbitrary.

Publicola: What, where there is no more than Hobson's choice, this or none?

Valerius: It is true that if they can have nothing else, they must at length have a commonwealth; but though they can have nothing else to be holding, yet they will be trying other things.

Publicola: There is all the mischief.

Valerius: And enough to ruin the nation.

Publicola: To hurt it very sore, but not to ruin it; nor yet to evade a commonwealth, except they expose us unto foreign invasion.

Valerius: I am glad of your confidence.

Publicola: You may let it pass for confidence, if you please; but if there be no other way, except that only of invasion, whereby the present balance can receive a change sudden enough to admit of any other form, the reason why we must have a commonwealth is coercive.

Valerius: And putting the case it be the will of God to defend us from foreign invasion, how long will it be ere they see at home the coerciveness of this reason, or, which is all one, that all power is in and from the people?

Publicola: Good Valerius, how long is it since this was both seen and declared in parliament?

Valerius: Perhaps, as they meant, it might be admitted as a principle even in monarchy.

Publicola: This with your pardon you will revoke, seeing you well remember that this their declaration of power in the people hath been exclusive unto king and lords, and that in express terms.

Valerius: But in this they related not at all unto the distribution of property.

Publicola: Why then, there is not such difference between the growing of a plant and of a commonwealth as you thought; seeing a commonwealth, knowing as little, doth no less.

Valerius: This of all other is unto me a consideration fullest of comfort.

Publicola: It will in time proceed accordingly, through mere necessity of nature, or by feeling; but your desire, I suppose, is to know how it should be rationally introduced, or by seeing; and that with more ease and better speed.

Valerius: If it might please God, I would live to have my share of it, though I fear I never shall.

Publicola: You carve yourself ill; for by hope a man enjoys even that which he never comes to attain, and by fear he is deprived even of that which he comes not to lose.

Valerius: I must confess that our army hath it now in their power to introduce a commonwealth.

Publicola: And there is no other action in their power that can excuse them.

Valerius: Putting the case they would hearken unto you, what course would you advise?

Publicola: The same that I have advised over and over.

Valerius: As how?

Publicola: As how! Is that yet a question? Let them divide the territory into fifty equal parts.

Valerius: They will never make a new division.

Publicola: Why then, they shall never have an equal commonwealth.

Valerius: What ill luck is this, that the first step should be so difficult?

Publicola: You speak as if never any territory had been divided, whereas there is none that hath not; and surveyors will tell you it is a work to be perfectly performed in two months, and with ease.

Valerius: Putting the case this were done, what is next?

Publicola: The next is that the commonwealth were complete.

Valerius: Say you so? This indeed makes amends; but how?

Publicola: With no more addition than that the people in every distinct division elect annually two knights and seven deputies.

Valerius: I dare say the people would never stick at this.

Publicola: Not sticking at this, they of their own power have instituted the two great assemblies of which every commonwealth consisteth.

Valerius: But in advising these things, you must advise men so that they may understand them.

Publicola: Valerius, could I as easily have advised men how to understand as what to do, there had been a common wealth ere this.

Valerius: Come, I will have you try something of this kind, and begin upon some known principle: as this, all power is in the people.

Publicola: Content. But the diffusive body of the people (at least in a territory of this extent) can never exercise any power at all.

Valerius: That is certain.

Publicola: Hence is the necessity of some form of government.

Valerius: That is, the people, of themselves being in a natural incapacity of exercising power, must be brought into some artificial or political capacity of exercising the same.

Publicola: Right. Now this may be done in three ways: as first, by a single person . . .

Valerius: How!

Publicola: Nay, I am not likely to trouble you much upon this point; but as you were intimating very now, there are royalists who derive the original right of monarchy from the consent of the people.

Valerius: There are so.

Publicola: And these hold the king to be nothing else but the representor of the people and their power.

Valerius: As the Turk.

Publicola: Yes, as the Turk.

Valerius: The people's power at that rate comes to the people's slavery.

Publicola: You say right; and so it may at other rates too.

Valerius: As how?

Publicola: Why, as I was about to say. The power of the people may be politically brought into exercise three ways: by a single person, by an assembly consisting of a few, or by an assembly consisting of many.

Valerius: Or by a mixture.

Publicola: Nay, I pray you let that alone yet a while; for which way soever you go, it must come at length to some mixture, seeing the single person you named but now, without his divan or council to debate and propose to him, would make but bad work even for himself. But as the government cometh to be pitched fundamentally upon one of these three, so it differs not only in name, but in nature.

Valerius: I apprehend you; as monarchy, aristocracy and democracy.[2]

Publicola: Nay, you are out with your learning, when you have forbidden it me. But in countries where there is not a nobility sufficiently balanced or enriched, there can be none of your aristocracy; and yet there may (as long as it will last) be a government in a few.

Valerius: What call you that?

Publicola: Nay, what say you?

Valerius: Come, it is oligarchy; when all is done, some words of art we must use.

Publicola: I thought you would come to it; and yet seeing I have promised, I will be sparing. But with your pardon, you have disordered my discourse, or by this I had shown that if the power of the people be committed to a single person, the common interest is submitted unto that of a family; and if it be committed to a few, it is submitted to the interest of a few families.

Valerius: Which, so many times as they are more than one, is so many times worse than monarchy.

Publicola: I am not sorry that you are of that mind. For there is no such thing as a commonwealth or, as you say, democracy in nature, if it be not pitched upon a numerous assembly of the people.

Valerius: What call you numerous?

Publicola: Why an assembly such, for number, as can neither go upon the interest of one single person or family, nor the interest of a few persons or families.

Valerius: How will you constitute such an assembly?

Publicola: Commonwealths, for the constitution of their popular assemblies, have had two ways. The first by enrolling all their citizens, and stating the quorum in such sort that all to and above the stated number, repairing at the time and place appointed, are empowered to give the vote of the whole commonwealth.

Valerius: The Athenian quorum was six thousand; which, towards the latter end of that commonwealth, came to five.

Publicola: So, so, you may quote authors. But you may remember also that Athens was a small commonwealth.

Valerius: How many would you advise for England?

Publicola: Put the case I should say ten thousand?

Valerius: They will laugh at you.

Publicola: What can I help that? Or how many would you advise?

Valerius: I would not go above five thousand.

Publicola: Mark you then: they only that are nearest would come; and so the city of London would give law unto the whole nation.

Valerius: Why really, that same now is clear; but would there be less danger of it in case you stated your quorum at ten, at twenty, or though it were at a hundred or two hundred thousand?

Publicola: No; for which cause, as to England, it is a plain case that this is no way for the institution of a popular assembly.

Valerius: Which way then?

Publicola: For England there is no way but by representative, to be made rise equally and methodically by stated election of the people throughout the whole nation.

Valerius: Need this be so numerous as the other?

Publicola: No.

Valerius: Why?

Publicola: Because it is not obnoxious unto a party, to any certain rank, or such as are soonest upon the spur, to make least account of their pains or of their money.

Valerius: Will you be so curious?

Publicola: Hold you this a curiosity? How else will you avoid improvement in the interest of the better sort, to the detriment of those of meaner rank, or in the interest of the few to the detriment of that of the many?

Valerius: Even this way then there is danger of that foul beast the oligarchy.

Publicola: Look about you. The parliament declares all power to be in the people; is that in the better sort only?

Valerius: Stay, the king was to observe *leges et consuetudines quas vulgus elegerit*;[a] that *vulgus* is to be understood of the parliament, and the parliament consisted wholly of the better sort.

Publicola: It is true; but then that commonwealth went for the rest accordingly.

Valerius: It was, you will say, no democracy.

Publicola: And will you say it was?

Valerius: No, truly; yet this derived in part from the free election of the people.

Publicola: How free? Seeing the people, then under lords, dared not to elect otherwise than as pleased those lords.

Valerius: Something of that is true; but I am persuaded that the people, not under lords, will yet be most addicted unto the better sort.

Publicola: That is certain.

Valerius: How then will you prevent the like in your institution?

Publicola: You shall see presently. The diffusive body of the people, in which the power is and is declared to be, consisteth in the far greater part of the lower sort; wherefore their representative, to rise naturally, and to be exactly comprehensive of the common interest, must consist also in the far greater part of the lower sort.

Valerius: Of what number will you have this representative?

Publicola: Say a thousand, or thereabout.

Valerius: What proportion will you have the meaner sort in it to hold unto the better?

Publicola: Say about six to four.

Valerius: How will you order it, that it shall be so constituted?

Publicola: Why thus: let the people in every precinct or shire at election choose four, under one hundred pounds a year in lands, goods, or money together with three at or above that proportion.[4]

Valerius: I see not but this representative must be exact.

Publicola: It is yet none at all, that is, unless you presume changes; for one thousand without change governing the whole people amounteth neither to a representative nor to a commonwealth, but comes still unto your hard name.

Valerius: How do you order your changes?

Publicola: By annual election of one third part for three years.

Valerius: So that every year one third part of your assembly falls out of it, and a new third part at the same time enters into the same.

Publicola: Even so.

Valerius: This causeth the representative to be perpetually extant.

---

[a] Laws and customs which the people shall choose.[3]

Publicola: It doth so. But to respite that a little, I should be glad, before I stir farther, to know which way the vote of a representative thus constituted can go one hair's beside the common and public interest of the whole diffusive body of the people.

Valerius: No way in the earth that I can imagine, except through ignorance.

Publicola: No human ordinance is infallible; and what is done through mere ignorance or mistake, at one time, will be found and amended at another.

Valerius: A thousand men, and six to four of the lower sort, perpetually extant! This must be a grievous charge to most of them; it will be hard to bring them, and impossible to hold them together.

Publicola: Upon such as are elected, and come not, considerable fines must be levied; and such as come and stay together must have good salaries.

Valerius: Salaries to so many! What will that come to?

Publicola: Not, with the rest of the pomp of the commonwealth, unto three hundred thousand pounds a year.

Valerius: Why? The kings have rarely had above six.

Publicola: And did England ever grudge them of that proportion?

Valerius: I must confess the quarrel grew, when they would not be contented with so little.

Publicola: Now if England never did nor needed grudge a king of six hundred thousand pounds a year, to be spent among courtiers; why should we imagine she should grudge a commonwealth of three hundred thousand pounds a year, to be spent among magistrates?

Valerius: But parliament men have taken nothing.

Publicola: Have the people given nothing?

Valerius: That was for the maintenance of armies.

Publicola: And whether had you rather maintain armies or magistrates?

Valerius: But putting the case that this assembly needed not to be perpetually extant, this charge in the whole or in the far greater part might be abated.

Publicola: I cannot tell; for how often think you fit that this assembly should convene?

Valerius: Parliaments at the most met not above once a year.

Publicola: If they had been perpetually extant, there would have been no king.

Valerius: No truly, except in name only.

Publicola: Therefore the popular assembly in a commonwealth ought not to be perpetually extant.

Valerius: To the end (you will say) that there may be some king.

Publicola: Mock not; or what other guard of liberty[5] is there in any commonwealth but the popular assembly?

Valerius: Come, let them assemble twice a year upon their ordinary guard.

Publicola: And what if there be extraordinary occasion?

Valerius: Then as often as there is any such occasion.

Publicola: How much will this abate of their necessary charge, or of the salaries? And how much better were it for a representative to lead the life of statesmen than of carriers?

Valerius: Commonwealths, whose assemblies have been of the former kind, have called them no otherwise than at stated times, or upon extraordinary occasions.

Publicola: But then their assemblies were not equal representatives, but consisted of such as, being next at hand, were still ready upon any occasion.

Valerius: That makes indeed a considerable difference. But were this representative always extant, I cannot see but it would have nothing to do.

Publicola: And in case it be not always extant, you imagine that it may have something to do.

Valerius: Yes.

Publicola: Then whether goeth it better with the commonwealth when the representative hath something to do, or when it hath nothing to do?

Valerius: This is very quaint.

Publicola: No truly, Valerius, it is plain that the guard of liberty, perpetually extant, in doing nothing must do much; and not perpetually extant, in doing much may do nothing.

Valerius: I am afraid that having nothing to do, they will make work.

Publicola: Such, I warrant you, as the parliament and the army made the other day.[6]

Valerius: Nay, I am not so wide. A civil council and a standing army must needs have interests much more distinct than two civil assemblies; and where there is not like cause, I know well enough there cannot be the like effect.

Publicola: I shall desire no more than that you will hold you to this; and then tell me what disputes there used to be between the senate of Venice and the great council, which is perpetually extant and consisteth of about two thousand.

Valerius: Nay, certain it is that between those two there never was any dispute at all.

Publicola: Then tell me for what cause such a thing should any more happen between the assemblies proposed; or according to your own rule, from the like causes expect like effects.

Valerius: You put me to it.

Publicola: Nay, it is you that put me to it; for you will be presuming that this assembly can have nothing to do, before we come to consider what are their proper businesses and functions.

Valerius: Cry you mercy, and what are those?

Publicola: Why surely, no small matters: for in every common-wealth truly popular, it is inseparable from the assembly of the people that, first, they wholly and only have the right of result in all matter of law-giving, of making peace and war, and in levying men and money. Secondly, that the ultimate result in judicature lie unto them; and thirdly, that they have right to call unto account and to punish their magistrates for all matter of maladministration of government.

Valerius: I assure you this must amount unto a great deal of business.

Publicola: Certain it is that in some commonwealths the popular assembly, by this means, hath been perpetually employed.

Valerius: And so I think it might be in England.

Publicola: It might but I do not think it would. However, if it be in the undoubted right of the popular assembly to proceed against their magistrates for maladministration, would you leave it upon the hand of those magistrates whether this representative should assemble or no?

Valerius: Come, you have said enough; it were not prudent; but as to the matter of appeals, it is certain that in Israel the ultimate resort was to the Sanhedrim or seventy elders.

Publicola: I know it very well; nevertheless you shall find that the congregation judged Benjamin; and if you mark the appeal unto the seventy elders, you shall find that it was not to an appeal of the party for relief, but of the judges in inferior courts for further light and direction in difficult cases of the law.

Valerius: Let me but know in what manner this assembly is to perform these functions, and I have done.

Publicola: Why, as to matter of lawgiving, I told you that they wholly and only have the right and power of result.

Valerius: But to result there must necessarily go precedent debate, seeing a man, much less an assembly, resolveth not upon anything without some considerations, motives or reasons thereunto conducing, which ought to be first orderly and maturely debated; and how will you bring a thousand men, especially being six to four of the lower sort, to debate anything with order and maturity?

Publicola: You say that the popular assembly in Athens consisted at the least of five thousand.

Valerius: And I said true.

Publicola: Yet this debated; why may not one thousand men debate as well as five thousand men?

Valerius: As well! Nay, Publicola, if they debate no better in your commonwealth than they did in that, you may know what will become of it. And to tell you true, I do not think that one thousand men can debate any whit more orderly and maturely than five thousand.

Publicola: And so I think too.

Valerius: How then?

Publicola: How then? Why, this is the reason of the senate in every commonwealth.

Valerius: So there must be a senate, which amounts unto thus much: without a senate there can be no commonwealth; and with a senate, there will always be practising upon the liberty of the people.

Publicola: How prove you that?

Valerius: Why, by the senate of Lacedaemon in the beginning, and by the senate of Rome throughout.

Publicola: But find you the like by the senates of Athens and Venice?

Valerius: No.

Publicola: Consider then that these were by election of the people and upon frequent removes; and that the former were defective in one or in both those circumstances.

Valerius: You intend your senate upon removes then?

Publicola: Right.

Valerius: And elective by the people?

Publicola: Yes.

Valerius: How? By the popular assembly, or by the body of the people in their precincts?

Publicola: By the body of the people in their precincts, at the same time when they elect their other deputies; and with the same circumstances, save that these be all elected out of such as have one hundred pounds a year real or personal.

Valerius: What hurt if they were elected by the popular assembly?

Publicola: They would not derive so immediately, nor rise so equally from the people, as chosen in the precincts; because this way every shire cometh necessarily to have a share in the senate; besides, wise men and understanding are better known in their tribes than they can be in an assembly out of their tribes, especially while they are newcomers; nor will the popular assembly afford so good choice as the whole people. There are other reasons.

Valerius: Enough, enough. Of what number constitute you this senate?

Publicola: Of three hundred.

Valerius: Why should not one hundred be full enough for a debating council; especially seeing debate is the more orderly, where the counsellors are fewer?

Publicola: You are to bear it in mind that this senate is upon annual change in one third part.

Valerius: That is, every year one hundred, having served three years, go out, and a new hundred come in.

Publicola: Right; for which cause, to have one hundred well practised in debate, your senate must consist of three hundred.

Valerius: May not those that go out come presently in again by new election?

Publicola: In no wise; for that were yet another way of continuing the government in a few.

Valerius: Mean you that no man serve in this capacity, or that of the popular assembly, but once in his life?

Publicola: I mean that a man, having served his term in one of these, may after a like vacation or interval be elected again to serve in either of them, and not before.

Valerius: At what age do you make a man capable of these elections?

Publicola: Not till thirty.

Valerius: He stays a great while ere he come to preferment, and is soon out again; at which rate a man should have much ado to attain unto sufficient knowledge for the leading of the commonwealth.

Publicola: This was never objected against parliaments.

Valerius: It is true; but then the election of parliament men was not obliged to any interval, and divers have been of every parliament that was summoned during their lives.

Publicola: Parliaments, when they were the most frequent, assembled not above once a year, very rarely so often; and how long, I pray you, did they usually sit?

Valerius: Some two or three months.

Publicola: I allow you with the most you ask: at which rate a man that had sat in twenty parliaments could not have sat above four years complete.

Valerius: And in your parliament, at one election he sits three.

Publicola: Mark you that?

Valerius: Yes, and more: whereas a parliament man without interval could in twenty years have sat but four complete, in your assemblies a man observing his intervals may in twenty years serve ten years complete.

Publicola: You allow that, I hope, to be some advantage towards acquiring knowledge in conduct; and yet anciently your parliament men were in this point thought able enough.

Valerius: Now would I desire no more than to be as fully satisfied that these senators must be honest enough.

Publicola: Which way can they be dishonest?

Valerius: Verily, I am not yet acquainted with their ways; but if nothing can be proposed unto the popular assembly save by these only, they methinks should propose nothing but what is for their own advantage.

Publicola: They are the senate; and in that, they have all the advantages that a well-ordered commonwealth can give unto a senate.

Valerius: But they will be still hankering after more.

Publicola: As what?

Valerius: Why, riches or power.

Publicola: All magistrates are accountable unto the popular assembly; and so, without acquisition of power, I cannot imagine which way they should turn themselves unto the acquisition of riches.

Valerius: They will drive then at power; they will be co-ordinate.

Publicola: In the world there hath never yet been any senate that durst so much as pretend unto power.

Valerius: No? Had not the senate of Israel and that of Lacedaemon power?

Publicola: Executive power they had, inasmuch as they were judicatories; but legislative or sovereign power (which is that whereof we speak) they had none at all.

Valerius: Other senates have had other power, as in the managing of foreign affairs and the like.

Publicola: Which still cometh not unto the point in hand, because in these and like matters, as the creation of divers magistrates, the senate useth to be made plenipotentiary by the popular assembly, that is by law.

Valerius: I hear them talk of making a co-ordinate senate first, and without the people, and then of assembling a parliament in the old way to govern with that senate.

Publicola: Things, Valerius, are soon said; but if any parliament whatever, so it be elected by the people (and, perhaps, if otherwise) do not make it one of their first works to pull down a co-ordinate senate, I ask no credit to my politics.

Valerius: This is to prophesy.

Publicola: Then to reason. I say that, the senate assuming power, the popular assembly falls immediately to debate; and, the popular assembly debating, the senate is *ipso facto* deposed, there being no other necessary use or function of the senate but debate only.

Valerius: You said but now that the popular assembly could not debate.

Publicola: Not orderly and maturely; but upon such an occasion as this, they will do as they can; nor is it avoidable.

Valerius: Nay, if there be some occasion in which you allow that the popular assembly must and ought to debate, there will hardly be any in which they will be persuaded that they may not. So this will come to the pulling down of the senate as often as the people please.

Publicola: Which is so much the rather to be feared, because you shall never find that popular assembly which did ever actually depose their senate.

Valerius: Our army hath pulled down a good many parliaments.

Publicola: What is that to the purpose? Is our army a popular assembly? Yet let them pull down a parliament as often as they please, they must set up another, and in this indeed there may be some resemblance; for let a popular assembly pull down the senate as often as they please, they must set up another.

Valerius: Or a single person.

Publicola: Right; for that holds both ways too, and (as to our case) will stand neither.

Valerius: The people of Athens debated, yet in that was not their senate deposed.

Publicola: Not formally; but it remained little better than a warren wherein great men did as it were start hares, to be hunted in the tumult of the popular assembly.

Valerius: Verily, Publicola, this model of yours is a most entire thing.

Publicola: This, with the necessary consequences, as the division of the senate into senatorian councils, the adorning and actuating of this and the other assembly with fit magistrates, whereof I have sufficiently discoursed in other places, amounteth unto an entire thing.

Valerius: And you offer it freely.

Publicola: I do.

Valerius: Would it not grieve you to see them crop a little of it and spoil it?

Publicola: They had better take it to some purpose.

Valerius: Nay, what they take will be to some purpose, I warrant you. Come, there is a party, a select, a refined party, a nation in a nation, must and will govern.

Publicola: That is it which I desire to see.

Valerius: You are of a rare temper; happy in unhappiness.

Publicola: O, I love often changes.

Valerius: Is that any of your virtues?

Publicola: Yes, where we are certain never to go right, while there remains a way to go wrong.

Valerius: They are confident men. They cannot be persuaded but they can govern the world.

Publicola: Till they have tried. Such as can govern the world are such as can be governed by reason. Now there is no party, refined, select, or what you will, in England, amounting to one twentieth part of the whole people.

Valerius: One twentieth part of the people, for aught I know, may amount unto one hundred thousand; there is no party anything near this account, I dare say.

Publicola: A twentieth part of the people can never govern the other nineteen, but by a perpetual army.

Valerius: They do not like that the worse.

Publicola: The people, having been governed by a king without an army, and being governed by a commonwealth with an army, will detest the government of a commonwealth and desire that of a king.

Valerius: Yes, such is the spirit of the nation.

Publicola: Such is the spirit in this case of any nation.

Valerius: And yet they make it a particular quarrel.

Publicola: They make everything particular: if you speak of Israel, Athens, Rome, Venice, or the like, they hear you with volubility of countenance, and will not have it that God ever minded the matter of government, till he brought them in play. Nay, though they have come heels over head for this very thing, I know not how often, yet they are resolved to take no warning.

Valerius: Publicola, you will be shent.[a]

Publicola: I am to perform my duty. To flatter is not my duty.

Valerius: But between you and me, do you not think that the spirit of the nation, or the main body of the people of this land, desires the restitution of their ancient government?

---

[a] Blamed or disgraced.

Publicola: I make little doubt of it.

Valerius: How then, in case of a commonwealth, are they to be trusted?

Publicola: In case of a commonwealth, it is not the people that are trusted, but the orders of the commonwealth.

Valerius: The commonwealth must consist of the people.

Publicola: The people under the monarchy, when that invaded them, invaded it.

Valerius: True, and in such manner as hath caused the ruin of it.

Publicola: What was the spirit of the people then?

Valerius: But it is now another thing.

Publicola: Nay, the very same; for then it invaded a government that invaded their liberty, and now it would invade a government that invadeth their liberty.

Valerius: But how should this be mended?

Publicola: Do you not see that this should not be mended, but encouraged?

Valerius: How should it be encouraged then?

Publicola: By giving them a form that must preserve their liberty.

Valerius: I little doubt but there is in your form a full security unto the people of their liberty; but do you think that there is in it any full security that the people shall not cast off this form?

Publicola: If it secure their liberty, why should they?

Valerius: My question is not why they should, but whether they can.

Publicola: They cannot, without going against their own interest.

Valerius: But they can go against their own interest.

Publicola: Nay, remember yourself, whether the form shown be not such as you have already granted can in no wise go besides the interest of the whole people.

Valerius: They that are now in power have no trust at all in forms.

Publicola: Do they sail in ships, not upon planks? Do they ride horses, not hogs? Do they travel in coaches, not upon hurdles? Do they live in houses, not in ditches? Do they eat bread, not stones?

Valerius: Enough, enough.

Publicola: But in so doing, they acknowledge such a form to be security for such a use or action. And must the form of a commonwealth be the only form in which they can allow no security for the proper use and action?

Valerius: They observe none of this.

Publicola: Do they observe that there is any security in men?

Valerius: That, especially in our times, were somewhat a hard matter.

Publicola: And how many securities are there?

Valerius: I know no more than one personal, or in men; another real, or in things.

Publicola: Choose you whether you would have.

Valerius: Well, be the necessary action or use of your form what it will, I would see it more plainly and particularly demonstrated how the spirit of the nation, or the whole people, being freely eligible into your assemblies, must presently lose that inclination, which now plainly they have, to set up monarchy or to persecute for conscience.

Publicola: You will allow no weight in the argument that a people in liberty, unless the orders of their commonwealth were first fundamentally ruined, that is, broken in the balance or foundation, did never do either of these.

Valerius: What weight soever I allow unto this argument, it is no wise to my present purpose.

Publicola: You will put me then besides experience, and to show by what reason it is that a pear tree must bear pears, or why men gather not grapes on thorns, or figs on thistles.

Valerius: Poor Publicola, be the task as hard as it will, I am for this time resolved to hold you to it.

Publicola: What is it then that any government can be sufficiently founded or balanced upon, but such an interest as is sufficiently able to bear it?

Valerius: Good sir, a government ought to be founded upon justice, I take it.

Publicola: Right; and is not that government, which is founded upon an interest not sufficiently able to bear it, founded upon injustice?

Valerius: I suspect whither this will go. A government founded upon the overbalance of property is legitimately founded, and so upon justice; but a government founded upon the underbalance of property must of necessity be founded upon force, or a standing army. Is not this that which you mean by interest sufficient or not sufficient to sustain a government?

Publicola: You have it right.

Valeius: Atheist, this damns the government of the saints.

Publicola: Look you now, how irreligious a thing it may be made, to speak but with common honesty. Do you think that such as are plainly oligarchists, or shall exercise by a force, and without election by the people, such power as is both naturally and declaredly in the people, and in them only, can establish their throne upon justice?

Valerius: No.

Publicola: Do you think that such as are truly saints can establish their throne upon injustice?

Valerius: No.

Publicola: Why then, you have granted that such as are plainly oligarchists cannot be truly saints. Again, do you still think, as you once intimated, that a government now introduced in England, exactly according unto the principles of prudence and justice, would rule the earth?

Valerius: Yes.

Publicola: Do you think that such as are truly saints, if they introduce government, ought to introduce it exactly according to the principles of prudence and justice?

Valerius: Yes.

Publicola: Why then, let such as are truly saints but see what it is to rule the earth, and take the rule of the earth.

Valerius: They will not approve of this way.

Publicola: How! Not the saints approve of prudence and justice! Who is the atheist now, Valerius?

Valerius: Good Publicola, let us keep unto the point at hand. You say that the security of liberty lieth not in the people, but in the form of their government; so I am yet to expect when you will show what there is in your form why it must be impossible for the people under it to restore monarchy, or to persecute for conscience.

Publicola: See you not that to do either of these under such a form must be point blank against their interest?

Valerius: But so either of these is now, and yet in this posture you will confess that they would do both.

Publicola: Mark how I am used. I speak of a form supported by an interest sufficiently able to bear it, and of an interest contained under a form sufficiently able to secure it; and you instance in a posture which is no form at all, but such a confusion among and force upon the people as createth an interest in them to rid themselves which way they can of such a misery.

Valerius: I did acknowledge and must confess that your popular assembly is such as cannot err, except through ignorance; but through this, you yourself have acknowledged, and must confess, that it may err.

Publicola: I retract nothing.

Valerius: Now, first or never, they will restore monarchy through ignorance.[7]

Publicola: But they cannot do this first, therefore they can never do it.

Valerius: Why cannot the popular assembly do this first?

Publicola: Because it must first be proposed by a senate, that can neither do any such thing through ignorance nor through knowledge.

Valerius: Nay then, have at you: I will set this same senate and representative of yours to work in such a manner, that you shall confess they may set up monarchy.

Publicola: Do your worst.

Valerius: Your senate being assembled (I will not have them make long speeches) . . .

Publicola: Nor I.

Valerius: Rises me up one of the senators, and saith: Mr. Speaker, this nation hath been long in labour, but now, through the mercy of God, the child is not only come to the birth, but there is also strength to bring forth; in the number of counsellors there is strength; the number of this house is good (far better than hath usually been of late) and their election hath been very free and fair. Here is also, I know not how (but the inventions of men are overruled by the providence of God), an extraordinary and exceeding great confluence of honest men, who are not so well here and, if you determine anything that is good for your country, will go home and pray for you. Now, sir, (to be brief) since our government consisted of king, lords and commons, the ancient, the only, the most happy government that this nation, nay, that the world ever knew, it is but too well known that we have had no government at all; wherefore my opinion is that we propose (as they call it) unto these honest men (who you need not doubt will receive it with glad hearts) the restitution of right, and of the government in this nation by king, lords and commons. As sure as you live, Publicola, thus much being said, your whole senate will immediately agree to propose it unto the representative; and thus much being proposed unto the representative, those people will throw up their caps for joy, and forthwith return unto their houses.

Publicola: But, Valerius, thus much hath been said in parliament when the house was fuller; when they who were for this restitution were backed by a single person in actual possession of the throne; when, over and above the zeal of presbyterians, there were parties that knew no other means of self-preservation; as without, divines adoperating the oak of every pulpit, and within, lawyers and salary-men; yet was it so far from being carried that the single person hath been forced to dissolve parliaments, and that through apparent danger of being overrun by the principles of a commonwealth not in being. But if this were so when a commonwealth could scarce be hoped, what will it be when the commonwealth shall be in such a condition as cannot be withstood? For the senate can never come to propose anything unto the people, without first agreeing upon debate what it is that they will propose; nor is it possible that such debate should be brought unto any end, but by reasons thereunto conducing. Now, it must not only be impossible to find reasons for the restitution of monarchy, but the reasons why monarchy ought not to be restored must be obvious, not only in regard that it is quite contrary to the interest of the nation and of these assemblies, but to the interest, ten to one, of every particular man in either of these assemblies; nor are or have the reasons been less obvious, or less ventilated in parliament, why monarchy as to this nation is impossible in itself.

Valerius: Will you say the like for liberty of conscience?

Publicola: Yes; because without liberty of conscience civil liberty cannot be perfect, and without civil liberty, liberty of conscience cannot be perfect.

Valerius: These things are true, but they will never see them, never, Publicola: you yourself say that the people cannot see, but they can feel.

Publicola: I mean that of the diffusive body of the people, not of the people under good orders; in which case they are the sharpest sighted of any kind of government whatsoever; and therefore it is not modest that you or I, or any particular man or party, blinded with self, should pretend to see with such a constitution; or show me that eye under the sun, that sees like that of Venice. But, putting the case it were otherwise as to seeing, these things are plainly palpable or obvious unto feeling.

Valerius: I have indeed observed that in commonwealths there are very few that see or understand them, and yet their affection unto that way of government is exceeding vigorous.

Publicola: Whence then can this otherwise be than from feeling? But one thing, Valerius, I take at your hands extreme heavily.

Valerius: What is that, Publicola?

Publicola: That you, with one little speech of a single senator, should run so regardlessly over these two assemblies, without taking any notice at all of the necessary course of them.

Valerius: What course, Publicola?

Publicola: Why, you might easily have thought that among three hundred senators there might have been at least one hundred as good speakers as yours.

Valerius: Have I said anything to the contrary?

Publicola: And do you or I what we can, ten to one of them will be longer-winded than you have allowed.

Valerius: For that matter, let them please themselves.

Publicola: Aye, but then you should not have made an end of your debate in a minute.

Valerius: What is all this?

Publicola: Why, I say, they would have been debating upon that point at least a fortnight.

Valerius: Well, and when that had been done, would never have agreed.

Publicola: No.

Valerius: Did not you say that before?

Publicola: Well, but I am now upon another point; that was to the matter in debate, this is to the manner of proceeding: imagine the matter had been such upon which they could have agreed.

Valerius: What then?

Publicola: Then such an agreement had been a decree of the senate.

Valerius: Is a decree of the senate binding?

Publicola: If it be upon law made, it is binding; if upon law to be made, it is to be proposed unto the people. Now, every proposition to the people is to be promulgated, that is, printed and published to the whole nation, six weeks before the time that the representative is to assemble and give the vote of the commonwealth, or that test without which no such proposition can be any law.

Valerius: By this means it must follow that the whole people, both by discourse and letters, debate six weeks together upon the matter.

Publicola: You are right.

Valerius: How is it then that you say the representative of the people must not debate? Allow you unto these less privilege than unto the whole people?

Publicola: No less, nor in this point any more.

Valerius: Yet amounteth this to debate in those that are of the representative.

Publicola: You say well, but not unto any debate at all in the representative.

Valerius: Why, this representative is nothing else but an instrument or method, whereby to receive the result of the whole nation, with order and expedition and without any manner of tumult or confusion.

Publicola: And is that anything the worse?

Valerius: No, but I am glad you have told it me; for that those of the representative would one way or other have debate, I knew certainly.

Publicola: In sum, are you satisfied that the spirit of the nation, or the people – however they may now, under no form at all, and in detestation of such as, having governed them by force, will let them see no way out of confusion, desire their old government, as having never yet known any other – yet under such a form as is proposed, can never go about to introduce monarchy, without obvious discovery that, as to their interest, it is quite contrary, and as to itself impossible?

Valerius: The satisfaction is pretty good.

Publicola: Pretty good! Give me but half so good that the spirit of the army, not formerly obedient unto parliaments, and now dreading or despising them, must apprehend the restitution of monarchy to be quite contrary to their interest.

Valerius: You surprise me; for if the army will have no parliament, and a king restored can now in England without an army have no government, they may imagine this their only way unto greatness and continuance.

Publicola: Had not the oligarchy then, if they meant well, better to have used sober expressions, and minded what those true and real interests are, which in the foundation and preservation of every kind of government are paramount, than to have overcast them with the mist of new-affected phrases, and fallen on conjuring up spirits?

Valerius: You have conjured up a spirit will keep me waking.

Publicola: Set him on pulling down the law and the ministry; when that is done, let him blow up Windsor Castle, Hampton Court, and throw Whitehall into the Thames.

Valerius: It is the only way, for then there can be no king.

Publicola: You may be sure of that, seeing the count of Holland's domain and his houses are yet not only standing, but diligently preserved by the Hollanders.

Valerius: Publicola, have you any more to tell me?

Publicola: Valerius, have you any more to ask me?

Valerius: No, except why you have not given the parliament to understand thus much.

Publicola: I have printed it over and over.

Valerius: They take no great notice of books; you should have laid it, as they say, in their dish, by some direct address, as a petition or so.

Publicola: I did petition the committee of government.

Valerius: What answer did they make you?

Publicola: None at all.

Valerius: I would have gone further, and have presented it unto the house.

Publicola: Towards this also I went as far as I could.

Valerius: How far was that?

Publicola: Why, I think my petition may have been worn out in the pockets of some two or three members.

Valerius: Have you a copy of it about you?

Publicola: Let me see – here are many papers; this same is it.

To the Parliament of the Commonwealth of
England, etc.
The humble petition, etc.

Showeth:

That what neither is, nor ever was in nature, can never be in nature.

That without a king and lords, no government either is, or ever was in nature (but in mere force), other than by a senate indued with authority to debate and propose, and by a numerous assembly of the people, wholly and only invested with the right of result in all matter of lawgiving, of making peace and war, and of levying men and money.

Wherefore your petitioner (to disburden his conscience in a matter of such concernment unto his country) most humbly and earnestly prayeth and beseecheth this parliament to take into speedy and serious consideration the irrefragable truth of the premises and what thereupon must assuredly follow: that is, either the institution of a commonwealth in the whole people of England (without exception, or with exception for a time of so few as may be) by way of a senate and a numerous assembly of the people, to the ends and for the respective functions aforesaid; or the inevitable ruin of this nation, which God of his mercy avert.

And your petitioner shall pray, etc.

Valerius: I would it had been delivered.

Publicola: Look you, if this had been presented to the house, I intended to have added this other paper, and to have printed them together.

The Petition to the Reader.

Reader:

I say not that the form contained in the petition (if we had it, and no more) would be perfect; but that without thus much (which, rightly introduced, introduceth the rest) there neither is, was, nor can be any such thing as a commonwealth, or government without a king and lords, in nature.

Where there is a co-ordinate senate, there must be a king, or it falleth instantly by the people; as, the king failing, the house of peers fell by the commons.

Where there is a senate not elective by the people, there is perpetual feud between the senate and the people, as in Rome.

To introduce either of these causes is certainly and inevitably to introduce one of these effects; and if so, then who are cavaliers, I leave you to judge hereafter.

But to add farther reason unto experience: all civil power among us (not only by declaration of parliament, but by the nature of property) is in and from the people.

Where the power is in the people, there the senate can legitimately be no more unto the popular assembly than my counsel at law is to me, that is, *auxilium, non imperium*; a necessary aid, not a competitor or rival in power.

Where the aids of the people become their rivals or competitors in power, there their shepherds become wolves; their peace, discord; and their government, ruin. But to impose a select or co-ordinate senate upon the people is to give them rivals and competitors in power.

Some perhaps (such is the temper of the times) will say that so much human confidence as is expressed, especially in the petition, is atheistical. But how were it atheistical if I should as confidently foretell that a boy must expire in nonage, or become a man? I prophesy no otherwise; and this kind of prophecy is also of God, by those rules of his providence which, in the known government of the world, are infallible. In the right observation and application of these consisteth all human wisdom; and we read (Ecclesiastes, 9: 14) that a poor man delivered a city by his wisdom; yet was this poor man forgotten. But if the premises of this petition fail, or one part of the conclusion come not to pass accordingly, let me hit the other mark of this ambitous address, and remain a fool upon record in parliament to all posterity.

Valerius: Thou boy! And yet I hope well of thy reputation.

Publicola: Would it were but as good now, as it will be when I can make no use of it.

Valerius: The major of the petition is in some other of your writings; and I remember some objections which have been made against it. As that *a non esse, nec fuisse, non datur argumentum ad non posse.*[a]

Publicola: Say that in English.

Valerius: What if I cannot? Are not you bound to answer a thing, though it cannot be said in English?

Publicola: No, truly.

Valerius: Well, I will say it in English then. Though there neither be any house of gold, nor ever were any house of gold, yet there may be a house of gold.

Publicola: Right; but then *a non esse nec fuisse in natura, datur argumentum ad non posse in natura.*[b]

Valerius: I hope you can say this in English too.

Publicola: That I can, now you have taught me. If there were no such thing as gold in nature, there never could be any house of gold.

Valerus: Softly. The frame of a government is as much in art, and as little in nature, as the frame of a house.

---

[a] From a thing's not being now, nor having been, it does not follow that it is not possible.

[b] From a thing's not being now nor having been, in nature, it follows that it is not possible in nature.

Publicola: Both softly and surely. The materials of a government are as much in nature, and as little in art, as the materials of a house. Now as far forth as art is necessarily disposed by the nature of her foundation or materials, so far forth it is in art as in nature.

Valerius: What call you the foundation or the materials of government?

Publicola: That which I have long since proved, and you granted: the balance, the distribution of property, and the power thence naturally deriving; which as it is in one, in a few, or in all, doth necessarily dispose of the form or frame of the government accordingly.

Valerius: Be the foundation or materials of a house what they will, the frame or superstructures may be diversely wrought up or shaped; and so may those of a commonwealth.

Publicola: True; but let a house be never so diversely wrought up or shaped, it must consist of a roof and walls.

Valerius: That's certain.

Publicola: And so must a commonwealth of a senate and of a popular assembly, which is the sum of the minor in the petition.

Valerius: The mathematicians say they will not be quarrelsome; but in their sphere there are things altogether new in the world, as the present posture of the heavens is, and as was the star in Cassiopeia.[8]

Publicola: Valerius, if the major of the petition extend as far as is warranted by Solomon – I mean, that there is nothing new under the sun – what new things there may be or have been above the sun will make little to the present purpose.

Valerius: It is true; but if you have no more to say, they will take this but for shifting.

Publicola: Where there is sea, as between Sicily and Naples, there was anciently land; and where there is land, as in Holland, there was anciently sea.

Valerius: What then?

Publicola: Why then, the present posture of the earth is other than it hath been, yet is the earth no new thing, but consisteth of land and sea, as it did always; so whatever the present posture of the heavens be, they consist of star and firmament, as they did always.

Valerius: What will you say then to the star in Cassiopeia?

Publicola: Why, I say: if it consisted of the same matter with other stars, it was no new thing in nature, but a new thing in Cassiopeia; as, were there a commonwealth in England, it would be no new thing in nature, but a new thing in England.

Valerius: The star (you will say) in Cassiopeia, to have been a new thing in nature, must have been no star, because a star is not a new thing in nature.

Publicola: Very good.

Valerius: You run upon the matter, but the newness in the star was in the manner of the generation.

Publicola: At Pozzuoli[9] near Naples, I have seen a mountain that rose up from under water in one night, and poured a good part of the lake anciently called Lucrine into the sea.

Valerius: What will you infer from hence?

Publicola: Why, that the new and extraordinary generation of a star, or of a mountain, no more causeth a star or a mountain to be a new thing in nature, than the new and extraordinary generation of a commonwealth causeth a commonwealth to be a new thing in nature. Aristotle reports[10] that the nobility of Tarentum being cut off in a battle, that commonwealth became popular. And if the powder plot in England had destroyed the king and the nobility, it is possible that popular government might have risen up in England, as the mountain did at Pozzuoli. Yet for all these, would there not have been any new thing in nature.

Valerius: Some new thing (through the blending of unseen causes) there may seem to be in shuffling; but nature will have her course, there is no other than the old game.

Publicola: Valerius, let it rain or be fair weather, the sun to the dissolution of nature shall ever rise; but it is now set, and I apprehend the mist.

Valerius: Dear Publicola, your health is mine own; I bid you goodnight.

Publicola: Goodnight to you, Valerius.

Valerius: One word more, Publicola: pray make me a present of those same papers and, with your leave and licence, I will make use of my memory to commit the rest of this discourse unto writing, and print it.

Publicola: They are at your disposing.

Valerius: I will not do it as hath been done, but with your name to it.

Publicola: Whether way you like best, most noble Valerius.

22 October

9. John Milton, 'The Readie and Easie Way to Establish A Free Commonwealth', April 1660

(second edition, enlarged)

The first edition was probably composed between 18 and 22 February 1660, and published at the end of that month (Thomason's copy is dated 3 March). The second edition, revised and expanded, was published not later than the first week of April, the absence of the printer's name from the title-page suggesting a fugitive printing. In translation the epigraph reads: 'We have advised Sulla himself, advise we now the people' (Juvenal, *Satires*, 1, 15–16).

On 26 December 1659 those members of the recently dissolved Rump that Speaker Lenthal could gather together had met in the Parliament-house, where they were just quorate. The Committee of Safety had lost the initiative, and for a final brief period the old-guard Republicans of the 'Good Old Cause' were back in the saddle. But by the New Year Monck was on the march from Scotland, and Fairfax was raising the Yorkshire gentry. Each was agreed on the need for a more moderate and comprehensive government in London though Monck was still formally committed to the Rump. Public opinion appears increasingly to have favoured a restoration.

The first edition seems to have been written in haste; it is not a carefully prepared statement of a republican ideal but a desperate attempt to show how a lasting republic could be built on the surviving foundation of the Rump. Milton's proposal is one of extreme simplicity: a 'Grand Councel of ablest men chosen by the people' to 'sit perpetual'. In direct contrast to Harrington's proposals there would be no regular rotation or election: membership would be for life. In this regard, and in both editions, Milton is openly contemptuous of majority opinion and sees no reason why its changes should necessarily be reflected in government. Thus he opposes the idea of 'A full and free parliament' in 1660 and rather supports the Rump's proposal that the vacant places left by the secluded members should be filled by candidates eligible only by the strictest qualifications stipulated by the Rump itself. Even before the publication of the first edition, however, events overtook him. On 21 February 1660 Monck allowed the secluded Members of Parliament to resume their seats, the decision to fill up the vacant places on the Rump's terms was rescinded, and writs were issued for a full new Parliament. This is referred to in the prefatory paragraph in each edition.

The prefatory paragraph of the second edition also alludes to its coming out 'in the midst of our Elections to a free Parliament': this and not the final deliberations of the Rump is the occasion of the second edition. Because, however, it might still be hoped that the new Parliament would bring in a republican majority (Milton even professes to think that the qualifications insisted on by the Rump are still in force), Milton's earlier proposal is enlarged upon and revised. He excises the comparison of Charles II with King Coniah (cf. Jeremiah, XXII, 28) at the end, but insists still that if it came to

The readie and easie way

to establish a

free Commonwealth;

*and the excellence therof com
par'd with the inconveniencies
and dangers of readmit-
ting Kingship in
this Nation.*

The second edition revis'd and
augmented.

The author J. M.

---

*——————— et nos
consilium dedimus Syl'æ, demus populo nunc.*

LONDON,
Printed for the Author, 1660.

force, 'a less number [should] compell a greater to retain their libertie': i.e. that form of government that 'the less number' thinks best. This 'terrible argument' evokes from the Wolfe editors (*Prose Works*, VII, p. 212) allusions to Hungary (1956), Czechoslovakia (1968), and comparisons with Robespierre on 'the despotism of liberty'.

The Readie and Easie Way is a contemptuous, often satirical and finally tragic diatribe against the mounting demand for a restoration of the Stuart monarchy quite as much as it is a republican programme. Milton risked his life to write it. It is certainly revolutionary. It is not, as most of the writers and speakers in this volume are, democratic.

The text is that of R. W. Ayers ed. (vol. 7, 1974) from *John Milton: Complete Prose Works*, ed. D. M. Wolfe (7 vols., New Haven, Conn., 1953–74).

Although since the writing of this treatise, the face of things hath had som change, writs for new elections have bin recall'd,[1] and the members at first chosen, readmitted from exclusion,[2] yet not a little rejoicing to hear declar'd the resolution of those who are in power,[a] tending to the establishment of a free Commonwealth, and to remove, if it be possible, this noxious humor of returning to bondage,[3] instilld of late by som deceivers,[4] and nourishd from bad principles and fals apprehensions among too many of the people, I thought best not to suppress what I had written,[b] hoping that it may now be of much more use and concernment to be freely published, in the midst of our Elections[5] to a free Parlament, or their sitting to consider freely of the Government; whom it behoves to have all things represented to them that may direct thir judgment therin; and I never read of any State, scarce of any tyrant grown so incurable, as to refuse counsel from any in a time of public deliberation; much less to be offended. If thir absolute determination be to enthrall us,[6] before so long a Lent of Servitude, they may permitt us a little Shroving-time[7] first, wherein to speak freely, and take our leaves of Libertie. And because in the former edition through haste, many faults escap'd, and many books were suddenly dispersd, ere the note to mend them could be sent, I took the opportunitie from this occasion to revise and somwhat to enlarge the whole discourse, especially that part which argues for a perpetual Senat. The treatise thus revis'd and enlarg'd, is as follows.

The Parliament of *England*, assisted by a great number of the people who appeerd and stuck to them faithfullest in defence of religion and thir civil liberties, judging kingship by long experience a government unnecessarie, burdensom and dangerous,[8] justly and magnanimously abolishd it; turning regal bondage into a free

---

[a] General Monck, the Army officers, and the Rump.
[b] The body of the present tract, now revised from its first edition.

Commonwealth, to the admiration and terrour of our emulous neighbours.[9] They took themselves not bound by the light of nature or religion, to any former covnant, from which the King himself by many forfeitures of a latter date or discoverie, and our own longer consideration theron had more & more unbound us, both to himself and his posteritie; as hath bin ever the justice and the prudence of all wise nations that have ejected tyrannie. They covnanted *to preserve the Kings person and autoritie in the preservation of the true religion and our liberties*;[10] not in his endeavoring to bring in upon our consciences a Popish religion,[a] upon our liberties thraldom, upon our lives destruction, by his occasioning, if not complotting, as was after discoverd, the *Irish* massacre,[b] his fomenting and arming the rebellion, his covert leaguing with the rebels against us, his refusing more then seaven times, propositions[12] most just and necessarie to the true religion and our liberties, tenderd him by the Parlament both of *England* and *Scotland*. They made not thir covnant concerning him with no difference between a king and a god, or promisd him as *Job* did to the Almightie, *to trust in him, though he slay us*:[13] they understood that the solemn ingagement, wherin we all forswore kingship, was no more a breach of the covnant, then the covnant was of the protestation[14] before, but a faithful and prudent going on both in the words, well weighd, and in the true sense of the covnant, *without respect of persons*, when we could not serve two contrary maisters,[15] God and the king, or the king and that more supreme law, sworn in the first place to maintain, our safetie and our libertie.[16] They knew the people of *England* to be a free people, themselves the representers of that freedom; & although many were excluded, & as many fled (so they pretended) from tumults to *Oxford*,[c] yet they were left a sufficient number to act in Parlament; therefor not bound by any statute of preceding Parlaments, but by the law of nature[17] only, which is the only law of laws truly and properly to all mankinde fundamental; the beginning and the end of all Government; to which no Parlament or people that will throughly reforme, but may and must have recourse; as they had and must yet have in church reformation (if they throughly intend it) to evangelic rules;[d] not to ecclesiastical

[a] Not Roman Catholicism but the Arminian form of Protestantism favoured by Charles I and Laud.[11]

[b] The Irish insurrection of October 1641 in which thousands of English Protestants were killed, and which had falsely claimed the specific authority of the King.

[c] Charles declared Parliament no longer free on 20 June 1643, after which a pro-Parliamentary mob demonstrated at Westminster. The King's Oxford Parliament, 22 Jan. 1644, consisted of Royalists willing to dissociate themselves from the Westminster Parliament.

[d] Faith and Charity: the general position of Luther on the church.

canons, though never so ancient, so ratifi'd and establishd in the land by Statutes, which for the most part are meer positive laws, neither natural nor moral, & so by any Parlament for just and serious considerations, without scruple to be at any time repeal'd. If others of thir number, in these things were under force, they were not, but under free conscience; if others were excluded[a] by a power which they could not resist, they were not therefore to leave the helm of government in no hands, to discontinue thir care of the public peace and safetie, to desert the people in anarchie and confusion; no more then when so many of thir members left them, as made up in outward formalitie a more legal Parlament[b] of three estates against them. The best affected also and best principl'd of the people, stood not numbring or computing on which side were most voices in Parlament, but on which side appeerd to them most reason, most safetie, when the house divided upon main matters: what was well motiond and advis'd, they examind not whether fear or perswasion carried it in the vote; neither did they measure votes and counsels by the intentions of them that voted; knowing that intentions either are but guessd at, or not soon anough known; and although good, can neither make the deed such, nor prevent the consequence from being bad: suppose bad intentions in things otherwise welldon; what was welldon, was by them who so thought, not the less obey'd or followd in the state; since in the church, who had not rather follow *Iscariot*[18] or *Simon* the magician,[19] though to covetous ends, preaching, then *Saul*,[20] though in the uprightness of his heart persecuting the gospell? Safer they therefore judgd what they thought the better counsels, though carried on by some perhaps to bad ends, then the wors, by others, though endevord with best intentions: and yet they were not to learn that a greater number[c] might be corrupt within the walls of a Parlament as well as of a citie; wherof in matters of neerest concernment all men will be judges; nor easily permitt, that the odds of voices in thir greatest councel, shall more endanger them by corrupt or credulous votes, then the odds of enemies by open assaults; judging that most voices ought not alwaies to prevail where main matters are in question; if others hence will pretend to disturb all counsels, what is that to them who pretend not, but are in real danger; not they only so judging, but a great though not the greatest, number of thir chosen Patriots, who might be more in

[a] The purged members of the Long Parliament.   [b] The Royal Parliament at Oxford.
[c] I.e. Presbyterians in Parliament and the City of London still anxious, in 1648, to negotiate with the King.

waight, then the others in number; there being in number little
vertue,[21] but by weight and measure wisdom working all things:
and the dangers on either side they seriously thus waighd: from the
treatie,[22] short fruits of long labours and seaven years warr;
securitie for twenty years, if we can hold it; reformation in the
church for three years: then put to shift again with our vanquishd
maister. His justice, his honour his conscience declar'd quite
contrarie to ours; which would have furnishd him with many such
evasions, as in a book entitl'd *an inquisition for blood*,[23] soon after
were not conceald: bishops not totally remov'd, but left as it were in
ambush, a reserve, with ordination in thir sole power; thir lands
alreadie sold,[24] not to be alienated[a] but rented, and the sale of them
call'd *sacrilege*; delinquents[b] few of many brought to condigne
punishment; accessories punishd; the chief author,[c] above pardon,
though after utmost resistance, vanquish'd; not to give, but to
receive laws; yet besought, treated with, and to be thankd for his
gratious concessions, to be honourd, worshipd, glorifi'd. If this we
swore to do, with what righteousness in the sight of God, with
what assurance that we bring not by such an oath the whole sea of
blood-guiltiness upon our own heads? If on the other side we
preferr a free government, though for the present not obtaind, yet
all those suggested fears and difficulties, as the event will prove,
easily overcome, we remain finally secure from the exasperated[d]
regal power, and out of snares; shall retain the best part of our
libertie, which is our religion, and the civil part will be from these
who deferr us, much more easily recoverd, being neither so suttle
nor so awefull as a King reinthron'd. Nor were thir actions less both
at home and abroad then might become the hopes of a glorious
rising Commonwealth; nor were the expressions both of armie and
people,[25] whether in thir publick declarations or several writings
other then such as testifi'd a spirit in this nation no less noble and
well fitted to the liberty of a Commonwealth, then in the ancient
Greeks or *Romans*. Nor was the heroic cause unsuccessfully defended
to all Christendom against the tongue of a famous and thought
invincible adversarie;[26] nor the constancie and fortitude that so
nobly vindicated our liberty, our victory at once against two the
most prevailing unsurpers over mankinde, superstition and tyrannie
unpraisd or uncelebrated in a written monument, likely to outlive

---

[a] Sold to others.
[b] Those who had supported the King in the civil wars, or who were ill-affected towards
Parliament.
[c] The King.   [d] Provoked to roughness.

detraction, as it hath hitherto convinc'd or silenc'd not a few of our detractors, especially in parts abroad. After our liberty and religion thus prosperously fought for, gaind and many years possessd, except in those unhappie interruptions, which God hath remov'd, now that nothing remains, but in all reason the certain hopes of a speedie and immediat settlement for ever in a firm and free Commonwealth, for this extolld and magnifi'd nation, regardless both of honour wonn or deliverances voutsaf't from heaven, to fall back or rather to creep back so poorly as it seems the multitude would to thir once abjur'd and detested thraldom of Kingship, to be our selves the slanderers of our own just and religious deeds, though don by som to covetous and ambitious ends, yet not therefor to be staind with their infamie, or they to asperse[a] the integritie of others, and yet these now by revolting from the conscience of deeds welldon both in church and state, to throw away and forsake, or rather to betray a just and noble cause for the mixture of bad men who have ill manag'd and abus'd it (which had our fathers don heretofore, and on the same pretence deserted true religion, what had long ere this become of our gospel and all protestant reformation so much intermixt with the avarice and ambition of som reformers?) and by thus relapsing, to verifie all the bitter predictions of our triumphing enemies, who will now think they wisely discernd and justly censur'd both us and all our actions as rash, rebellious, hypocritical and impious, not only argues a strange degenerate contagion suddenly spread among us fitted and prepar'd for new slaverie, but will render us a scorn and derision to all our neighbours. And what will they at best say of us and of the whole *English* name, but scoffingly as of that foolish builder, mentioned by our Saviour, who began to build a tower, and was not able to finish it.[27] Where is this goodly tower of a Commonwealth, which the English boasted they would build to overshaddow kings, and be another *Rome* in the west? The foundation indeed they laid gallantly; but fell into a wors confusion, not of tongues, but of factions, then those at the tower of *Babel*;[28] and have left no memorial of thir work behinde them remaining, but in the common laughter of *Europ*. Which must needs redound the more to our shame, if we but look on our neighbours the United Provinces, to us inferior in all outward advantages; who notwithstanding, in the midst of greater difficulties, courageously, wisely, constantly went through with the same

[a] Calumniate.

work, and are setl'd in all the happie enjoinments of a potent and flourishing Republic[29] to this day.

Besides this, if we returne to Kingship, and soon repent, as undoubtedly we shall, when we begin to finde the old encroachments coming on by little and little upon our consciences, which must necesarily proceed from king and bishop united inseparably in one interest,[30] we may be forc'd perhaps to fight over again all that we have fought, and spend over again all that we have spent, but are never like to attain thus far as we are now advanc'd to the recoverie of our freedom, never to have it in possession as we now have it, never to be voutsaf't heerafter the like mercies and signal assistances from heaven in our cause, if by our ingratefull backsliding we make these fruitless; flying now to regal concessions from his divine condescensions and gratious ansers to our once importuning praiers against the tyrannie which we then groand under: making vain and viler then dirt the blood of so many thousand faithfull and valiant *English* men, who left us in this libertie, bought with thir lives; losing by a strange after game of folly, all the battels we have wonn, together with all *Scotland*[31] as to our conquest, hereby lost, which never any of our kings could conquer, all the treasure we have spent, not that corruptible treasure[32] only, but that far more precious of all our late miraculous deliverances; treading back again with lost labour all our happie steps in the progress of reformation; and most pittifully depriving our selves the instant fruition of that free government which we have so dearly purchased, a free Commonwealth, not only held by wisest men in all ages the noblest, the manliest, the equallest, the justest, government, the most agreeable to all due libertie and proportiond equalitie, both human, civil, and Christian, most cherishing to vertue and true religion, but also (I may say it with greatest probabilitie) planely commended, or rather enjoind by our Saviour himself, to all Christians, not without remarkable disallowance,ᵃ and the brand of *gentilism* upon kingship. God in much displeasure gave a king to the *Israelites*, and imputed it a sin to them that they sought one:[33] but *Christ* apparently forbids his disciples to admitt of any such heathenish government: *the kings of the gentiles*, faith he, *exercise lordship over them*; and they that *exercise authoritie upon them, are call'd benefactors: but ye shall not be so; but he that is greatest among you let him be as the younger; and he that is chief, as he that serveth.*[34] The occasion of these his words was the ambitious desire of *Zebede's* two sons, to be exalted above thir

---

ᵃ Prohibition.

brethren in his kingdom, which they thought was to be ere long upon earth. That he speaks of civil government, is manifest by the former part of the comparison, which inferrs the other part to be alwaies in the same kinde. And what government coms neerer to this precept of Christ, then a free Commonwealth; wherin they who are greatest, are perpetual servants and drudges to the public at thir own cost and charges, neglect thir own afairs; yet are not elevated above thir brethren; live soberly in thir families, walk the streets as other men, may be spoken to freely, familiarly, friendly, without adoration. Whereas a king must be ador'd like a Demigod, with a dissolute and haughtie court about him, of vast expence and luxurie, masks and revels, to the debaushing[a] of our prime gentry both male and female; not in thir passetimes only, but in earnest, by the loos imploiments of court service, which will be then thought honorable. There will be a queen also of no less charge; in most likelihood outlandish[b] and a Papist; besides a queen mother[c] such alreadie; together with both thir courts and numerous train: then a royal issue, and ere long severally thir sumptuous courts; to the multiplying of a servile crew, not of servants only, but of nobility and gentry, bred up then to the hopes not of public, but of court offices; to be stewards, chamberlains, ushers, grooms, even of the closestool;[d] and the lower thir mindes debas'd with court opinions, contrarie to all vertue and reformation, the haughtier will be thir pride and profuseness: we may well remember this not long since at home; or need but look at present into the *French* court,[35] where enticements and preferments daily draw away and pervert the Protestant Nobilitie. As to the burden of expence, to our cost we shall soon know it; for any good to us, deserving to be termd no better than the vast and lavish price of our subjection and their debausherie; which we are now so greedily cheapning, and would so fain by paying most inconsideratly to a single person; who for any thing wherin the public really needs him, will have little els to do, but to bestow the eating and drinking of excessive dainties, to set a pompous face upon the superficial actings of State, to pageant himself up and down in progress among the perpetual bowings and cringings of an abject people, on either side deifying and adoring him for nothing don that can deserve it. For what can hee more then another man? who even in the expression of a late court-poet,[e] sits

---

a Debauching.   b Foreign.

c Queen Henrietta Maria, Roman Catholic and originally French, widow of Charles I, remained an influential figure.

d Chamber-pot; lavatory.

e Probably Sir William Davenant (1606–68); cf. his *Gondibert* (1651), II, ii, 14.

only like a great cypher set to no purpose before a long row of other significant figures. Nay it is well and happy for the people if thir King be but a cypher, being oft times a mischief, a pest, a scourge of the nation, and which is wors, not to be remov'd, not to be controul'd, much less accus'd or brought to punishment, without the danger of a common ruin, without the shaking and almost subversion of the whole land. Wheras in a free Commonwealth, any governor or chief counselor offending, may be remov'd and punishd without the least commotion. Certainly then that people must needs be madd or strangely infatuated, that build the chief hope of thir common happiness or safetie on a single person: who if he happen to be good, can do no more then another man, if to be bad, hath in his hands to do more evil without check, then millions of other men. The happiness of a nation must needs be firmest and certainest in a full and free Councel[36] of thir own electing, where no single person, but reason only swaies. And what madness is it, for them who might manage nobly thir own affairs themselves, sluggishly and weakly to devolve all on a single person; and more like boyes under age then men, to commit all to his patronage and disposal, who neither can performe what he undertakes, and yet for undertaking it, though royally paid, will not be thir servant, but thir lord? how unmanly must it needs be, to count such a one the breath of our nostrils, to hang all our felicity on him, all our safetie, our well-being, for which if we were aught els but sluggards or babies, we need depend on none but God and our own counsels, our own active vertue and industrie; *Go to the Ant, thou sluggard,* saith *Solomon; consider her waies, and be wise; which having no prince, ruler, or lord, provides her meat in the summer, and gathers her food in the harvest:*[37] which evidently shews us, that they who think the nation undon without a king, though they look grave or haughtie, have not so much true spirit and understanding in them as a pismire: neither are these diligent creatures hence concluded to live in lawless anarchie, or that commended, but are set the examples to imprudent and ungovernd men, of a frugal and self-governing democratie or Commonwealth; safer and more thriving in the joint providence and counsel of many industrious equals, then under the single domination of one imperious Lord. It may be well wonderd that any Nation styling themselves free, can suffer any man to pretend hereditarie right over them as thir lord; when as by acknowledging that right, they conclude themselves his servants and his vassals, and so renounce thir own freedom. Which how a people and thir leaders especially can do, who have fought so gloriously for liberty, how they can change thir noble words and actions, heretofore so becoming the majesty of a free people, into the base necessitie of court flatteries and prostrations, is not only strange and admirable,[a] but lamentable to think on. That a nation should be so valorous and courageous to winn thir liberty in the field, and when they have wonn it, should be so heartless and unwise in thir counsels, as not to know how to use it, value it, what to do with it or with themselves; but after ten or twelve years prosperous warr and contestation with tyrannie, basely and besottedly to run their necks again into the yoke which they have broken, and prostrate all the fruits of thir victorie for naught at the feet of the vanquishd, besides our loss of glorie, and such an example as kings or tyrants never yet had the like to boast of, will be an ignomine if it befall us, that never yet befell any nation possessd of thir libertie; worthie indeed themselves, whatsoever they be, to be for ever slaves: but that part of the nation which consents not with them, as I perswade me of a great number, far worthier then by their means to be brought into the same bondage. Considering these things so plane, so rational, I cannot but yet furder admire on the other side, how any man who hath the true principles of justice and religion in him, can presume or take upon him to be a king and lord over his brethren, whom he cannot but know whether as men or Christians, to be for the most part every way equal or superior to himself: how he can display with such vanitie and ostentation his regal splendor so supereminently above other mortal men; or being a Christian, can assume such extraordinarie honour and worship to himself, while the kingdom of Christ our common King and Lord, is hid to this world, and such *gentilish* imitation forbid in express words by himself to all his disciples. All Protestants[38] hold that Christ in his church hath left no vicegerent of his power, but himself without deputie, is the only head therof, governing it from heaven: how then can any Christian-man derive his kingship from Christ, but with wors usurpation then the Pope his headship over the church, since Christ not only hath not left the least shaddow of a command for any such vicegerence from him in the State, as the Pope pretends for his in the Church, but hath expressly declar'd, that such regal dominion is from the gentiles, not from him, and hath strictly charg'd us, not to imitate them therin.

I doubt not but all ingenuous and knowing men will easily agree with me, that a free Commonwealth without single person or house of lords, is by far the best government, if it can be had; but we have all

[a] Astonishing.

this while, say they, bin expecting it, and cannot yet attain it. Tis true indeed, when monarchie was dissolvd, the form of a Commonwealth should have forthwith bin fram'd; and the practice therof immediatly begun; that the people might have soon bin satisfi'd and delighted with the decent order, ease and benefit therof: we had bin then by this time firmly rooted past fear of commotions or mutations, & now flourishing: this care of timely setling a new government instead of yᵉ old, too much neglected, hath bin our mischief. Yet the cause therof may be ascrib'd with most reason to the frequent disturbances, interruptions and dissolutions which the Parlament hath had partly from the impatient or disaffected people, partly from som ambitious leaders in the Armie; much contrarie, I beleeve, to the mind and approbation of the Armie it self and thir other Commanders, once undeceivd, or in thir own power. Now is the opportunitie, now the very season wherein we may obtain a free Commonwealth and establish it for ever in the land, without difficulty or much delay. Writs are sent out for elections, and which is worth observing in the name, not of any king, but of the keepers of our libertie,[39] to summon a free Parlament: which then only will indeed be free, and deserve the true honor of that supreme title, if they preserve us a free people. Which never Parlament was more free to do; being now call'd, not as heretofore, by the summons of a king, but by the voice of libertie: and if the people, laying aside prejudice and impatience, will seriously and calmly now consider thir own good both religious and civil, thir own libertie and the only means thereof, as shall be heer laid before them, and will elect thir Knights and Burgesses able men, and according to the just and necessarie qualifications[a] (which for aught I hear, remain yet in force unrepeald, as they were formerly decreed in Parlament) men not addicted to a single person or house of lords, the work is don; at least the foundation firmly laid of a free Commonwealth, and good part also erected of the main structure. For the ground and basis of every just and free government (since men have smarted so oft for commiting all to one person) is a general councel of ablest men,[40] chosen by the people to consult of public affairs from time to time for the common good. In this Grand Council must the sovrantie, not transferrd, but delegated only, and as it were deposited, reside; with this caution they must have the forces by sea and land committed to them for preservation of the common peace and libertie; must raise and manage the public revenue, at least with som

---

[a] The resolution of the Rump, 4 Feb. 1659, which disqualified from election any who had advocated a king, rule by a single person, or a house of lords.

inspectors deputed for satisfaction of the people, how it is imploid; must make or propose, as more expressly shall be said anon, civil laws; treat of commerce, peace, or warr with foreign nations, and for the carrying on som particular affairs with more secrecie and expedition, must elect, as they have alreadie out of thir own number and others, a Councel of State.

And although it may seem strange at first hearing, by reason that mens mindes are prepossessed with the notion of successive Parliaments,[41] I affirme that the Grand or General Councel being well chosen, should be perpetual:[42] for so thir business is or may be, and oft times urgent; the opportunitie of affairs gaind or lost in a moment. The day of counsel cannot be set as the day of a festival; but must be readie alwaies to prevent or answer all occasions. By this continuance they will become everie way skilfullest, best provided of intelligence from abroad, best acquainted with the people at home, and the people with them. The ship of the Commonwealth is alwaies under sail; they sit at the stern; and if they stear well, what need is ther to change them; it being rather dangerous? Add to this, that the Grand Councel is both foundation and main pillar of the whole State; and to move pillars and foundations, not faultie,[43] cannot be safe for the building. I see not therefor, how we can be advantag'd by successive and transitorie Parlaments; but that they are much likelier continually to unsettle rather then to settle a free government; to breed commotions, changes, novelties and uncertainties; to bring neglect upon present affairs and opportunities, while all mindes are suspense with expectation of a new assemblie, and the assemblie for a good space taken up with the new setling of it self. After which, if they finde no great work to do, they will make it, by altering or repealing former acts, or making and multiplying new; that they may seem to see what thir predecessors saw not, and not to have assembld for nothing: till all law be lost in the multitude of clashing statutes. But if the ambition of such as think themselves injur'd that they also partake not of the government, and are impatient till they be chosen, cannot brook the perpetuitie of others chosen before them, or if it be feard that long continuance of power may corrupt sincerest men, the known expedient is, and by som lately propounded, that annually (or if the space be longer, so much perhaps the better) the third part of Senators may go out according to the precedence of thir election, and the like number be chosen in thir places, to prevent the setling of too absolute a power,[44] if it should be perpetual: and this they call *partial rotation*. But I could wish that this wheel or partial wheel in State, if it be possible, might be avoided; as having too much affinitie with the wheel of fortune. For it appeers not how this can be don, without danger and mischance of putting out a great number of the best and ablest: in whose stead new elections may bring in as many raw, unexperienc'd and otherwise affected, to the weakning and much altering for the wors of public transactions. Neither do I think a perpetual Senat, especially chosen and entrusted by the people, much in this land to be feard, where the well-affected either in a standing armie, or in a setled militia have thir arms in thir own hands.[45] Safest therefor to me it seems and of least hazard or interruption to affairs, that none of the Grand Councel be mov'd, unless by death or just conviction of som crime: for what can be expected firm or stedfast from a floating foundation? however, I forejudge not any probable expedient, any temperament that can be found in things of this nature so disputable on either side. Yet least this which I affirme, be thought my single opinion, I shall add sufficient testimonie. Kingship it self is therefor counted the more safe and durable, because the king and, for the most part, his councel, is not chang'd during life: but a Commonwealth is held immortal; and therin firmest, safest and most above fortune: for the death of a king, causeth ofttimes many dangerous alterations; but the death now and then of a Senator is not felt; the main bodie of them still continuing permanent in greatest and noblest Commonwealths, and as it were eternal.[46] Therefor among the *Jews*, the supreme councel of seaventie, call'd the *Sanhedrim*, founded by *Moses*, in *Athens*, that of *Areopagus*, in *Sparta*, that of the Ancients, in *Rome*, the Senat, consisted of members chosen for term of life; and by that means remaind as it were still the same to generations. In *Venice* they change indeed ofter then every year som particular councels of State, as that of six, or such other; but the true Senat, which upholds and sustains the government, is the whole aristocracie immovable. So in the United Provinces, the States General, which are indeed but a councel of state deputed by the whole union, are not usually the same persons for above three or six years; but the States of every citie, in whom the sovrantie hath bin plac'd time out of minde, are a standing Senat, without succession, and accounted chiefly in that regard the main prop of thir liberty. And why they should be so in every well orderd Commonwealth, they who write of policie, give these reasons; "That to make the Senat successive, not only impairs the dignitie and lustre of the Senat, but weakens the whole Commonwealth, and bring it into manifest danger; while by this means the secrets of State are frequently divulgd, and matters of greatest consequence committed to inexpert and novice counselors, utterly to seek in the full and intimate knowledge of affairs past." I know not therefore what should be peculiar in *England* to make successive Parlaments thought safest, or convenient here more then in other nations, unless it be the fickl'ness which is attributed to us as we are Ilanders: but good education and acquisit wisdom ought to correct the fluxible fault, if any such be, of our watry situation. It will be objected, that in those places where they had perpetual Senats, they had also popular remedies against thir growing too imperious: as in *Athens*, beside *Areopagus*, another Senat of four or five hunderd; in *Sparta*, the *Ephori*;[a] in *Rome*, the Tribunes of the people. But the event tels us, that these remedies either little availd the people, or brought them to such a licentious and unbridl'd democratie, as in fine ruind themselves with thir own excessive power. So that the main reason urg'd why popular assemblies are to be trusted with the peoples libertie, rather then a Senat of principal men, because great men will be still endeavoring to inlarge thir power, but the common sort will be contented to maintain thir own libertie, is by experience found false; none being more immoderat and ambitious to amplifie thir power, then such popularities; which was seen in the people of *Rome*; who at first contented to have thir Tribunes, at length contended with the Senat that one Consul, then both; soon after, that the Censors and Praetors also should be created Plebeian, and the whole empire put into their hands; adoring lastly those, who most were advers to the Senat, till *Marius*[b] by fulfilling thir inordinat desires, quite lost them all the power for which they had so long bin striving, and left them under the tyrannie of *Sylla*: the ballance therefor must be exactly so set, as to preserve and keep up due autoritie on either side, as well in the Senat as in the people. And this annual rotation of a Senat to consist of three hunderd, as it lately propounded,[48] requires also another popular assembly upward of a thousand, with an answerable rotation. Which besides that it will be liable to all those inconveniencies found in the foresaid remedies, cannot but be troublesom and chargeable, both in thir motion and thir session, to the whole land; unweildie with thir own bulk, unable in so great a number to mature thir consultations as they ought, if any be allotted them, and that they meet not from so many parts remote to sit a whole year lieger[c] in

a Political overseers or leading magistrates.[47]
b Gaius Marius (157–86 BC), soldier, tribune, consul and opponent of Sulla; leader of the *optimates* (aristocracy) as Sulla was of the *populares* (people).
c One who stays as a representative.

one place, only now and then to hold up a forrest of fingers, or to convey each man his bean or ballot into the box, without reason shewn or common deliberation; incontinent of secrets, if any be imparted to them, emulous and always jarring with the other Senat.[49] The much better way doubtless will be in this wavering condition of our affairs, to deferr the changing or circumscribing of our Senat, more then may be done with ease, till the Commonwealth be throughly setl'd in peace and safetie, and they themselves give us the occasion.[50] Militarie men hold it dangerous to change the form of battel in view of an enemie: neither did the people of *Rome* bandie with thir Senat while any of the *Tarquins*[a] livd, the enemies of thir libertie, nor sought by creating Tribunes to defend themselves against the fear of thir Patricians, till sixteen years after the expulsion of thir kings, and in full securitie of thir state, they had or thought they had just cause given them by the Senat. Another way will be, to wel-qualifie and refine elections: not committing all to the noise and shouting of a rude multitude, but permitting only those of them who are rightly qualifi'd,[51] to nominat as many as they will; and out of that number others of a better breeding, to chuse a less number more judiciously, till after a third or fourth sifting and refining of exactest choice, they only be left chosen who are the due number, and seem by most voices the worthiest. To make the people fittest to chuse, and the chosen fittest to govern, will be to mend our corrupt and faulty education, to teach the people faith not without vertue, temperance, modestie, sobrietie, parsimonie, justice; not to admire wealth or honour; to hate turbulence and ambition; to place every one his privat welfare and happiness in the public peace, libertie and safetie. They shall not then need to be much mistrustfull of thir chosen Patriots in the Grand Councel; who will be then rightly call'd the true keepers of our libertie, though the most of thir business will be in foreign affairs. But to prevent all mistrust, the people then will have thir several ordinarie assemblies (which will henceforth quite annihilate the odious power and name of Committies) in the chief towns of every countie, without the trouble, charge, or time lost of summoning and assembling from far in so great a number, and so long residing from thir own houses, or removing of thir families, to do as much at home in thir several shires, entire or subdivided, toward the securing of thir libertie, as a numerous assembly of them all formd and conven'd on purpose with the wariest rotation. Wherof I shall

---

[a] Kings of Rome until their expulsion in 510 BC.

speak more ere the end of this discourse: for it may be referred to time, so we be still going on by degrees to perfection. The people well weighing and performing these things, I suppose would have no cause to fear, though the *Parlament*, abolishing that name, as originally signifying but the *parlie* of our Lords and Commons with thir *Norman* king when he pleasd to call them, should, with certain limitations of thir power, sit perpetual, if thir ends be faithfull and for a free Commonwealth, under the name of a Grand or General Councel. Till this be don, I am in doubt whether our State will be ever certainly and throughly setl'd; never likely till then to see an end of our troubles and continual changes or at least never the true settlement and assurance of our libertie. The Grand Councel being thus firmly constituted to perpetuitie, and still, upon the death or default of any member, suppli'd and kept in full number, ther can be no cause alleag'd why peace, justice, plentiful trade and all prosper-itie should not thereupon ensue throughout the whole land; with as much assurance as can be of human things, that they shall so continue (if God favour us, and our wilfull sins provoke him not) even to the coming of our true and rightfull and only to be expected King, only worthie as he is our only Saviour, the Messiah, the Christ, the only heir of his eternal father, the only by him anointed and ordaind since the work of our redemption finished, Universal Lord of all mankinde. The way propounded is plane, easier and open before us; without intricacies, without the introducement of new or obsolete forms, or terms, or exotic models; idea's that would effect nothing, but with a number of new injunctions to manacle the native liberty of mankinde;[52] turning all vertue into prescription, servitude, and necessities, to the great impairing and frustrating of Christian libertie: I say again, this way lies free and smooth before us; is not tangl'd with inconveniencies; invents no new incumbrances; requires no perilous, no injurious alteration or circumscription of mens lands and proprieties; secure, that in this Commonwealth, temporal and spiritual lords remov'd, no man or number of men can attain to such wealth or vast possession, as will need the hedge of an Agrarian law[53] (never succesful, but the cause rather of sedition, save only where it began seasonably with first possession) to confine them from endangering our public libertie; to conclude, it can have no considerable objection made against it, that it is not practicable: least it be said hereafter, that we gave up our libertie for want of a readie way or distinct form propos'd of a free Commonwealth. And this facilitie we shall have above our next neighbouring Commonwealth (if we can keep us from the fond conceit of something like a duke of *Venice*,[a] put lately into many mens heads, by som one or other sutly driving on under that notion his own ambitious ends to lurch[b] a crown) that our liberty shall not be hamperd or hoverd over by any ingagement to such a potent familie as the house of *Nassau*[c] of whom to stand in perpetual doubt and suspicion, but we shall live the cleerest and absolutest free nation in the world.

On the contrarie, if ther be a king, which the inconsiderate multitude[54] are now so madd upon, mark how far short we are like to com of all those happinesses, which in a free state we shall immediately be possessd of. First, the Grand Councel, which, as I shewd before, should sit perpetually (unless thir leisure give them now and then som intermissions or vacations, easilie manageable by the Councel of State left sitting) shall be call'd, by the kings good will and utmost endeavor, as seldom as may be. For it is only the king's right, he will say, to call a parlament; and this he will do most commonly about his own affairs rather then the kingdom's, as will appeer planely so soon as they are call'd. For what will thir business then be and the chief expence of thir time, but an endless tugging between petition of right and royal prerogative, especially about the negative voice, militia, or subsidies, demanded and oft times extorted without reasonable cause appeering to the Commons, who are the only true representatives of the people, and thir libertie, but will be then mingl'd with a court faction; besides which within thir own walls, the sincere part of them who stand faithful to the people, will again have to deal with two troublesom counter-working adversaries from without, meer creatures of the king, spiritual, and the greater part, as is likeliest, of temporal lords, nothing concernd with the peoples liberties. If these prevail not in what they please, though never so much against the peoples interest, the Parlament shall be soon dissolvd, or sit and do nothing; not sufferd to remedie the least greevance, or enact aught advantageous to the people. Next, the Councel of State shall not be chosen by the Parlament, but by the king, still his own creatures, courtiers and favorites; who will be sure in all thir counsels to set thir maister's grandure and absolute power, in what they are able, far above the peoples libertie. I denie not but that ther may be such a king, who may regard the

---

[a] The Doge of Venice was elected for life. Milton may have had in mind Richard Cromwell, or General Monck.

[b] Steal.

[c] The family of the Princes of Orange, which slowly came to dominate the republic of the United Provinces, under the title of Stadtholders, as the Medici family had come to dominate republican Florence and finally become hereditary Grand Dukes of Tuscany.

common good before his own, may have no vitious favorite, may hearken only to the wisest and incorruptest of his Parlament: but this rarely happens in a monarchie not elective; and it behoves not a wise nation to committ the summ of thir welbeing, the whole state of thir safetie to fortune. What need they; and how absurd would it be, when as they themselves to whom his chief vertue will be but to hearken, may with much better management and dispatch, with much more commendation of thir own worth and magnanimitie govern without a maister. Can the folly be paralleld, to adore and be the slaves of a single person for doing that which it is ten thousand to one whether he can or will do, and we without him might do more easily, more effectually, more laudably our selves? Shall we never grow old anough to be wise to make seasonable use of gravest authorities, experiences, examples? Is it such an unspeakable joy to serve, such felicitie to wear a yoke? to clink our shackles, lockt on by pretended law of subjection more intolerable and hopeless to be ever shaken off, then those which are knockt on by illegal injurie and violence? *Aristotle*, our chief instructer in the Universities, least this doctrine be though *Sectarian*, as the royalist would have it thought, tels us in the third of his Politics,[55] that certain men at first, for the matchless excellence of thir vertue above others, or som great public benefit, were created kings by the people; in small cities and territories, and in the scarcitie of others to be found like them: but when they abus'd thir power and governments grew larger, and the number of prudent men increasd, that then the people soon deposing thir tyrants, betook them, in all civilest places, to the form of a free Commonwealth. And why should we thus disparage and prejudicate[a] our own nation, as to fear a scarcitie of able and worthie men united in counsel to govern us, if we will but use diligence and impartiality to finde them out and chuse them, rather yoking our selves to a single person, the natural adversarie and oppressor of libertie, though good, yet far easier corruptible by the excess of his singular power and exaltation, or at best, not comparably sufficient to bear the weight of government, nor equally dispos'd to make us happie in the enjoyment of our libertie under him.

But admitt, that monarchie of it self may be convenient to som nations; yet to us who have thrown it out, receivd back again, it cannot but prove pernicious. For kings to com, never forgetting thir former ejection, will be sure to fortifie and arm themselves

---

[a] Prejudge.

sufficiently for the future against all such attempts hereafter from the people: who shall be then so narrowly watchd and kept so low, that though they would never so fain and at the same rate of thir blood and treasure, they never shall be able to regain what they now have purchasd and may enjoy, or to free themselves from any yoke impos'd upon them: nor will they dare to go about it; utterly disheartn'd for the future, if these thir highest attempts prove unsuccesfull; which will be the triumph of all tyrants heerafter over any people that shall resist oppression; and thir song will then be, to others, how sped the rebellious *English*? to our posteritie, how sped the rebells your fathers? This is not my conjecture, but drawn from God's known denouncement against the gentilizing[a] *Israelites*; who though they were governd in a Commonwealth of God's own ordaining, he only thir king, they his peculiar people, yet affecting rather to resemble heathen, but pretending the misgovernment of *Samuel's* sons, no more a reason to dislike thir Commonwealth, then the violence of *Eli's* sons[56] was imputable to that priesthood or religion, clamourd for a king. They had thir longing; but with this testimonie of God's wrath; *ye shall cry out in that day because of your king whom ye shall have chosen, and the Lord will not hear you in that day.*[57] Us if he shall hear now, how much less will he hear when we cry heerafter, who once deliverd by him from a king, and not without wondrous acts of his providence, insensible and unworthie of those high mercies are returning precipitantly, if he withhold us not, back to the captivitie from whence he freed us. Yet neither shall we obtain or buy at an easie rate this new guilded yoke which thus transports us: a new royal-revenue must be found, a new episcopal; for those are individual: both which being wholy dissipated or bought by privat persons or assign'd for service don, and especially to the Armie, cannot be recovered[58] without a general detriment and confusion to mens estates, or a heavie imposition on all mens purses; benifit to none, but to the worst and ignoblest sort of men, whose hope is to be either the ministers of court riot and excess, or the gainers by it: But not to speak more of losses and extraordinarie levies on our estates; what will then be the revenges and offences rememberd and returnd, not only by the chief person, but by all his adherents; accounts and reparations that will be requir'd, suites, inditements, inquiries, discoveries, complaints, informations, who knows against whom or how many, though perhaps neuters,[b] if not to utmost infliction, yet to imprisonment, fines, banishment, or

[a] Wishing to become like Gentiles. [b] People who have been neutral.

molestation; if not these, yet disfavor, discountnance, disregard and contempt on all but the known royalist or whom he favors, will be plenteous: nor let the new royaliz'd presbyterians[59] perswade themselves that thir old doings, though now recanted, will be forgotten; what ever conditions be contriv'd or trusted on. Will they not beleeve this; nor remember the pacification,[60] how it was kept to the *Scots*; how other solemn promises many a time to us? Let them but now read the diabolical forerunning libells, the faces, the gestures that now appeer foremost and briskest in all public places; as the harbingers of those that are in expectation to raign over us; let them but hear the insolencies, the menaces, the insultings of our newly animated common enemies crept lately out of thir holes, thir hell,[61] I might say, by the language of thir infernal pamphlets, the spue of every drunkard, every ribald; nameless, yet not for want of licence, but for very shame of thir own vile persons, not daring to name themselves, while they traduce others by name; and give us to foresee that they intend to second thir wicked words, if ever they have powers, with more wicked deeds. Let our zealous backsliders forethink now with themselves, how thir necks yok'd with these tigers of Bacchus,[a] these new fanatics of not the preaching but the sweating-tub,[b] inspir'd with nothing holier then the Venereal pox, can draw one way under monarchie to the establishing of church discipline with these new-disgorg'd atheismes: yet shall they not have the honor to yoke with these, but shall be yok'd under them; these shall plow[62] on their backs. And do they among them who are so forward to bring in the single person,[c] think to be by him trusted or long regarded? So trusted they shall be and so regarded, as by kings are wont reconcil'd enemies; neglected and soon after discarded, if not prosecuted for old traytors; the first inciters, beginners, and more then to the third part actors of all that followd; it will be found also, that there must be then as necessarily as now (for the contrarie part will be still feard) a standing armie; which for certain shall not be this, but of the fiercest Cavaliers, of no less expence, and perhaps again under *Rupert*:[d] but let this armie be sure they shall be soon disbanded, and likeliest without arrear or pay; and being disbanded, not be sure but they may as soon be question for being in arms against thir king: the same let them fear, who have contributed monie; which will amount to no small number that

---

[a] Orgiastic god of wine.   [b] Used for the treatment of venereal disease.
[c] Charles II, Monck, or Richard Cromwell once more.
[d] Prince Rupert (1619–82), nephew of Charles I, general of his cavalry, and of the royal army after the Battle of Marston Moor.

must then take thir turn to be made delinquents and compounders. They who past reason and recoverie are devoted to kingship, perhaps will answer, that a greater part by far of the Nation will have it so; the rest therefor must yield. Not so much to convince these, which I little hope, as to confirm them who yield not, I reply; that this greatest part have both in reason and the trial of just battel, lost the right of their election what the government shall be: of them who have not lost that right, whether they for kingship be the greater number,[63] who can certainly determin? Suppose they be; yet of freedom they partake all alike, one main end of government: which if the greater part value not, but will degenerately forgoe, is it just or reasonable, that most voices against the main end of government should enslave the less number that would be free? More just it is doubtless, if it com to force, that a less number compell a greater to retain, which can be no wrong to them, thir libertie, then that a greater number for the pleasure of thir baseness, compell a less most injuriously to be thir fellow slaves. They who seek nothing but thir own just libertie, have alwaies right to winn it and to keep it, when ever they have power, be the voices never so numerous that oppose it. And how much we above others are concernd to defend it from kingship, and from them who in pursuance therof so perniciously would betray us and themselves to most certain miserie and thraldom, will be needless to repeat.

Having thus far shewn with what ease we may now obtain a free Commonwealth, and by it with as much ease all the freedom, peace, justice, plentie that we can desire, on the other side the difficulties, troubles, uncertainties, nay rather impossibilities to enjoy these things constantly under a monarch, I will now proceed to shew more particularly wherin our freedom and flourishing condition will be more ample and secure to us under a free Commonwealth then under kingship.

The whole freedom of man consists either in spiritual or civil libertie. As for spiritual, who can be at rest, who can enjoy any thing in this world with contentment, who hath not libertie to serve God and to save his own soul, according to the best light which God hath planted in him to that purpose, by the reading of his reveal'd will and the guidance of his holy spirit? That this is best pleasing to God, and that the whole Protestant Church allows no supream judge or rule in matters of religion, but the scriptures, and these to be interpreted by the scriptures themselves, which necessarily inferrs liberty of conscience, I have heretofore prov'd at large in another treatise,[64] and might yet furder by the public declarations, confessions and admoni-

tions of whole churches and states, obvious in all historie since the
Reformation.

This liberty of conscience which above all other things ought to
be to all men dearest and most precious, no government more
inclinable not to favor only but to protect, then a free Commonwealth; as being most magnanimous, most fearless and confident of
its own fair proceedings. Wheras kingship, though looking big, yet
indeed most pusillanimous, full of fears, full of jealousies, startl'd at
every ombrage, as it hath bin observd of old to have ever suspected
most and mistrusted them who were in most esteem for vertue and
generositie of minde, so it is now known to have most in doubt and
suspicion them who are most reputed to be religious. Queen
Elizabeth though her self accounted so good a Protestant, so
moderate, so confident of her Subjects love would never give way
so much as to Presbyterian reformation in this land, though once
and again besought, as *Camden* relates,[65] but imprisond and
persecuted the very proposers therof; alleaging it as her minde &
maxim unalterable, that such reformation would diminish regal
autoritie. What liberty of conscience can we then expect of others,
far wors principl'd from the cradle, traind up and governd by *Popish*
and *Spanish* counsels, and on such depending hitherto for subsistence? Especially what can this last Parlament expect, who having
reviv'd lately and publishd the covnant,[a] have reingag'd themselves,
never to readmitt Episcopacie: which no son of *Charls* returning,
but will most certainly bring back with him, if he regard the last and
strictest charge of his father, *to persevere in not the doctrin only, but
government of the church of* England; *not to neglect the speedie and
effectual suppressing of errors and schisms*;[66] among which he accounted Presbyterie one of the chief: or if notwithstanding that
charge of his father, he submitt to the covnant, how will he keep
faith to us with disobedience to him; or regard that faith given,
which must be founded on the breach of that last and solemnest
paternal charge, and the reluctance, I may say the antipathie which
is in all kings against Presbyterian and Independent discipline? for
they hear the gospel speaking much of libertie; a word which
monarchie and her bishops both fear and hate, but a free Commonwealth both favors and promotes; and not the word only, but the
thing it self. But let our governors beware in time, least thir hard
measure to libertie of conscience be found the rock wheron they
shipwrack themselves as others have now don before them in the

---

[a] The Solemn League and Covenant, on 5 March 1660 ordered to be published and read in every
church, by the House of Commons to which the secluded members had returned.

cours wherin God was directing thir stearage to a free Commonwealth, and the abandoning of all those whom they call *sectaries*, for
the detected falshood and ambition of som, be a wilfull rejection of
thir own chief strength and interest in the freedom of all Protestant
religion, under what abusive name soever calumniated.

The other part of our freedom consists in the civil rights and
advancements of every person according to his merit: the enjoyment of those never more certain, and the access to these never
more open, then in a free Commonwealth. Both which in my
opinion may be best and soonest obtaind, if every countie in the
land were made a kinde of subordinate Commonaltie[67] or Commonwealth, and one chief town or more, according as the shire is in
circuit, made cities, if they be not so call'd alreadie; where the
nobilitie and chief gentry from a proportionable compas of territorie annexd to each citie, may build, houses or palaces, befitting
thir qualitie, may bear part in the government, make thir own
judicial laws, or use these that are, and execute them by thir own
elected judicatures and judges without appeal, in all things of civil
government between man and man. so they shall have justice in thir
own hands, law executed fully and finally in thir own counties and
precincts, long wishd, and spoken of, but never yet obtaind; they
shall have none then to blame but themselves, if it be not well
administerd; and fewer laws to expect or fear from the supreme
autoritie; or to those that shall be made, of any great concernment
to public libertie, they may without much trouble in these commonalties or in more general assemblies call'd to thir cities from the
whole territorie on such occasion, declare and publish thir assent or
dissent by deputies within a time limited sent to the Grand Councel:
yet so as this thir judgment declar'd shal submitt to the greater
number of other counties or commonalties, and not avail them to
any exemption of themselves, or refusal of agreement with the rest,
as it may in any of the United Provinces, being sovran within it self,
oft times to the great disadvantage of that union. In these imploiments they may much better then they do now, exercise and fit
themselves, till thir lot fall to be chosen into the Grand Councel,
according as thir worth and merit shall be taken notice of by the
people. As for controversies that shall happen between men of
several counties, they may repair, as they do now, to the capital
citie, or any other more commodious, indifferent[a] place and equal
judges. And this I finde to have bin practisd in the old *Athenian*

[a] Impartial.

Commonwealth, reputed the first and ancientest place of civilitie in all *Greece*; that they had in thir several cities, a peculiar; in *Athens*, a common government;[68] and thir right, as it befell them, to the administration of both. They should have heer also schools and academies at thir own choice, wherin thir children may be bred up in thir own sight to all learning and noble education not in grammar only, but in all liberal arts and exercises. This would soon spread much more knowledge and civilitie, yea religion through all parts of the land, by communicating the natural heat of government and culture more distributively to all extreme parts, which now lie numm and neglected,[69] would soon make the whole nation more industrious, more ingenuous at home, more potent, more honorable abroad. To this a free Commonwealth will easily assent; (nay the Parlament hath had alreadie som such thing in designe) for of all governments a Commonwealth aims most to make the people flourishing, vertuous, noble and high spirited. Monarchs will never permitt: whose aim is to make the people, wealthie indeed perhaps and well fleec't, for thir own shearing and the supplie of regal prodigalitie; but otherwise softest, basest, vitiousest, servilest, easiest to be kept under; and not only in fleece, but in minde also sheepishest; and will have all the benches of judicature annexd to the throne, as a gift of royal grace that we have justice don us; whenas nothing can be more essential to the freedom of a people, then to have the administration of justice and all public ornaments in thir own election and within thir own bounds, without long travelling or depending on remote places to obtain thir right or any civil accomplishment; so it be not supreme, but subordinate to the general power and union of the whole Republic.[70] In which happy firmness as in the particular above mentiond, we shall also far exceed the United Provinces, by having, not as they (to the retarding and districting oft times of thir counsels or urgentest occasions) many Sovranties united in one Commonwealth, but many Commonwealths under one united and entrusted Sovrantie. And when we have our forces by sea and land, either of a faithful Armie or a setl'd Militia, in our own hands[71] to the firm establishing of a free Commonwealth, publick accounts under our own inspection, general laws and taxes with thir causes in our own domestic suffrages, judicial laws, offices and ornaments at home in our own ordering and administration, all distinction of lords and commoners, that may any way divide or sever the publick interest, remov'd, what can a perpetual senat have then wherin to grow corrupt, wherin to encroach upon us or unsurp; or if they do, wherin to be formidable? Yet if all this avail not to remove the fear or envie of a perpetual sitting, it may be easilie provided, to change a third part of them yearly or every two or three years,[72] as was above mentiond; or that it be at those times in the peoples choice, whether they will change them, or renew thir power, as they shall finde cause.

I have no more to say at present: few words will save us, well considerd; few and easie things, now seasonably don. But if the people be so affected, as to prostitute religion and libertie to the vain and groundless apprehension, that nothing but kingship can restore trade, not remembering the frequent plagues and pestilences that then wasted this citie, such as through God's mercie we never have felt since, and that trade flourishes no where more then in the free Commonwealths of *Italie, Germanie*, and the Low-Countries before thir eyes at this day; yet if trade be grown so craving and importunate through the profuse living of tradesmen, that nothing can support it, but the luxurious expences of a nation upon trifles or superfluities, so as if the people generally should betake themselves to frugalitie, it might prove a dangerous matter, least tradesmen should mutinie for want of trading, and that therefor we must forgoe & set to sale religion, libertie, honor, safetie, all concernments Divine or human to keep up trading, if lastly, after all this light among us, the same reason shall pass for current to put our necks again under kingship, as was made use of by the *Jews* to returne back to *Egypt*[73] and to the worship of thir idol queen, because they falsly imagind that they then livd in more plentie and prosperitie, our condition is not sound but rotten, both in religion and all civil prudence; and will bring us soon, the way we are marching, to those calamities which attend alwaies and unavoidably on luxurie, all national judgments under forein or domestic slaverie: so far we shall be from mending our condition by monarchizing our government, whatever new conceit now possesses us. However with all hazard I have ventur'd what I thought my duty to speak in season, and to forewarne my countrey in time: wherin I doubt not but ther be many wise men in all places and degrees, but am sorrie the effects of wisdom are so little seen among us. Many circumstances and particulars I could have added in those things wherof I have spoken; but a few main matters now put speedily in execution, will suffice to recover us, and set all right: and ther will want at no time who are good at circumstances; but men who set thir mindes on main matters and sufficiently urge them, in these most difficult times I finde not many. What I have spoken, is the language of that

which is not call'd amiss *the good Old Cause*:ᵃ if it seem strange to
any, it will not seem more strange, I hope, then convincing to
backsliders. Thus much I should perhaps have said though I were
sure I should have spoken only to trees and stones; and had none to
cry to, but with the Prophet, *O earth, earth, earth!*[74] to tell the very
soil it self, what her perverse inhabitants are deaf to. Nay though
what I have spoke, should happn' (which Thou suffer not, who
didst create mankinde free; nor Thou next, who didst redeem us
from being servants of men!) to be the last words of our expiring
libertie. But I trust I shall have spoken perswasion to abundance of
sensible and ingenuous men: to som perhaps whom God may raise
of these stones to become children of reviving libertie; and may
reclaim, though they seem now chusing them a captain back for
Egypt, to bethink themselves a little and consider whether they are
rushing; to exhort this torrent also of the people, not to be so
impetuos, but to keep thir due channell; and at length recovering
and uniting thir better resolutions, now that they see alreadie how
open and unbounded the insolence and rage is of our common
enemies, to stay these ruinous proceedings; justly and timely fearing
to what a precipice of destruction the deluge of this epidemic
madness would hurrie us through the general defection of a
misguided and abus'd multitude.

THE END

ᵃ I.e. Republicanism.

'Queres and Conjectures, Concerning the present state of this Kingdome', 1643

Published in 1643, the second year of the First Civil War, one of many such anonymous 'Queries' that appeared during the period. Some have an obvious party-commitment; others, like this, unideological and apparently neutral, are unresigned to the miseries of a continued war, and argue strongly for a settlement.

Our text is taken from the copy in the Cambridge University Library.

I. QUERY

What issue may probably be expected of these great differences amongst us?

CONJECTURE

There are but three conditions that can possibly befall us; *Accommodation, Victory*, or the *continuance* of these *civil wars*.

As for Accommodation, there are but slender hopes of that, if a man seriously weighs these particulars.

1. The confidence which both sides have of their own strength together with their several successes.

2. The mutual sufferings, whereby they have exasperated one another.

3. The deep engagements of both parties, not only of their fortunes, friends, persons, but the tie of an Oath (according to several interpretations), the bond of religion, which of all other do make men more eager and zealous in their prosecution.

4. The great distance of terms on which they stand, each side expecting that of the other, which according to their own suppositions cannot be imagined possible, *viz.*

1. That such Delinquents should be delivered up, who by their own acknowledgment are so prevalent, and of such authority on each side, that they carry all businesses as they themselves please. As if men would consent to their own ruins.

2. That they may have the chief power and places of the Kingdom at their own disposal, which neither side can enjoy with any sufficient security to the other.

As for victory, it is not easily conceivable upon what ground any judicious man and lover of his Country can rationally desire it; or if he should, yet it seems still as difficult to imagine what grounds he can have to hope for it; The strength of both parties being late more equally poised than before. 'Tis commonly granted, that with his Majesty there are the generality of the Nobility, Gentry, Clergy, throughout the whole Kingdom, and a great part of the people everywhere, who of late do fall off from the other side every day more and more; So that if he should perhaps have the worst in one battle, yet the estates, reputations, abilities, multitudes of those that are engaged on his side in several places, (especially considering his dispersed Armies) would be able to repair it again, and to hold out for a lasting war. As for supply of moneys, 'tis as easily imaginable, how he should get more, as how he should get so much.

On the Parliament's side, there are, beside some Nobility, Gentry, Clergy, the greatest part of the Commonalty, the Corporations, Forts, and Navy. Nor is it without ground suspected, that many of those who fall off from them, do it to save charges, and for fear of future payments. In which kind when his Majesty shall expect their assistance, they are like to prove as useless to him, as they were before to the Parliament. So that though we should suppose, as many of the people to fall off from this side, as may probably be suspected, yet those that are cordially engaged, with such advantages as they are like to keep, will be able to hold out so long in a Civil war, till the whole Kingdom be ruined.

Since therefore there is so little likelihood either of *Accommodation* or *Victory*, it must necessarily follow, that the most probable expectation is the continuance of these wars.

2. QUERY

Where lies the fault of this unhappy division?

CONJECTURE

Since both parties do in this difference appeal to every man's judgment, therefore I hope 'tis no great presumption to venture upon the determination of this *Query*, and I am sure no extraordinary thing to mistake in it.

1. Some there are who attribute all to a great design, which hath been a long time acting amongst us for the introducing of Popery. In the prosecution of which, they conceive all these troubles to be

raised: But this others disrelish as groundless, because his Majesty is sufficiently known to be a resolved Protestant, being naturally of such a disposition as will strongly adhere unto those principles which he hath once embraced.

As for the Bishops (to whose former violences we owe much of our present miseries) though they might perhaps affectionately incline to Popery, in those points which seem to promote their own greatness; yet for other things, 'tis likely they did only connive at it in opposition to Puritans, whom they esteemed their greatest enemies; so that though that religion might consequently by this means have increased and stolen in amongst us; yet 'tis not probable that it was by them directly intended and upon design.

2. Others there are, who (according as they are severally engaged) do ascribe the fault of this division to the several parties of it. The relations of both sides concerning the occasions and passages of this difference being so fair and plausible, that either of them alone were enough to insinuate into the belief of any indifferent man.

His Majesty tells us, that at the beginning of this Parliament he did in everything comply with their advice for the promoting of the public good, granting unto them so many acts of grace (beyond any example of his Progenitors) as might abundantly repair those oppressions and grievances, under which they have formerly suffered. But when he had such strong reasons to suspect that there was a prevalent Faction amongst them, combin'd together for the utter subversion of government, and that they would make Laws without his assent, when as first by threats and tumults they had frighted away the major part of both Houses, who were otherwise affected, not without some danger to his own person; then he was forced to withdraw himself, and to provide for his own person in remoter places.

On the other side, the *Parliament* acknowledge those many good Laws which they have propounded, and his Majesty hath passed; But withal they say, that there is great reason to suspect that all these acts were but unwillingly assented unto, only in satisfaction to the exigency of those times, His Majesty's bad Councillors being still as prevalent with him as before, who might afterwards as easily persuade him to the breach of these new acts, as they had formerly done to the breach of others: so that all they had done was nothing worth, unless there might be some further course taken for the removal of these evil Councillors, and the settling of the power of the Kingdom in such hands as might preserve the Laws, and not destroy them: It being very probable, that those Councillors, who have now persuaded his Majesty to this opposition of his Parliament, if the *Militia* had been at their disposal, would themselves have used the power of it, for the suppressing of the Parliament.

Such plausible pretences are there on both sides, that an honest man may very excusably mistake, especially if he understand these things only by Relation from others, and be not himself an inquisitive looker on upon the several passages of them.

3. To me it seems the most probable conjecture, that mutual jealousy did first make this wound, and mutual bitterness hath since festered and enlarged it.

Where the truest ground of this jealousy lies, must be found by examining the several parties, whether that change which hath produced our present troubles hath been in the people, or in the Governors. This may seem hard to determine in this particular case, though if a man speak abstractly and in the general: the truth is, it is not so common nor so likely for people to rise up without cause, as for Governors to oppress without cause. And on the other side, when the people have been much intrenched upon in their properties or liberties, it may probably be expected, that when they do show themselves, they should appear exasperated unto a high degree of fear and impatience.

The bitterness on both sides hath been occasioned by 1. Violence in opinion. 2. Unusual practices.

There are too many on both sides who are so eager and violent in their opinions, as scarce to allow him for an honest man, who is of a different judgment from them, as if it were possible, that there should be so great a difference betwixt men of the same Religion, where persons of Learning and Piety should not be engaged on both sides.

Though a man had as good Judgment and Affections as he is capable of, yet still they would be liable to the frailties of human nature. Injuries and hard dealing might exasperate him, hopes and preferment might seduce him; conversation, Dependencies, friends, calling, have a great influence upon the mind, and may unawares insinuate strong prejudices. As for the lawfulness of being engaged on either side, I suppose this case hath been so thoroughly discussed *pro* and *con*, that it is now grown as endless as other controversies, and that men of honest affection may be on both sides, on both parties. So that for matter of opinion, there should be a liberty granted for everyone to go according to his own evidence.

But for matter of outward practice, as levying taxes upon the estates of others, and the like; it cannot be reasonably expected, but that everyone should be forced unto a conformity to that side, under whose power he is. If a man will not willingly contribute, he must look to have it taken from him; if he will be active in speaking or preaching against them, he must think to be silenced and imprisoned, though in other respects he may be of never so much known honesty and credit, yet he cannot reasonably imagine, that others should prefer his private ways or opinions before that which to them seems most conducible to the public welfare. So that such proceedings by either party (supposing the case undecided, and that these proceedings be not made odious by circumstances) are in themselves excusable upon the grounds of common reason and policy: Which if men would equally consider, it would abate much of that bitterness and violence on either side.

3. QUERY

What is the best cure and remedy for our distempers?

CONJECTURE

If mutual jealousy be the disease, then mutual confidence must be the cure, which is in his power only to effect, in whose hands are the hearts of all men.

But for outward applications, the best way of prescribing is to accommodate this difference by some middle way, wherein either party shall remit somewhat of the rigour of those terms on which now they stand. Only here will be the difficulty, how to frame such an accommodation as may by both sides be esteemed safe and honourable. This perhaps would not be so difficult, if it were not for that which seems to make it very easy, I mean that near relation betwixt King and people, whose mutual concernments should be so entwined, that the honour and safety of the one should be so to the other.

But as the case now stands, these two must be considered according to their divided interests: And under this notion the chief enquiry must be (supposing the case undecided) which side may suffer with least prejudice to itself; and to the public welfare.

And here to me it seems for matter of power and safety, that there is less danger in the King's yielding too much, than in the Parliament's; for experience tells us, (as hath been often observed) that what the people once lose, is scarce ever recovered again; whereas what the King parts with, is afterwards by the subtlety of Statists easily regained.

And for matter of honour, it is considerable:

1. That where the fault is least, the dishonour must be least. But now the fault must needs be less in his Majesty, who is but one, and may more easily be deceived by mis-information, than in the Parliament, which being an assembly of so many choice persons, cannot be so liable to mistakes, and consequently are not so excusable for them.

2. It seems necessary, for the public welfare, that the honour of that assembly should be preserved most inviolable, and with the greatest caution, which is so the supreme, that from it there can be no appeal: If this once lose its respect, it will presently lose its power: And then the very constitution of this Kingdom is utterly ruined.

But what then (may some say) shall those persons suffer that are declared Delinquents, for being active on the King's side? I answer, it cannot stand with his Majesty's honour to give them wholly over to punishment, nor with the Parliament's to let them wholly escape. In this difficulty therefore it may perhaps be some satisfaction in the formality of Law, that they should be tried and censured, though they were afterwards pardoned.

If this may seem too hard and unequal, let it be considered, that 'tis no dishonour to yield to necessity, especially such desperate necessity, as that whereunto this Kingdom is now reduced.

4. QUERY

Whether the likely inconveniences of such an Accommodation as may probably be obtained, be not much to be preferred before those great mischiefs, that may accompany victory, or the continuance of these wars?

CONJECTURE

If the Protestant Religion may be secured, the Doctrine ratified, and the Discipline in some things reformed, for satisfaction to tender consciences, as is intended and proffered on both sides; If our Liberties and properties may be ensafed according to those new Acts which have been lately made: then methinks men should rather content themselves with thus much, than hazard all by further contentions.

The chief inconveniences of such an Accommodation would be:

1. *The coming short of so full a Reformation as some men aim at.*

2. *The countenancing of those persons that have been the chief instruments and occasions of these miseries, and the discountenancing of others that have been active for the public good.*

The miseries that may ensue upon a victory (not considering the great charges, difficulty, and uncertainty of it) are briefly these:

Epilogue

1. *The effusion of so much blood as it will cost for the present; besides the mischief of a lasting and desperate division for the future.*

2. *The extremities and violence which further opposition may provoke unto, and each success encourage.*

If it be said, that 'tis better to be cured by a Fever than to die of a Lethargy; I answer, 'tis true where the Fever is a likely cure, and the Lethargy is certain death, but not when both seem equally mortal, or it may be, the cure more dangerous than the disease.

The mischiefs that will befall us upon the continuance of these civil wars will be as many, as pressing, as our own fears can create, or as our enemies can curse us with. It may deprive us of our arts, learning, our liberties and properties, our Laws, and (it may be) our Religion too; so that we shall have nothing left us to be preserved. Many of our neighbours can by their own experience, tell us sad stories of the miseries they have suffered by it already: And if the beginnings of it are so cruel, what may be expected when it shall more generally rage through the whole Kingdom, producing famine as it needs must, when the husbandman dares not sow, or cannot reap, and consequently all pestilential diseases which will follow upon coarse and unwholesome diets?

Both these particulars have been excellently amplified by the Moderator,[1] in whom you may see this Query strongly and fully resolved. Both sides do pretend to a defensive war, it will now appear who have least ground for this pretence by the Averseness to Accommodation; since doubtless if peace and safety be their chief end, it must needs be far better for them to enjoy this with some inconveniences, than to want it with many more.

FINIS

'An Agreement of the People', composed October 1647

This document, constantly invoked by the Levellers, was presented to the Army Council on 28 October 1647 and published early in November. Lilburne, although still in the Tower, may well have had a hand in its composition; it is unlikely that it was written by the five Agitators, as stated. It sets out shortly and clearly the Leveller–Agitator position on the present and future Parliaments, and in particular their determination to limit Parliament's legislative power.

Our text is taken from D. M. Wolfe, ed. *Leveller Manifestoes of the Puritan Revolution* (New York, 1944).

AN
AGREEMENT
OF THE
PEOPLE
FOR

A firme and present Peace, upon
grounds of common-right and freedome;

As it was proposed by the Agents of the five
Regiments of Horse; and since by the generall approbation of the Army, offered to the joynt concurrence of all the free COMMONS of
ENGLAND.

The names of the Regiments which have already appeared for the Case, of *The Case of the Army truly stated*,
and for this present Agreement, *viz.*

	Of Horse			Of Foot
1. *Gen. Regiment.*		1. *Gen. Regiment.*		
2. *Life-Guard.*		2. *Col. Sir Hardrese Wallers Reg.*		
3. *Lieut. Gen. Regiment.*		3. *Col. Lamberts Reg.*		
4. *Com. Gen. Regiment.*		4. *Col. Rainboroughs Regiment.*		
5. *Col. Whaleyes Reg.*		5. *Col. Overtons Reg.*		
6. *Col. Riches Reg.*		6. *Col. Lilburns Reg.*		
7. *Col. Fleetwoods Reg.*		7. *Col. Backsters Reg.*		
8. *Col. Harrisons Reg.*				
9. *Col. Twisldens Reg.*				

Printed *Anno. Dom.* 1647.

Having by our late labours and hazards made it appeare to the world at how high a rate wee value our just freedome, and God having so far owned our cause, as to deliver the Enemies thereof into our hands: We do now hold our selves bound in mutual duty to each other, to take the best care we can for the future, to avoid both the danger of returning into a slavish condition, and the chargable remedy of another war: for as it cannot be imagined that so many of our Country-men would have opposed us in this quarrel, if they had understood their owne good; so may we safely promise to our selves, that when our Common Rights and liberties shall be cleared, their endeavours will be disappointed, that seek to make themselves our Masters: since therefore our former oppressions, and scarce yet ended troubles have beene occasioned, either by want of frequent Nationall meetings in Councell, or by rendring those meetings ineffectuall; We are fully agreed and resolved, to provide that hereafter our Representatives be neither left to an uncertainty for the time, nor made uselesse to the ends for which they are intended: In order whereunto we declare,

I

That the People of England being at this day very unequally distributed by Counties, Cities, & Burroughs, for the election of their Deputies in Parliament, ought to be more indifferently proportioned, according to the number of the Inhabitants: the circumstances whereof, for number, place, and manner, are to be set down before the end of this present Parliament.

II

That to prevent the many inconveniences apparently arising from the long continuance of the same persons in authority, this present Parliament be dissolved upon the last day of September, which shall be in the year of our Lord, 1648.

III

That the People do of course chuse themselves a Parliament once in two yeares, viz. upon the first Thursday in every 2d. March, after the manner as shall be prescribed before the end of this Parliament, to begin to sit upon the first Thursday in Aprill following at Westminster, or such other place as shall bee appointed from time to time by the preceding Representatives; and to continue till the last day of September, then next ensuing, and no longer.

IV

That the power of this, and all future Representatives of this Nation, is inferiour only to theirs who chuse them, and doth extend, without the consent or concurrence of any other person or persons; to the enacting, altering, and repealing of Lawes; to the erecting and abolishing of Offices and Courts; to the appointing, removing, and calling to account Magistrates, and Officers of all degrees; to the making War and peace, to the treating with forraign States: And generally, to whatsoever is not expresly, or implyedly reserved by the represented to themselves.

Which are as followeth,

1. That matters of Religion, and the wayes of Gods Worship, are not at all intrusted by us to any humane power, because therein wee cannot remit or exceed a tittle of what our Consciences dictate to be the mind of God, without wilfull sinne: neverthelesse the publike way of instructing the Nation (so it be not compulsive) is referred to their discretion.

2. That the matter of impresting and constraining any of us to serve in the warres, is against our freedome; and therefore we do not allow it in our Representatives; the rather, because money (the

sinews of war) being alwayes at their disposall, they can never want numbers of men, apt enough to engage in any just cause.

3. That after the dissolution of this present Parliament, no person be at any time questioned for anything said or done, in reference to the late publike differences, otherwise then in execution of the Judgments of the present Representatives, or House of Commons.

4. That in all Laws made, or to be made, every person may be bound alike, and that no Tenure, Estate, Charter, Degree, Birth, or place, do confer any exemption from the ordinary Course of Legall proceedings, whereunto others are subjected.

5. That as the Laws ought to be equall, so they must be good, and not evidently destructive to the safety and well-being of the people.

These things we declare to be our native Rights, and therefore are agreed and resolved to maintain them with our utmost possibilities, against all opposition whatsoever, being compelled thereunto, not only by the examples of our Ancestors, whose bloud was often spent in vain for the recovery of their Freedomes, suffering themselves, through fraudulent accommodations, to be still deluded of the fruit of their Victories, but also by our own wofull experience, who having long expected, & dearly earned the establishment of these certain rules of Government are yet made to depend for the settlement of our Peace and Freedome, upon him that intended our bondage, and brought a cruell Warre upon us.

For the noble and highly honoured the Free-born People of ENGLAND, in their respective Counties and Divisions, these.

Deare Country-men, and fellow-Commoners,

For your sakes, our friends, estates and lives, have not been deare to us; for your safety and freedom we have cheerfully indured hard Labours and run most desperate hazards, and in comparison to your peace and freedome we neigher doe nor ever shall value our dearest bloud and wee professe, our bowells are and have been troubled, and our hearts pained within us, in seeing & considering that you have been so long bereaved of these fruites and ends of all our labours and hazards, wee cannot but sympathize with you in your miseries and oppressions. It's greife and vexation of heart to us; to receive your meate or moneyes, whilest you have no advantage, nor yet the foundations of your peace and freedom surely layed: and therefore upon most serious considerations, that your principall right most essentiall to your well-being is the clearnes, certaintie, sufficiencie and freedom of your power in your representatives in Parliament, and considering that the original of most of your oppressions & miseries hath been either from the obscuritie and doubtfulnes of the power you have committed to your representatives in your elections, or from the want of courage in those whom you have betrusted to claime and exercise their power, which might probably proceed from their uncertaintie of your assistance and maintenance of their power, and minding that for this right of yours and ours wee engaged our lives; for the King raised the warre against you and your Parliament, upon this ground, that hee would not suffer your representatives to provide for your peace safetie and freedom that were then in danger, by disposing of the *Militia* and otherwise, according to their trust; and for the maintenance and defense of that power and right of yours, wee hazarded all that was deare to us, and God hath borne witnesse to the justice of our Cause. And further minding that the only effectual meanes to settle a just and lasting peace, to obtaine remedie for all your greivances, & to prevent future oppressions, is the making clear & secure the power that you betrust to your representatives in Parliament, that they may know their trust, in the faithfull execution whereof you wil assist them. Upon all these grounds, we propound your joyning with us in the agreement herewith sent unto you; that by vertue thereof, we may have Parliaments certainly cal'd and have the time of their sitting & ending certain & their power or trust cleare and unquestionable, that hereafter they may remove your burdens, & secure your rights, without oppositions or obstructions, & that the foundations of your peace may be so free from uncertainty, that there may be no grounds for future quarrels, or contentions to occasion warre and bloud-shed; & wee desire you would consider, that as these things wherein we offer to agree with you, are the fruites & ends of the Victories which God hath given us: so the settlement of these are the most absolute meanes to preserve you & your Posterity, from slavery, oppression, distraction, & trouble; by this, those whom your selves shall chuse, shall have power to restore you to, and secur you in, all your rights; & they shall be in a capacity to tast of subjection, as well as rule, & so shall be equally concerned with your selves, in all they do. For they must equally suffer with you under any common burdens, & partake with you in any freedoms; & by this they shal be disinabled to defraud or wrong you, when the lawes shall bind all alike, without priviledge or exemption; & by this your Consciences shall be free from tyrannie & oppression, & those occasions of endlesse strifes & bloudy warres, shall be perfectly removed: without controversie by your joyning with us in this Agreement, all your particular & common grievances will be redressed forthwith without delay; the Parliament must then make your reliefe and common good their only study.

Now because we are earnestly desirous of the peace and good of all our Country-men, even of those that have opposed us, and would to our utmost possibility provide for perfect peace and freedome, & prevent all suites, debates, & contentions that may happen amongst you, in relation to the late war: we have therefore inserted it into this Agreement, that no person shall be questionable for any thing done, in relation to the late publike differences, after the dissolution of this present Parliament, further then in execution of their judgment; that thereby all may be secure from all sufferings for what they have done, & not liable hereafter to be troubled or punished by the judgment of another Parliament, which may be to their ruine, unlesse this Agreement be joyned in, whereby any acts of indempnity or oblivion shalbe made unalterable, and you and your posterities be secure.

But if any shall enquire why we should desire to joyn in an Agreement with the people, to declare these to be our native Rights, & not rather petition to the Parliament for them; the reason is evident: No Act of Parliament is or can be unalterable, and so cannot be sufficient security to save you or us harmlesse, from what another Parliament may determine, if it should be corrupted; and besides Parliaments are to receive the extent of their power, and trust from those that betrust them; and therefore the people are to declare what their power and trust is, which is the intent of this Agreement; and its to be observed, that though there hath formerly been many Acts of Parliament, for the calling of Parliaments every yeare, yet you have been deprived of them, and inslaved through want of them; and therefore both necessity for your security in these freedomes, that are essentiall to your well-being, and wofull experience of the manifold miseries and distractions that have been lengthened out since the war ended, through want of such a settlement, requires this Agreement and when you and we shall be joyned together therein, we shall readily joyn with you, to petition the Parliament, as they are our fellow Commoners equally concerned, to joyn with us.

And if any shall inquire, Why we undertake to offer this Agreement, we must professe, we are sensible that you have been so often deceived with Declarations and Remonstrances, and fed with vain hopes that you have sufficient reason to abandon all confidence in any persons whatsoever, from whom you have no other security of their intending your freedome, then bare Declaration: And therefore, as our consciences witnesse, that in simplicity and integrity of heart, we have proposed lately in the Case of the

An Agreement of the People

Army stated, your freedome and deliverance from slavery, oppression, and all burdens: so we desire to give you satisfying assurance thereof by this Agreement wherby the foundations of your freedomes provided in the Case, &c. shall be setled unalterable, & we shall as faithfully proceed to, and all other most vigorus actings for your good that God shall direct and enable us unto; And though the malice of our enemies, and such as they delude, would blast us by scandalls, aspersing us with designes of Anarchy, and community; yet we hope the righteous God will not onely by this our present desire of setling an equall just Government, but also by directing us unto all righteous undertakings, simply for publike good, make our uprightnesse and faithfulnesse to the interest of all our Countreymen, shine forth so clearly, that malice it selfe shall be silenced, and confounded. We question not, but the longing expectation of a firme peace, will incite you to the most speedy joyning in this Agreement: in the prosecution whereof, or of any thing that you shall desire for publike good; you may be confident, you shall never want the assistance of

Your most faithfull fellow-Commoners, now in Armes for your service.

Edmond Bear	Lieut. Gen. Regiment.
Robert Everard	
George Garret	Com. Gen. Regiment.
Thomas Beverley	
William Pryor	Col. Fleetwoods Regiment.
William Bryan	
Matthew Weale	Col. Whalies Regiment.
William Russell	
John Dover	Col. Riches Regiment.
William Hudson.	

Agents coming from other Regiments unto us, have subscribed the Agreement to be proposed to their respective Regiments, and you. For Our much honoured, and truly worthy Fellow-Commoners, and Souldiers, the Officers and Souldiers under Command of His Excellencie Sir THOMAS FAIRFAX.

Gentlemen and Fellow Souldiers;

The deepe sense of many dangers and mischiefes that may befall you in relation to the late War, whensoever this Parliament shall end, unlesse sufficient prevention be now provided, hath constrained Us to study the most absolute & certain means for your security; and upon most serious considerations, we judge that no Act of Indempnity can sufficiently provide for your quiet, ease, and safety; because, as it hath formerly been, a corrupt Party (chosen into the next Parliament by your Enemies meanes) may possibly surprize the house, and make any Act of Indemnity null, seeing they cannot faile of the Kings Assistance and concurrence, in any such actings against you, that conquered him.

And by the same meanes, your freedome from impressing also, may in a short time be taken from you, though for the present, it should be granted; wee apprehend no other security, by which you shall be saved harmlesse, for what you have done in the late warre, then a mutuall Agreement between the people & you, that no person shall be questioned by any Authority whatsoever, for any thing done in relation to the late publike differences, after the dissolution of the present house of Commons, further then in execution of their judgment; and that your native freedome from constraint to serve in warre, whether domestick or forraign, shall never be subject to the power of *Parliaments*, or any other; and for this end, we propound the Agreement that we herewith send to you, to be forthwith subscribed.

And because we are confident, that in judgment and Conscience, ye hazarded your lives for the settlement of such a just and equall Government, that you and your posterities, and all the free borne people of this Nation might enjoy justice & freedome, and that you are really sensible that the distractions, oppressions, and miseries of the Nation, and your want of your Arreares, do proceed from the want of the establishment, both of such certain rules of just Government, and foundations of peace, as are the price of bloud, and the expected fruites of all the peoples cost: Therefore in this Agreement wee have inserted the certaine Rules of equall Government, under which the Nation may enjoy all its Rights and Freedomes securely; And as we doubt not but your love to the freedome and lasting peace of the yet distracted Country will cause you to joyn together in this Agreement.

So we question not: but every true English man that loves the peace and freedome of England will concurre with us; and then your Arrears and constant pay (while you continue in Armes) will certainly be brought in out of the abundant love of the people to you, and then shall the mouthes of those be stopped, that scandalize you and us, as endeavouring Anarchy, or to rule by the sword; & then will so firm an union be made between the people and you, that neither any homebred or forraigne Enemies will dare to disturbe our happy peace. We shall adde no more but this; that the knowledge of your union in laying this foundation of peace, this Agreement, is much longed for, by

Yours, and the Peoples most faithful Servants.

Postscript.

GENTLEMEN.

We desire you may understand the reason of our extracting some principles of common freedome out of those many things proposed to you in the Case truly stated, and drawing them up into the forme of an Agreement. Its chiefly because for these things wee first ingaged gainst the King, He would not permit the peoples Representatives to provide for the Nations safety, by disposing of the Militia, and otherwayes, according to their Trust, but raised a Warre against them, and we ingaged for the defence of that power, and right of the people, in their Representatives. Therefore these things in the Agreement, the people are to claime as their native right, and price of their bloud, which you are obliged absolutely to procure for them.

And these being the foundations of freedom, its necessary, that they should be setled unalterably, which can be by no meanes, but this Agreement with the people.

And we cannot but mind you, that the ease of the people in all their Grievances, depends upon the setling those principles or rules of equal Government for a free people, & were but this Agreement established, doubtlesse all the Grievances of the Army and people would be redressed immediately, and all things propounded in your Case truly stated to be insisted on, would be forthwith granted.

Then should the House of Commons have power to helpe the oppressed people, which they are now bereaved of by the chiefe Oppressors, and then they shall be equally concerned with you and all the people, in the settlement of the most perfect freedome: for they shall equally suffer with you under any Burdens, or partake in any Freedome. We shall onely adde, that the summe of all the Agreement which we herewith offer to you, is but in order to the fulfilling of our Declaration of June the 14. wherein we promised to the people, that we would with our lives vindicate and cleare their right and power in their Parliaments.

Edmond Bear Robert Everard	Lieut. Gen. Reg.
George Garret Thomas Beverley	Com. Gen. Reg.
William Pryor William Bryan	Col. Fleetwood Reg.
Matthew Weale William Russell	Col. Whaley Reg.
John Dover William Hudson	Col. Rich Reg.

Agents coming from other Regiments unto us, have subscribed the Agreement, to be proposed to their respective Regiments and you.

Notes

INTRODUCTION

1 Clarendon used it in this sense, as may be seen from the fact that he applied it to the Restoration at 1660 (*The History of the Rebellion and Civil Wars in England*, ed. W. D. Macray (6 vols., Oxford, 1888), IV, p. 467). Colonel Nathaniel Rich used the word in the same sense in the Army Debates: 'I remember there were many workings and revolutions, as we have heard, in the Roman Senate; and there was never a confusion that did appear (and that indeed *was* come to) till the state came to know this kind of distribution of election. That is how the people's voices were bought and sold' (A. S. P. Woodhouse, ed., *Puritanism and Liberty, Being the Army Debates (1647–49)* from the *Clarke Manuscripts* (London, 1938), p. 64).

2 See Keith Thomas, 'The Levellers and the Franchise' in G. E. Aylmer, ed., *The Interregnum: The Quest for a Settlement, 1646–60* (London, 1972), pp. 57–78.

3 S. R. Gardiner, *History of the Great Civil War* (London, 1893), III, p. 379.

4 Conrad Russell, ed., *The Origins of the English Civil War* (London, 1973), p. 7.

5 J. Rushworth, *Historical Collections of Private Passages of State* (8 vols., London, 1682–92), III, pt i, p. 86.

6 Clarendon, *History of the Rebellion*, ed. Macray, I, p. 93. Bryan Manning, *The English People and the English Revolution 1640–1649* (London, 1976).

7 J. H. Hexter, *The Reign of King Pym* (Cambridge, Mass., 1941), p. 7.

8 Quoted *ibid.*, p. 8.

9 See J. S. Morrill, ed., *The Revolt of the Provinces: Conservatives and Radicals in the English Civil War, 1630–1650* (London, 1976); and *Queres and Conjectures*, pp. 230–6, below.

10 Conrad Russell, *The Crisis of Parliaments: English History 1509–1660* (Oxford, 1971), p. 354.

11 Quoted in Aylmer, ed., *The Interregnum*, p. 2.

12 Opinion has veered as to the nature and extent of the Leveller franchise; it is a subtle matter probably not yet settled. For a persuasive recent view see Keith Thomas, 'The Levellers and the Franchise' in Aylmer, ed., *The Interregnum*, pp. 57–78.

13 We are indebted to Dr Richard Tuck for advice on Henry Parker.

14 Pauline Gregg, *Free-born John. A Biography of John Lilburne* (London, 1961), pp. 52–69.

15 Gardiner, *History of the Great Civil War*, IV, p. 296.

16 *Ibid.*, p. 317.

17 Quoted in Blair Worden, *The Rump Parliament, 1648–1653* (Cambridge, 1974), p. 2.

18 Cf. some words of Christopher Hill: 'Perhaps the radicals simply did not have long enough to propagate their democratic ideas, so revolutionary in their novelty ... To break the centuries-old crust of custom would have needed longer' (*Some Intellectual Consequences of the English Revolution* (London, 1980), p. 9). It may be thought that the word 'revolution' begins to change its dominant meaning as it becomes associated with notions of fulfilment and progress. Cf.

Tom Paine: 'The name of a Revolution is diminutive of its character [i.e. the exordium to the French Declaration of Rights] and it rises into a REGENERATION OF MAN'; and 'It appears to general observation, that revolutions create genius and talents; but those events do no more than bring them forward. There is existing in man a mass of talent lying in a dormant state' (*The Rights of Man* (1791–2); introduction by Arthur Selden (London, 1915; reprint of 1969), pp. 99, 172).

19 See Quentin Skinner, 'Conquest and Consent: Thomas Hobbes and the engagement controversy' in Aylmer, ed., *The Interregnum*, pp. 79–98.

20 Conrad Russell, *Crisis of Parliaments*, p. 387.

21 *Ibid.*, p. 395.

22 Godfrey Davies, *The Restoration of Charles II, 1658–1660* (Oxford, 1955), p. 333.

23 Bevil Higgons, *A Short View of English History* (London, 1726; 3rd edn, 1728), p. 252.

24 See W. K. Jordan, *Men of Substance* (Chicago, 1942), pp. 73, 85–6.

25 See Lucy Hutchinson, *Memoirs of the Life of Colonel Hutchinson*, ed. J. Sutherland (London, 1973), p. 62.

26 See Clarendon, *History of the Rebellion,* ed. Macray, v, p. 264.

27 See A. S. P. Woodhouse, ed., *Puritanism and Liberty*, p. 13.

28 See M. A. Gibb, *John Lilburne, the Leveller* (London, 1947), p. 259.

29 See Gerrard Winstanley, *The Law of Freedom and Other Writings*, ed. Christopher Hill (London, 1973), p. 10.

30 *A Watch-word to the City of London and the Armie*, 1649 in *The Works of Gerrard Winstanley*, ed. G. H. Sabine (Ithaca, New York, 1941), p. 315.

31 See the new evidence given by James Alsop, 'Gerrard Winstanley's Later Life', *Past and Present* (Feb. 1979), 73–81.

32 See *The Political Works of James Harrington*, ed. J. G. A. Pocock (Cambridge, 1977), p. 5.

33 J. P. Kenyon, *The Stuart Constitution, 1603–1688* (Cambridge, 1966), p. 7.

34 J. N. Figgis, *Political Thought from Gerson to Grotius, 1414–1625* (New York, 1960), p. 81; Quentin Skinner, *The Foundations of Modern Political Thought* (2 vols., Cambridge, 1978), II, p. 113.

35 Romans, XIII, 1–2. Skinner, *Foundations*, II, pp. 15–19.

36 *Ibid.*, p. 300. *The six bookes of a Commonweale . . . Written by J. Bodin . . . done into English, by Richard Knolles* was published in 1606.

37 Bodin fully recognised the *de jure* status of Augustus's principate as a republic, and also that many of the emperors who succeeded Augustus ruled tyrannously. Nevertheless he concludes his discussion of the Triumvirate: 'Whereafter ensued the sure state of the empire, established under one man's gouernment' (*The six bookes of a Commonweale . . .*, vol. II, pt ii, p. 199).

38 *The Political Works of James I*, ed. C. H. McIlwain (Cambridge, Mass., 1918), pp. 53–5, 61.

39 *Ibid.*, p. 68.

40 Cf. Parker's *Observations*, pp. 36–7, 45–6, below.

41 M. A. Judson, *A Crisis of the Constitution . . . 1603–1645* (New Brunswick, New Jersey, 1949), p. 212.

42 *Ibid.*, pp. 81–2.

43 Peter Laslett, ed., *Patriarcha and Other Political Works of Sir Robert Filmer* (Oxford, 1949), pp. 13, 57.

44 *Ibid.*, pp. 81–2.

45 Skinner, *Foundations*, II, p. 199.

46 Laslett, ed., *Filmer*, p. 53.
47 Skinner, *Foundations*, II, pp. 338–47.
48 *Ibid.*, pp. 199–200.
49 *Ibid.*, p. 348.
50 'An Horatian Ode on Cromwel's Return from Ireland', lines 35–6, *The Poems and Letters of Andrew Marvell*, ed. H. M. Margoliouth (2 vols, Oxford, 1927), I, p. 88.
51 The subject of Joan Webber's study of seventeenth-century prose-style, *The Eloquent 'I'* (Madison, Wisconsin, 1968).
52 *Ibid.*, pp. 55–79.
53 See Margot Heinemann, *Puritanism and Theatre* (Cambridge, 1980), pp. 237–52.
54 Parker, *The True Grounds of Ecclesiasticall Regiment* (London, 1641), p. 30.

1. HENRY PARKER, 'OBSERVATIONS UPON SOME OF HIS MAJESTIES LATE ANSWERS AND EXPRESSES', 1642

1 Generally true of the King's Answers, but not invariably: cf. 'that preeminence and Authority, which God, the Law, the custom and consent of this Nation, had placed in Us' (*His Majesties Declaration . . . Published . . . at York, 16 June 1642*, p. 2). Behind Charles's affirmation of 'Our Regall Authoritie (which God hath intrusted Us with for the good of Our People)' (*His Majesties Answer to the nineteen Propositions*, p. 12) lies James I's statement that 'Kings are not onely Gods Lieutenants upon earth, and sit upon Gods throne, but even by God himselfe they are called Gods' (McIlwain, ed., *The Political Works of James I*, p. 307); Luther's Pauline argument that secular powers are ordained of God; and Jean Bodin's influential theories of royal absolutism in his *Six Livres de la République* (1576).
2 A view propounded by both Calvinists and Jesuits in the Renaissance, but taking its origin from William of Occam, Jacques Almain, and the fourteenth-century Conciliar movement (see Skinner, *Foundations*, II, pp. 123–7).
3 The movement towards a centralised absolute monarchy had gone much further in France than anything Charles I, Strafford or Laud had achieved in England.
4 As Ixion, attempting to embrace Juno, whom Jupiter had turned into a cloud: Pindar, *Pythian*, II.
5 A maxim disputed by Parker's opponents, as Selden: 'This does not hold. For if I have 1000l. per annum, and give it to you, and leave myself never a penny, I made you; but when you have my land you are greater than I . . . The answer to all these doubts is, Have you agreed so? If you have, then it must remain until you have altered it.' (Quoted in Tuck, *Natural Rights Theories*, p. 100.)
6 The first English translation of Machiavelli's *The Prince, Nicholas Machiavel's Prince. Translated . . . into English by E. D. [Edward Dacres] With Some Animadversions Noting and Taxing His Errors*, had been published in 1640. Parker may have had Chapter 7 particularly in mind, but he is more concerned to associate royalist views with Machiavelli than to cite Machiavelli accurately.
7 Of Duke Cesare Borgia, bastard son of Pope Alexander VI, Machiavelli wrote: 'I could not well blame him, but rather . . . set him as a pattern to be followed by all those who by fortune and by others armes have been exalted to an Empire. For he being of great courage, and having lofty designes, could not carry himself otherwise.' (*The Prince*, translated by Edward Dacres, Ch. 7.)
8 Strafford would be the great recent example.
9 '. . . the great businesse of the Oath, which is to protect them [i.e. other men]' (*His Majesties Answer, to a printed Book*, p. 15).

10 Among the concessions made by the King to the Long Parliament prior to the outbreak of the Civil War were: the abolition of Ship Money; of the royal right to levy customs without Parliamentary consent; of Arminianist measures in the Church (see Introduction, p. 4); and of the High Commission and the Star Chamber; and an agreement to hold Triennial Parliaments.

11 Charles had agreed to the exclusion of bishops from the House of Lords, after some delay and when, perhaps, he was only playing for time. *His Majesties Answer to the nineteen Propositions* noted that the Popish Lords had withdrawn voluntarily from the House, and argued that they should not be deprived of their votes by law, but not admitted, and allowed to have their votes cast for them by proxy.

12 To this affirmation Selden responded: 'There is not anything in this world more abused than this sentence, *Salus populi suprema lex esto*, for we apply it, as if we ought to forsake the known law, when it may be for the most advantage of the people, when it means no such thing. For first, 'tis not *salus populi suprema lex est*, but *esto* . . . that is, in all the laws you make, have a special eye to the good of the people' (Tuck, *Natural Rights Theories*, p. 99).

13 The argument that the power and right of kings derived from original conquest was well-known and respectable: in *The Trew Law of Free Monarchies* (1598) James I had advanced it as a specific historical refutation of the view that the Crown of Scotland derived authority from any contract with the people.

14 The belief that the Norman Conquest suppressed earlier freedoms of the English people. Much referred to in controversies of the period, it was propounded in strong form by Cowling in the Army Debates: 'Since the Conquest the greatest part of the kingdom was in vassalage' (Woodhouse, ed. *Puritanism and Liberty*, p. 53). Milton gives the argument a different turn in *The Tenure of Kings and Magistrates* (see p. 122, below).

15 King Rehoboam succeeded Solomon (as Charles I succeeded James I, sometimes praised as the British Solomon). By alienating the northern tribes and introducing heathen religious practices, he exposed his kingdom to invasion, and must have seemed a compelling parallel to Charles I in 1642.

16 The Magna Carta, granted under King John.

17 The Coronation Oath was sometimes regarded as a contract between King and people. In *A Remonstrance, Or the Declaration of the Lords and Commons . . . 26 May 1642* Parliament spoke of 'the Oath that is or ought to be taken by the Kings of this Realm at their CORONATION . . . to confirm by their Royall assent such good Lawes as their people shall choose' (p. 6) and quoted: '. . . justas leges & consuetudines . . . quas vulgus eligerit' (p. 9). *His Majesties Answer, to a printed Book, intituled, A Remonstrance . . .* protested: 'We cannot possibly imagine, The Assertion that Declaration makes, can be deduced from the Words, or the Matter of that Oath; For, unless they have a power of declaring Latine, as well as Law, sure *Eligerit* signifieth, *Hath chosen*, as well as *Will chuse*; and that it signifieth so here . . . is evident by the Reference it hath to Customes . . .' (pp. 14–15).

18 Parker here sees King and Parliament as complementary.

19 To this statement the authors of *An Answer to a Printed Book* (Nov. 1642) – according to George Thomason, Falkland, Chillingworth and Digges – responded by saying: 'He cannot meane any people contracting to their owne certain ruine; there never was Government guilty of this madnesse: therefore hee must understand a contract to a possible ruine; as for example, an agreement patiently to submit themselves to the ordinary tryall of Law, and to suffer, if it should so fall out, though under an undeserved Sentence. In this case, he that doth not make resistance, and preferre his preservation to his contract, is

pronounced *Felo de se*; and a rebell to nature. Unhappy thiefe who for felony is condemned to be hanged, and will be guilty of another felony in being hanged! . . . The Observor takes no notice, that it is in our power to part with this right of self-defence, yet doe nothing contrary to nature, if reason tells us, wee shall thereby obtaine a more excellent good, the benefit of Peace and Society' (quoted in Tuck, *Natural Right Theories*, p. 104).

20 *His Majesties Answer, to a printed Book* stated that Parliament was called 'to be our Councellours, not commanders' (p. 10).

21 From Edward I's summons to his people to defend the State – a point Parker has discussed in the first section here omitted: he argued that not only the advice but the consent of the people was sought.

22 *His Majesties Answer* (York, 17 May 1642) declared, with regard to the Militia Bill which the King had refused to sign, 'that there is no legall power in either, or both houses, upon any pretence whatsoever, without Our consent' (pp. 18–19).

23 Cf. for example, *The Prince*, Ch. 3.

24 When the Long Parliament first assembled at Westminster.

25 The King withdrew from London at the end of 1641, and from Windsor to the North in March 1642. He could claim that Parliament had grown arbitrary if not illegal (see B. H. G. Wormald, *Clarendon: Politics, History and Religion*, pp. 97–9). On 20 June 1642, after Parliament had covenanted to raise forces against him, Charles declared it to be no longer free. Parker reverts to the significance of the King's withdrawal, at the conclusion of the pamphlet, in a tone of high irony.

26 Denzil Holles (1599–1680), M.P. and one of the five members the King had sought to arrest in 1641. He was a prominent statesman of this and the Restoration period. Parker refers to his recent marriage, 12 March 1642, to the twice-widowed Jane Shirley, daughter and co-heir of Sir John Shirley of Isfield, Sussex.

27 Thomas Wentworth, First Earl of Strafford, the King's Lieutenant in the North and in Ireland, one of the most distinguished servants of the Crown, was attainted by Parliament on the charge that he had attempted to subvert the laws, and beheaded on 12 May 1641. The signing of the Bill by the King, after a period of agonising indecision, was an act that he later came to regard as a betrayal and a sin.

28 Parker's argument here may be thought disingenuous. The King was indeed not 'sole Judge', but Strafford was not legally condemned to death until the King had signed the Bill.

29 The magazine and port of Hull were long recognised as of strategic importance in the event of war. The King especially needed an east-coast port to receive assistance from the continent. After the King's withdrawal from London Parliament sent Sir John Hotham to take control of Hull on its behalf. His orders were not to deliver it up save on the King's authority *as signified* by Parliament. Hotham's refusal to admit the King (who had not yet set up his standard) brought civil war much closer.

30 The heart of Parker's contractual theory of government, as Filmer recognised when he excerpted a long passage beginning with these words in his treatise, *The Anarchy of a Limited or Mixed Monarchy* (1648). Parker's case may be thought vulnerable in so far as it is taken to be historical: Filmer's challenge to him 'to name but one kingdom that hath either now or heretofore found out this art or peacable order [by which the people limit their king by contract]' is part of his own case that patriarchal government stretched back to the creation of man (Peter Laslett, ed., *Filmer*, p. 309). At the same time it should be noted that Parker

holds man to be innately social before the Fall: fallen man required magistracy to uphold society.

31 James I's answer was: God alone.

32 The Ephors in Sparta were powerful magistrates, five in number and annual in office, said to have been created by Lycurgus in order to check and restrain the authority of the kings. They safeguarded the liberty of the people, convened and dissolved the assemblies, controlled public money, and were arbiters of peace and war. The Ephors imprisoned King Agis for unconstitutional behaviour. Tribunes were magistrates at Rome established after a quarrel between the Senate and the people. Their office was annual, their number at first two, then five, and finally ten. Their power grew steadily, and they not only safeguarded the liberties of the people, but could summon assemblies, propose laws, stop consultations of the Senate and, if in agreement with one another, veto its legislation. They could imprison a Consul if he pursued measures hostile to the peace of Rome. Sulla attempted to check their power, but it was Augustus who finally did so, by himself becoming *tribunitia potestate donatus*. *Curatores:* guardians. The significance of these classical offices for Parker was that they seemed to afford a precedent for inferior magistrates limiting and resisting kings, and thus linked with the constitutional defence of resistance propounded by the Lutherans (see Skinner, *Foundations,* II, pp. 230–5; and Introduction, p. 26). Filmer was at pains to argue that Parker had mistaken the historical character of the Ephors and Tribunes.

33 The passage excerpted by Filmer ended here.

34 There was bitter disputation between King and Parliament as to the legality of their different methods of raising armies.

35 Alluding to the patriarchalist view that the King had authority over his subjects analogous to that of a father over his family.

36 The Turkish Emperor who was absolute.

37 The co-ordinated rebellion in Ireland which, after the fall of Strafford, broke out at the end of 1641. Sir Phelim O'Neil boasted that he was no rebel but the faithful servant of the King against his enemies in England and Scotland. To support his claim he produced a forged commission purporting to bear the King's great seal.

38 See p. 249, note 1, above.

39 Cf. 'Our Power of Treaties . . . not oneley as a King but as a father' (*His Majesties Answer to the nineteen Propositions*, p. 43). In *The Trew Law of Free Monarchies* James I said that kings were called gods by God himself, and in his 1603 Speech to Parliament he affirmed: 'I am the Husband, and the whole Isle is my lawful Wife; I am the Head, and it is my Body; I am the Shepherd, and it is my flocke' (McIlwain, ed., *The Political Works of James I*, p. 272).

40 Cf. Aristotle, *Politics*, v, iii; Shakespeare, *Coriolanus*, I, i.

41 From *His Majesties Answer to the nineteen Propositions*, pp. 35, 39 (three short passages run together). While in its constitutional analysis this *Answer* was so concessive to the Parliamentary ultimatum that even the moderate Clarendon felt it gave too much away, its tone was one of bitter resentment and sometimes defiance: on p. 35 the King declared his resolution 'not to make Our Self of a King of *England* a Duke of *Venice*, and this of a Kingdom a Republique'.

42 Parker turns the conciliatory analysis of the *Answer to the nineteen Propositions* to his own purpose. It is notable that he finds these notions of a balanced constitution acceptable, and that J. G. A. Pocock should regard them as the language of republicanism (Pocock, ed. *The Political Works of James Harrington*, pp. 19–22).

43 The *Answer to the nineteen Propositions*, p. 38.

44 As France and Spain had developed into modern absolute monarchies, the French Estates General and the Spanish Cortes had sunk into subordinate positions.

45 When the Long Parliament assembled.

46 That Parliament had connived at the riots in Westminster which took place shortly before the King withdrew from his capital was one of the most bitterly repeated charges in the royal Answers. They complained of 'the barbarous and seditious Tumults at *Westminster* and *Whitehall,* which were indeed so full of scandall to Our Government, and danger to Our Person' (*His Majesties Answer to a Book,* pp. 18–19).

47 *His Majesties Answer, to a printed Book,* p. 28.

48 The five members of the Commons, Pym, Hampden, Hazelrig, Holles and Strode whom the King had attempted to arrest on 3 Jan. 1642, but who had escaped and taken refuge in the City.

49 An allusion chiefly to 1533 when Anabaptists led by John Matthys and John Beukels ousted the Lutheran leadership of the imperal city of Münster and assumed control. Under siege from the Prince Bishop, Matthys ordered the sharing of all goods. On the death of Matthys, Beukels took over, added the sharing of wives to that of property, and had himself crowned king of righteousness. In 1534 the city was betrayed and the inhabitants slaughtered. Skinner comments that 'the spectres of communism and revolution had been terrifyingly raised' (*Foundations,* II, p. 81). Thus *His Majesties Answer, to a printed Book* alleged that Parliament 'would revive that Tragedie which Mr. *Hooker* relates of the Anabaptists in *Germany,* who talking of nothing but Faith, and of the true Fear of God . . . [ended by enriching themselves] with all kinds of spoil and pillage' (pp. 7–8).

50 Cited in *His Majesties Answer, to a printed Book,* p. 5. The Thirty Tyrants ruled Athens after her defeat in the Peloponnesian War until she recovered her liberty.

51 Here in a nutshell is Parker's statement of Parliamentary sovereignty. By comparison his repeated statements that he wishes to save the monarchy from evil councillors and itself are peripheral if prudent aspects of his argument.

52 Hooker, *Of The Laws of Ecclesiastical Polity,* Preface, VIII, vii–xii, from the last section of which the royal Answer had quoted.

53 The Carthaginian general who had such extraordinary success against Rome in the Second Punic War.

54 Scipio Africanus, the Roman general who finally beat Hannibal, at the Battle of Zama.

55 Alexander III, the Great, of Macedon, conqueror of most of the near east, of Persia and part of India. His death was premature, but it was rumour alone which ascribed it to poison.

56 King of Epirus, a restless and ambitious general and ruler who modelled himself on Alexander the Great and died in battle.

57 As King of Scots Charles I had singularly failed to impose his will on Estates (Parliament) and Kirk Assembly.

58 The Emperor Antoninus Pius, long considered a model of a virtuous prince, fought no aggressive wars during his long reign and was noted for his civility and benevolence.

59 The King spoke of 'such entrances made upon a Reall War against Us, upon pretence of an imaginarie war against you' (*His Majesties Answer to the nineteen Propositions,* p. 27).

60 The Turkish Emperor.

61 The royal veto, one of the great controversial issues in the Army Debates.

62 In *His Majesties Answer, to a printed Book*, p. 10, the King had argued that Parliament was called 'to be our Councellours, not Commanders . . . not in all things, but in some things, *De quibusdam arduis, &c.*'.

2. EXTRACTS FROM THE ARMY DEBATES, OCTOBER 1647

1 A prayer-meeting had just been arranged for the next day, so that God's guidance might be sought before the main attempt to settle the outstanding issues. Immediately, it seems, some suspected a political manoeuvre.

2 John Wildman (1623–93), a civilian Leveller brought to the Council by the Agitators to assist them in presenting their case. He seems to have had legal training and certainly skill in debate. He made a fortune by speculating in the confiscated estates of Royalists. He remained a Republican all his life.

3 *The Case of the Army truly stated*, signed by the ten Agitators of the five regiments on 9 Oct. 1647, published on the 15th and presented to General Fairfax for consideration by the Army Council on 18 Oct. 1647, was the work of several hands. Its most striking proposal was for biennial parliaments and something like manhood suffrage (see Introduction, p. 8 and p. 247 n. 12, above). It was not a strictly republican document, though it opposes the conceding to the King of any veto or Negative Voice. Fairfax and his advisors did not approve of it; it was sent back and became the basis for the better drafted and more conciliatory *Agreement of the People* (see Appendix) which omitted, perhaps only temporarily and tactically, the great question of the franchise. The rôle of this document could hardly have been more ambitiously conceived. It was to be an affirmation of the sovereign people, whose authority was to supersede that of the existing Parliament.

4 Wildman paraphrases *The Representation of the Army* (14 June 1647).

5 *An Agreement of the People*, first read at the Army Council on 29 Oct. 1647 and to be published on 3 Nov. (See Appendix.)

6 I.e. the prayer-meeting.

7 Wildman's phrase had in fact been: 'the Laws of Nature and Nations' – a formulation that might have been thought consistent with the position of Henry Parker, and acceptable to Ireton. Ireton, however, who is about to accuse Wildman of equivocation, evidently feels the hostile thrust of Wildman's remarks to lie behind the words: 'Law of Nature'.

8 Ireton makes it clear that by 'Covenants freely made' he understands the legitimate inheritance of property: he brings forward this crucial issue more plainly as the debate goes on.

9 Captain Lewis Audley.

10 Rainborough's younger brother.

11 *An Agreement of the People*.

12 Commissary Nicholas Cowling.

13 The notion, as Cowling soon makes clear, that fundamental liberties were usurped at the Norman Conquest and never regained.

14 Probably Henry Denne (d. ?1660), 'Judas Denne' to the Levellers. A Baptist clergyman, he was imprisoned in 1644, obtained the living of Eltisley, Cambridgeshire in 1645, and was one of the arrested Army officers who escaped execution at Burford in May 1649, when Cromwell put down the Leveller mutiny there. Denne was condemned to death, but staged a dramatic repentance and was pardoned. In the same month he published *The Leveller's Design Discovered*.

15 Maximilian Petty, with Wildman the other civilian Leveller introduced into the debate by the Agitators.

16 The seventeenth-century franchise, to which Rainborough makes several allusions in this speech, varied widely. In county elections the franchise had since 1430 been limited to freeholders of forty shillings a year or more. Boroughs elected their M.P.s either by choice of their corporation; or freemanship or special property-holders of the town; or all ratepayers; or all householders. At its widest, then, the borough franchise could include labourers of all kinds. The House of Commons, which had settled election disputes since 1604, had tended to widen the franchise, taking the view that where no clear custom of election could be shown, the right of election belonged to the commoners of the borough. Nevertheless the great magnates wielded great influence over county and borough elections, to which Rainborough chiefly refers in his remarks on 'the election of burgesses' (i.e. M.P.s for boroughs). His views are similar to those in the Commons who argued for franchise reform in 1640–1, when two reform bills were promoted but overwhelmed by pressure of other business (see Keith Thomas, 'The Levellers and the Franchise' in Aylmer, ed., *The Interregnum*, pp. 60–3).

17 In this formidable exchange between the chief speakers of the two sides it is to be noted that the preservation of property is common ground between them. Ireton says that the trend of Rainborough's argument is to question property – as indeed often seems to be the case; certainly he questions the justice of its distribution – while Rainborough repudiates this claim as a damaging aspersion upon his proposals for a franchise not based on property. H. N. Brailsford notes helpfully that: 'Landed property was much more widely diffused in the England of the seventeenth century than it is today' (*The Levellers and the English Revolution* (London, 1961; Spokesman Books edn, 1976), p. 277).

18 Cromwell, while endeavouring to lower the temperature of the exchange, sides unequivocally with Ireton.

19 Ireton thus accepts the notion of an inherited and binding contract, assent to which is implicit in receiving any protection deriving from it.

20 Colonel Nathaniel Rich.

21 'Cromwell's man-of-all-work' (Brailsford, *The Levellers and the English Revolution*, p. 280). In proposing a committee he probably had in mind a compromise that he was to propose later in the debate: the addition to the existing franchise of votes for those who had served Parliament in the Army.

22 Perhaps Cromwell and Ireton.

23 Ireton had suggested that unless the Levellers could produce 'evidence of history upon record by law', they should 'insist upon things of common safety' rather than issues of constitutional right.

24 Cf. Parker, *Observations*, pp. 53–4. The articles against Richard II were the terms upon which Parliament agreed to his deposition.

25 Constitutional proposals read out by Ireton for discussion and objection earlier in this debate.

26 Ireton charged that Wildman had not shown 'any evidence what was the ancient constitution' nor of how it had been usurped. Wildman replied that Rainborough's allusion to the deposition of Richard II was such evidence.

27 One of the besetting problems of these debates, as Ireton was well aware: terms such as 'the Law of Nature', 'just government' and even 'safety' were too broad to be brought easily to bear upon specific, immediate and practical proposals.

28 Shortly after this, the third Army Debate at Putney to be recorded was adjourned 'till to-morrow, and so from day to day till the proposals be all debated.' It must be stressed that nothing like a comprehensive record of the Army Debates has

survived. It is known, however, that at meetings on 4 and 5 November a motion supporting the Leveller view of the franchise was carried overwhelmingly against Cromwell and Ireton; and Rainborough's proposal for a general rendezvous (suggested on 29 October) was also passed. This was to have been a meeting to which a large body of London weavers, with whom John Lilburne was allied, was invited to commence the signing of the *Agreement of the People* (in Leveller eyes England's new contract and covenant) by the people of England. Cromwell and Ireton now took tough measures to regain control of the Army. First, the rendezvous was split into three, on different days and at different places. Secondly, officers and Agitators were ordered back to their regiments. Thirdly, Cromwell refused to allow debate of the royal powers at the Army Council, a conservative manifesto was drawn up embodying his and Ireton's point of view, and the great authority of Lord General Fairfax was brought into play, to preside over an Army Council, and to be present at the rendezvous. It was even threatened that the highly respected Fairfax might resign if the Army did not unite and comply. At the first of the rendezvous two regiments attempted mutiny by attending against orders and wearing copies of the *Agreement of the People* in their hats. A mixture of rebuke from Fairfax and browbeating from their officers reduced them to obedience. The Leveller Party continued influential for some time; but its power in the Army had been checked by military authority – and by an event which few had expected: the escape, on 11 November, of King Charles from Hampton Court. This presaged the Second Civil War. Social revolution gave way to the winning of another military contest.

5. JOHN MILTON, 'THE TENURE OF KINGS AND MAGISTRATES', FEBRUARY 1649

1 Aristotle's principle in *Politics*, v.
2 Jer. XLVIII, 10.
3 Prov. XII, 10.
4 Claude de Seissel, in *La Grande Monarchie de France*, 1519.
5 Milton had particularly in mind the republican government in Venice.
6 In the *Nicomachean Ethics*, VIII, x.
7 In *On the Crown* (AD 201)
8 See 2 Sam. XI, 2–17.
9 *Heraclidae*, 418–21.
10 Dio Cassius, Roman History, LXVIII, xvi.
11 *Roman History*, II.
12 St John Chrysostom, in his 23rd Homily.
13 St Basil, in *Works*, I, p. 456.
14 *Hercules Furens*, 922–4, spoken after killing the tyrant Lycus – a favourite quotation of the Regicides.
15 Judges III, 14–15.
16 1 Sam. XV, 33.
17 Saul (1 Sam. XXIV, 6).
18 Luke XXII, 25
19 In his commentary on the Book of Judges (1571), ch. 3.
20 *The Commonwealth of England* (1583), (V, p. 4).
21 From Gildass's *De excidio et conqueste Britanniae*; English trans., 1638.
22 The debate is given in *The Works of John Knox*, 1846–8, II, pp. 441–2.
23 Knox's *The History of the Reformation of the Church of Scotland* (1644), bk IV.

24 Buchanan, *History of Scotland*, bk xx, p. 243.
25 In 1 Sam. XXIV, 6 and XXVI, 11.
26 From the Song of Deborah:

> 'Curse Meroz, says the
>   angel of the Lord,
> Curse bitterly its
>   inhabitants,
> because they came not to the
>   help of the Lord,
> to the help of the Lord
>   against the mighty.'
>   (Judges v, 23).

6. RICHARD OVERTON, 'THE BAITING OF THE GREAT BULL OF BASHAN', JULY 1649

1 'Whu – all my brave Levelling Bull dogs and Bear Dogs, where are you? Siz – , ha – looe – ha – looe – all fly at him at once: There at him, at him; O brave Jockey with the sea-green ribbond in his eare! that Dog and his fellow for fourty shillings a Dog; Hold, hold, he hath caught him by the Gennitals, stave him off, give the Bull fair play. – A pox – they have burnt my Dog's mouth' (*Overton's Defyance of the Act of Pardon*, 1649; copy in Thomason Collection, British Museum).
2 1 Kings XVIII, 27.
3 It was first worn by Colonel Rainborough's supporters at his funeral the previous November, in recognition of his earlier command of the fleet.
4 The Baptists had recently repudiated the Levellers, their former allies, in *The Humble Petition and Representation of Several Churches of God in London*, 2 April 1649.
5 1 Sam. v, 3–4: the story of the statue of the Philistine god, Dagon, falling upon his face before the ark of the Covenant, at Ashdod.
6 Matt. v, 16.

7. GERRARD WINSTANLEY, 'A NEW-YEERS GIFT SENT TO THE PARLIAMENT AND ARMIE', DECEMBER 1649

1 Anti-enclosure Acts under the Tudors had ended some of the social distress caused, and the advantages of additional cultivation were being realised. But there were still angry attacks on the system.
2 After attacks by Parliament, the Statute of Monopolies, 1624, had put new patents under Parliament's control; but there were still exemptions.
3 For the legal controversy over the rights to commons and waste land see Christopher Hill, *The World Turned Upside Down* (London, 1972), p. 44.
4 A reference to the events of 1649. On 1 April of that year a small group of poor labourers collected on St George's Hill in the parish of Walton-on-Thames and began to dig the waste land there, sowing it with corn, parsnips, carrots, and beans. Their number soon rose to twenty or thirty. It was a symbolic claim to ownership. Local property-owners brought an action of trespass against the Diggers in the court of Kingston-upon-Thames. The Diggers were not allowed to plead unless they hired an attorney, which they refused to do, and so were condemned unheard. The jury imposed a fine of £10 a man against the Diggers,

plus 29s. 1d. costs. By August the colony had transferred to Cobham Heath, a mile or two away. Winstanley was arrested and fined £4 for trespass. The troops were called in and their presence emboldened the local gentry and freeholders. The troops stood by while houses were pulled down, tools and implements destroyed, the corn trampled, men beaten and imprisoned. By March 1650, their summer's crop destroyed, the colony was in dire financial straits, and by April it had been dispersed.

5 Winstanley attacked the Ranters in his *Vindication* of the Diggers, 20 Feb. 1650.

6 The Court of Wards and Liveries, a Royal Prerogative Court established in 1540–1, was abolished by Parliament in 1646, after mounting agitation against it by land-owning families. It was not re-established at the Restoration. 'Bearing in mind how many of the Parliament party had lands in chief of the crown, it is not unfair to include the Court as an important subsidiary cause of the Civil War' (H. E. Bell, *An Introduction to the History and Records of the Court of Wards and Liveries* (Cambridge, 1953), p. 149).

8. JAMES HARRINGTON, 'VALERIUS AND PUBLICOLA', 1659

1 In 1658 Cromwell had been offered the crown, but had refused it at least in name. On his death in September his son Richard succeeded him as Lord Protector, but resigned in May 1659 so as to allow the Army to recall the Rump in the name of renewed republicanism. When in October the Rump declared illegal all acts and ordinances since their dissolution, and cashiered General Lambert, Lambert dissolved them.

2 The three basic forms of government distinguished by Aristotle in his *Politics*.

3 Cf. the discussion of these words in Parker's *Observations*, pp. 39–40 and n. 17.

4 This is a new proposal of Harrington.

5 Cf. Machiavelli, *Discourses*, I, v.

6 12 October 1659 when Lambert dissolved the Rump.

7 It seems often to have been accepted in 1659 that the people would restore the Stuart monarchy if they could: cf. Milton's *Readie and Easie Way*, p. 228, below.

8 In 1572 the most brilliant Nova (temporary star) broke out in the constellation of Cassiopeia, and was observed by the astronomer Tycho Brahe.

9 The immediate region of the seaport Pozzuoli is highly volcanic.

10 *Politics*, v, iii.

9. JOHN MILTON, 'THE READIE AND EASIE WAY TO ESTABLISH A FREE COMMONWEALTH', APRIL 1660

1 The Rump had proposed to fill the vacant seats in Parliament by new members acceptable to itself.

2 Those members of Parliament, still willing to negotiate with the King, whom Colonel Pride had purged on 6 Dec. 1648.

3 'The surging tide of public sentiment for monarchy' (R. W. Ayers). The re-admission of the secluded members was generally seen as a prelude to a legal dissolution, and an election of a free parliament, which in turn seemed to promise successive parliaments, and a return of the King.

4 E.g. Matthew Griffith, author of *Fear God and the King* (1660).

5 As decreed by the Long Parliament (the Rump together with the secluded members) on 16 March 1660.

6 Milton's black irony, absent from the first edition, which had appeared before the calling of the free Parliament that the author so opposed.

7 Formerly a period for confession as well as recreation.

8 The language of the Act of 17 March 1649 which abolished the monarchy.

9 The first edition shows that Milton was thinking of the wars of the Fronde in France.

10 In the Solemn League and Covenant with the Scots (25 Sept. 1643).

11 The religion of Charles I and his Archbishop was a strict, ceremonious and episcopal Anglicanism, influenced by the Dutch Protestant Arminius, averse to the more extreme forms of Calvinism, and tolerant of the more conciliatory forms of Roman Catholicism. It may be seen as an Anglican equivalent of the Counter-Reformation.

12 From the Nineteen Propositions of 1 June 1642 to the Three Propositions (Treaty of Newport) 1648, seven sets of proposals had been put to the King.

13 Job XIII, 15.

14 The Engagement (11 Oct. 1649) to be true to the Commonwealth without King or House of Lords: the Protestation of 3 May 1641, pledged to defend Protestantism, King and Parliament.

15 Matt. VI, 24.

16 Phrases from the Solemn League and Covenant.

17 Cf. Aristotle, *Nichomachean Ethics*, v, vii.

18 John XII, 3–6.

19 Simon Magus (Acts VIII, 9–24).

20 Acts XXVI, 4–6, 9–11.

21 Milton attaches little significance to majorities.

22 Final negotiations with the King in Sept. 1648.

23 An Inquisition After Blood (July 1649) hinted that the King was not fully bound to his offer.

24 Church lands sold during the Interregnum.

25 Milton wishes to suggest that the two were as one in the best days of 'the Commonwealth'.

26 Salmasius published his attack on the regicides, *Defensio Regia pro Carolo I* . . . in 1649. Milton replied in *Pro Populo Anglicano Defensio* . . . in 1651.

27 Luke XIV, 28–30.

28 Genesis XI, 1–9.

29 The successful struggle (1558–1648) of the United Provinces to establish a republic independent of the crown of Spain.

30 One of the most conspicuous policies of the earlier Stuarts, affirmed by James I at the Hampton Court Conference on 16 Jan. 1604.

31 Added in the second edition. Milton refers to the union of Scotland with England, by the Act of Parliament of 26 June 1657, the result of Cromwell's victorious Scottish campaign.

32 1 Peter I, 18–19. Milton qualifies by this religious reference his unembarrassed satisfaction at the conquest of Scotland.

33 1 Sam. VIII, a crucial Old Testament text, cited by both Royalists and Republicans in their own support (see James I, *The Trew Law of Free Monarchies*, pp. 56–9).

34 Luke XXII, 25–6.

35 At present presided over by Cardinal Mazarin, and Anne of Austria, the Queen Mother.

36 'Full and free' were current words for the new parliament so much in demand. Milton does not yet make it clear that he is arguing for a *perpetual* Council.

37 Proverbs VI, 6–8.

38 Many Protestant Royalists in the Civil War controversies would deny Milton's statement; and Luther had argued, basing himself on Paul, that 'the powers that be are ordained of God' (see Quentin Skinner, *Foundations*, II, 15–16): if they command what is contrary to God's will they must be disobeyed, but never be actively resisted.

39 Parliament, first so styled in an act against treason, 17 July 1649. Cf. *Valerius and Publicola*, p. 185, above.

40 Milton comes here to his central constitutional proposal.

41 Milton here rejects a widespread current demand.

42 Though not necessarily always in session.

43 Cf. Dryden, *Absalom and Achitophel*, Part I, lines 801–4.

44 A concession to Harringtonian criticism of the first edition of this tract: 'the most readie & easie way to establish downright slaverie'.

45 Milton prefers a check by the military to that given by elections.

46 A very Harringtonian argument, from the traditions of Italian republicanism.

47 See Parker's *Observations*, p. 46 and n. 32 above.

48 By Harrington and his followers: cf. *The Rota: Or, A Model of the Free State* (9 Jan. 1660) and *Valerius and Publicola*, pp. 177–202 above.

49 Harrington had, of course, already given answers to these objections. Cf. *Valerius and Publicola*, pp. 197–8

50 In other words, opinion should not be consulted too fully until the great issue is settled.

51 Milton does not enlarge, but see footnote a on p. 214, above (on 'just and necessarie qualifications').

52 Cf. *Tenure of Kings and Magistrates*: 'No man is so stupid' p. 121, above. Many intelligent men, Sir Robert Filmer for one, denied the concept of 'native libertie'.

53 The great provision against imbalance in property and consequent civil discord, in Harrington's *Oceana*, and assumed in *Valerius and Publicola*.

54 Milton acknowledges the growing royalist sentiment.

55 *Politics*, III, ix, 7.

56 1 Sam. II, 12–17.

57 1 Sam. VIII, 18.

58 See n. 24, p. 208, above. Milton's appeal is to those who have profited from the disestablishing of the episcopal English Church.

59 An oversimplification: the goals of the Presbyterians were part of the first rather than the second revolution of the Civil War period. They wished to secure substantial concessions from the King, but not to execute him and establish a republic. As in *Tenure of Kings and Magistrates*, Milton is bitter against the church which was a political ally of the more extreme trends up to a point only, and then drew back.

60 Probably the Pacification of Berwick, 18 June 1639, by which Charles agreed to place ecclesiastical affairs in Scotland under the control of free parliaments and assemblies of the Kirk: an undertaking he soon went back on.

61 Probably a pun: after their expulsion the secluded members were conveyed to 'that place under the Exchequer which is commonly called Hell; where they might eat and drink at their own charge' (Clarendon, *History*, ed. Macray, IV, p. 466); 'Every body now drinks the King's health without any fear' (Samuel Pepys's *Diary*, 6 March 1660).

62 Psalm 129, 2–3.

63 Milton opposes the 'full and free' parliament which might reveal the extent of that support.

64 *A Treatise of Civil Power in Ecclesiastical Causes* (15 Feb. 1659).

65 *Annales Regnante Elizabetha ad annum . . . 1589* (1627), I, p. 23.

66 Cf. *Eikon Basiliké*, commonly then and sometimes still thought to have been written by Charles I, Ch. 27.

67 Milton's programme of decentralisation to chief cities has the aspect of civic republicanism, and offers encouragement to the 'nobilitie and chief gentrie' of the regions.

68 Cf. Aristotle, *Athenian Constitution*, XXI, iii, 22.

69 The introduction of this metaphor in the second edition greatly contributes to the idea of culture expressed in this important passage.

70 Milton writes in the spirit of Machiavelli and Harrington at their most admirable: cf. the *Art of War*, Book II (conclusion); and *Oceana* (The Preliminaries, showing the Principles of Government, Part I).

71 An essential feature of Machiavelli's Republicanism.

72 Milton's concession to Harrington's principle of rotation.

73 Exodus XXI, 3: captivity under alien rule.

74 Jer. XXII, 29 (the source of a more specific allusion at the corresponding point in the first edition); Matt III, 7–9; Luke III, 8.

EPILOGUE. 'QUERES AND CONJECTURES, CONCERNING THE PRESENT STATE OF THIS KINGDOME', 1643

1 *The Moderator Expecting Sudden Peace, or Certaine Ruine*, by Thomas Povey, was first published in 1642, and republished in 1643. It was one of the chief peace pamphlets of the Civil War period. The author was M.P. for Liskeard in 1647; after the Restoration was a Master of Requests; and was a friend of Evelyn and Pepys.

A select booklist

This is intended as a guide to further reading rather than as a comprehensive bibliography.

The place of publication is London, unless otherwise stated.

PRIMARY SOURCES

All the texts given here, with the exception of the Army Debates, are among the great collection of nearly 23,000 books, pamphlets and broadsides of the period, formed by George Thomason (d. 1666), London bookseller, between 1641 and 1662; bought by George III for £300 in 1761 and presented to the British Museum the following year. Henry Parker's *Observations Upon Some of his Majesties late Answers and Expresses* and the short *Queres and Conjectures* have been edited from the original copies in the Cambridge University Library. The remaining texts have been taken from the collections given below.

MODERN COLLECTIONS

W. C. Abbott, ed., *The Writings and Speeches of Oliver Cromwell* (4 vols., Cambridge, Mass., 1937–47): the standard scholarly edition.

William Haller, ed., *Tracts on Liberty in the Puritan Revolution, 1638–1647* (3 vols., New York, 1934). Texts in facsimile, with introduction and somewhat sparse commentary in each case.

W. Haller and G. Davies, eds., *The Leveller Tracts 1647–1653* (Gloucester, Mass., 1964): a major collection, with a full and valuable introduction.

J. Max Patrick, ed, *The Prose of John Milton* (New York, 1967): a well-chosen selection of the most important texts, with separate editors' forewords and notes.

A. L. Morton, ed., *Freedom in Arms: A Selection of Leveller Writings* (1975): it includes the only modern edition of Overton's *The Baiting of the Great Bull of Bashan* and several other lesser-known pamphlets.

Charles Petrie, ed., *The Letters of Charles I* (London, 1935).

J. G. A. Pocock, ed., *The Political Works of James Harrington* (Cambridge, 1977); the standard scholarly edition, with a full and important introduction.

G. H. Sabine, ed., *The Works of Gerrard Winstanley* (Ithaca, New York, 1941): the standard complete edition.

D. M. Wolfe, ed., *John Milton: Complete Prose Works*, (7 vols., New Haven, Conn., 1953–74): the standard scholarly edition, with very full introductions and notes.

Leveller Manifestoes of the Puritan Revolution (New York, 1944); a large collection, covering the years 1646–9, and including *An Agreement of the People, Nov 1647*.

A. S. P. Woodhouse, ed., *Puritanism and Liberty, Being the Army Debates (1647–49)* (from the *Clarke Manuscripts*) (1938); a modernised text of the Debates, together with a wide selection of related radical writings and a valuable introduction.

A select booklist

SECONDARY MATERIAL

Biographical studies

Lives of Cromwell are too numerous to list; C. H. Firth, *Oliver Cromwell and the Rule of the Puritans in England* (New York, 1900), in the 'Heroes of the Nations' series, is a short, readable account by a distinguished historian; Antonia Fraser, *Cromwell Our Chief of Men* (1973), the most recent scholarly – and sympathetic – biography. Maurice Ashley, *Cromwell's Generals* (1954), includes the fullest biographical sketch of Henry Ireton. Of the recent biographies of Milton, W. R. Parker, *Milton; a Biography* (2 vols., Oxford, 1968) is the fullest; Christopher Hill, *Milton and the English Revolution* (1977), the most original and, to many, provocative. M. A. Radzinowicz, *Towards Samson Agonistes* (1978), is an outstanding critical and intellectual biography. W. K. Jordan, *Men of Substance* (Chicago, 1942), discusses Parker's thought in the context of his career. Of the Levellers, Lilburne has had two full-scale biographies: M. A. Gibb, *John Lilburne, the Leveller* (1947) and Pauline Gregg, *Free-born John* (1961). The most famous biography of the period is Lucy Hutchinson, *Memoirs of the Life of Colonel Hutchinson*, the Puritan Governor of Nottingham and regicide, first published from her MS. in 1806; the most recent edition is that of J. Sutherland (1973). At the opposite end of the political spectrum stand H. R. Trevor-Roper, *Archbishop Laud* (1940), a brilliant study of him as a politician, and C. V. Wedgwood, *Thomas Wentworth, first Earl of Strafford: A Revaluation* (1961). A recent biography of the King is John Bowle, *Charles I* (1975).

Historical and political background

Studies of both the historical and political background of the period abound. All draw to a greater or lesser extent on S. R. Gardiner, *History of the Great Civil War 1642–1649* (4 vols., 1893), the classic account; and Gardiner himself drew widely on Edward Hyde (later Earl of Clarendon). The best edition of his *History of the Rebellion and Civil Wars in England* is that edited by W. D. Macray (6 vols., Oxford, 1888); and the best study of it and of Clarendon's ideas, is B. H. G. Wormald, *Clarendon; Politics, History and Religion, 1640–1660* (Cambridge, 1951). The most readable and reliable short history of the period is J. P. Kenyon, *Stuart England* (1978), which includes a full annotated bibliography; his *Stuart Constitution, 1603–1688* (Cambridge, 1966) is an indispensable collection of documents, with commentary, covering the period 1603–88. Conrad Russell, ed., *The Origins of the English Civil War* (1973), contains a collection of essays on the political, religious and economic issues leading up to the Civil War. *The Crisis of Parliaments* (Oxford, 1971), also by Russell, covers the period 1509–1660; the section, 'England's New Chains Discovered', deals with the years 1642–60. A work which has re-oriented seventeenth-century historiography is J. G. A. Pocock, *The Ancient Constitution and the Feudal Law* (Cambridge, 1957).

The Levellers and the Diggers have received considerable attention over the last forty years. A pioneering study of Winstanley's social philosophy was D. W. Petegorsky, *Left-Wing Democracy in the English Civil War* (1940). Wilhelm Schenk, *The Concern for Social Justice in the Puritan Revolution* (1948), contains essays on Lilburne, Walwyn and Winstanley; Joseph Frank, *The Levellers . . . J. Lilburne, R. Overton, W. Walwyn* (Cambridge, Mass., 1955), gives the history of the Leveller Party through the writings of their three leaders; H. N. Brailsford, *The Levellers and the English Revolution* (1961; Spokesman Books edn, 1976) is a full and sympathetic study; Christopher Hill, *The World Turned Upside Down* (1972), gives a comprehensive and

A select booklist

valuable account of the Levellers, Diggers and other revolutionary groups. Readers of the Army Debates may consult Leo F. Solt, *Saints in Arms: Puritanism and Democracy in Cromwell's Army* (Stanford, 1959) for a different perspective. G. E. Aylmer, ed., *The Interregnum: The Quest for a Settlement, 1646–60* (1972), contains a helpful study of the Leveller Franchise by Keith Thomas, besides studies of Hobbes by Quentin Skinner and of the part played in the period by the City of London, by Valerie Pearl. Other more specialised historical studies are J. H. Hexter, *The Reign of King Pym* (Cambridge, Mass., 1941), an account of John Pym's leadership of the House of Commons, 1640–3; Blair Worden, *The Rump Parliament, 1648–1653* (Cambridge, 1974); J. S. Morrill, ed., *The Revolt of the Provinces: Conservatives and Radicals in the English Civil War, 1630–1650* (1976), a collection of documents, with a long introduction, to illustrate the interaction of national and local politics in the Civil War; Brian Manning, *The English People and the English Revolution 1640–1649* (1976), a study of the rôle of popular movements in the period; and Godfrey Davies, *The Restoration of Charles II, 1658–1660* (Oxford, 1955), the fullest and most careful study of this remarkable political change.

Political and religious thought

William Haller devoted two important studies to the part played by Puritan preachers and their disciples both before and during the Civil War; *The Rise of Puritanism* (New York, 1938), and *Liberty and Reformation in the Puritan Revolution* (New York, 1955). Christopher Hill, *Puritanism and Revolution* (1958), is a collection of essays concerned with the interpretation of the Revolution; his *Intellectual Origins of the English Revolution* (Oxford, 1965), the Oxford Ford Lectures, claims, as influences upon it, Bacon, Raleigh and Edward Coke. M. A. Judson, *A Crisis of the Constitution . . . 1603–45* (New Brunswick, New Jersey, 1949), studies the conflicts in political thought of the period; Richard Tuck, *Natural Rights Theories. Their Origin and Development* (Cambridge, 1979), contains a valuable discussion of the exchanges between Parker and the King's advisers. C. H. McIlwain, ed., *The Political Works of James I* (Cambridge, Mass., 1918), Gordon J. Schochet, *Patriarchalism in Political Thought* (Oxford, 1975), Peter Laslett, ed., *Patriarcha and Other Political Works of Sir Robert Filmer* (Oxford, 1949), and J. N. Figgis, *Political Thought from Gerson to Grotius, 1414–1625* (repr. New York, 1960) and *The Divine Right of Kings*, 2nd edn (Cambridge, 1914), show the direction of royalist thought before and after the period illustrated in this volume. Quentin Skinner, *The Foundations of Modern Political Thought* (2 vols., Cambridge, 1978), is an authoritative study of political theory in its context from the thirteenth century to the end of the sixteenth, to show the origins of the concept of State that was ultimately fought over in the Civil War.

Style

The most helpful study is Joan Webber, *The Eloquent 'I'; Style and Self in Seventeenth-Century Prose* (Madison, Winsconsin, 1968); it contains essays on the styles of both Milton and Lilburne. K. W. Stavely, *The Politics of Milton's Prose Style* (New Haven, Conn., 1975) has helpful sections on the two Milton pamphlets given here. A. L. Morton, in *The Matter of Britain* (1966), contains an essay on 'the Leveller style'. G. R. Owst, *Literature and Pulpit in Medieval England* (Cambridge, 1933) is a very useful discussion of the popular sermon. Margot Heinemann, *Puritanism and Theatre. Thomas Middleton and Opposition Drama under the Early Stuarts* (Cambridge, 1980), has an interesting 'Postscript', showing the influence of popular drama on the Levellers' style and on Overton's in particular.